AT LAST

SHE SAID IT

Jackie,
keep saying it!
♡ Cynthia
Susan

SHE SAID IT

honest conversations about faith,
church, and everything in between

SUSAN HINCKLEY &
CYNTHIA WINWARD

SIGNATURE BOOKS | 2025 | SALT LAKE CITY

For all the women who have shared their stories with us,
and those who can only share in their hearts.

© 2025 Signature Books. All rights reserved. Signature Books is a registered trademark of Signature Books Publishing, LLC. Printed in the USA using paper from sustainably harvested sources.

Join our mailing list at signaturebooks.com for details on events and related titles we think you'll enjoy.

Design by Jason Francis

FIRST EDITION | 2025

LIBRARY OF CONGRESS CONTROL NUMBER: 2025932277

Paperback ISBN: 978-1-56085-521-7
Ebook ISBN: 978-1-56085-502-6

CONTENTS

INTRODUCTION

"I have both a thousand regrets, and none at all."
—Susan Hinckley

I begin by quoting myself because in the years since we started our podcast, so many listeners have repeated that line from the first episode back to us. I guess those words landed with a thud of truth.

Cynthia Winward and I got serious about starting the At Last She Said It project in late 2019. We had two very different personalities and a decade or so between us, but as our friendship developed, we kept stumbling onto what felt like an uncanny amount of common ground in our church experiences. Our conversations often ended with, "Why isn't anyone talking about this? Someone should do a podcast!" You can only say a thing so many times before it becomes an inside joke, or you do something about it. We were ready to go the next spring. YouTube videos provided the know-how, and a pandemic quarantine provided the captive audience. We didn't know whether anyone would listen, but we had a hunch we weren't the only women wishing we had a place to discuss the things we were thinking about, a lot of which we'd never said—or heard—out loud. If we've learned one thing from this project, it's that our hunch was right.

We're writing this book to share some of our favorite topics with another audience. We ask people to think about old ideas in new ways. That kind of stretching can be uncomfortable, but we call it "holy discomfort." The willingness to consider diverse perspectives—even on the things we hold most dear—feels essential in an evolving world. We've learned that sometimes we have to be open to changing our minds, including how we think about ourselves. Faith is alive when it's growing, and growing means change.

Our project goal was to amplify Latter-day Saint women's voices, and the natural place to start was with a couple of mics and our own.

We didn't have any particular expertise, but as lifetime members of The Church of Jesus Christ of Latter-day Saints, we had plenty of experiences. At the time of this writing, our 200-and-counting recorded conversations have been downloaded nearly two million times. We've learned, right along with our listeners, that there's no power quite like finding out you're not alone.

Here's the rest of what I said in that first episode:

> Douglas Adams wrote, "All you really need to know for the moment is that the universe is a lot more complicated than you might think, even if you start from a position of thinking it's pretty damn complicated in the first place."
>
> As a girl growing up in the church, I sensed from a young age that the answer to most everything about my life as a woman was likely to be, "It's complicated." As I've gotten older, I've realized that the young me—who knew enough to know that—didn't know the half of it.
>
> I saw married women, single women, women with children, women without, all working in their homes, many also working outside them. I saw vocal women, women who hardly spoke, women of all ages, shapes, sizes, and colors. I saw that women ran nothing in the church, but seemed to run everything in the world, if only behind the scenes. I saw men get bigger paychecks, watched women do the dishes after feeding them. Good men, and women who truly loved them. Bad men, and women who loved them too.
>
> I saw myself make choices I didn't fully understand. As a girl, I dreamed of being a single career woman making my way in a big city, then chose to marry at eighteen. I vowed to wait until I was in my thirties to have children, then had three before I turned twenty-five. I believed deeply in a woman's right to personal development and fulfillment, but never went to graduate school, even when I could have. I yearned to shatter cultural norms, but somehow determined to live happily within them. My thoughts were wildly rebellious and outspoken, my lips mostly silent. If you looked at how often my choices failed to line up with my opinions, you might wonder who was in charge. I've sometimes wondered that myself.
>
> But of course, all of that is complicated. And how I love my deeply messy woman's life, the peculiar mix of choices and lack thereof that have brought so much love, beauty, relationship and experience to my days! I have both a thousand regrets, and none at all. Things I'd do over, and things I never would, but most of all, these days, I feel optimistic and excited to meet everything I have yet to choose, and not choose, for myself.

"Women of faith, discussing complicated things." That's how we describe At Last She Said It, and we don't expect any of it to untangle itself. What a privilege it has been to pick at even our most stubborn knots in the company of what feels like thousands of kindred spirits. We truly mean it when we say: *Thanks for listening.* —Susan

ACKNOWLEDGMENTS

We would like to thank:

Russ and Paul for embracing our journeys and their own.

Lindsay, Chelsea, Hannah, Ilene, and Hallie whose lives needed a bigger world than Mormonism could offer.

And Nathan, who can help bring about a bigger Mormonism.

Trina Caudle for helping us write better.

Barbara Jones Brown and Beth Reeve for encouraging us to create this book and everyone at Signature who helped it become real.

Jeralee Renshaw, whose mentorship and support have been invaluable.

Blakelee Ellis, Katie Groberg, and Tiffany Wilhelm for their work behind the curtain.

Dan Wotherspoon for handing us a mic and encouraging us to use it.

Richard Rohr for giving us the second half of life and the language to talk about it.

All the feminists—especially Mormon ones—upon whose words and work we stand.

Every listener who has reached out to say: 1) Now I know I'm not crazy, and 2) I'm not alone.

DANCING WITH THE PATRIARCHY

WHAT WOMEN DON'T GET IN OUR CHURCH

"What happens when women are outnumbered? After years spent analyzing lab and real-life settings to determine what it takes for a woman to really be heard—to truly be perceived as competent and influential—these professors have found the same truth: for women, having a seat at the table does not mean having a voice."
—Brittany Karford Rogers[1]

Cynthia:

I once lamented to a friend over dinner how I wish women could have more leadership opportunities in the church. Her reply was that she liked sleeping in on Sundays and would prefer to have her husband be the one to get up early and attend bishopric meetings instead of her. On the surface this doesn't sound so bad.

What woman, or man, would want more responsibility? What normal person would want to attend more meetings? I am always up for less work as well, but this isn't about a *willingness* to attend early church meetings. It is about women having a voice at every table. It is about the ability to affect decisions that affect women. It's about making decisions that take into account the needs and perspectives of *all* Latter-day Saints, not just the male ones. It is about hearing and being heard, but just as important, it's about seeing women in charge. It is important to see women lead, not just leading women and children, but all members.

1 Corinthians 12:21 reads, "And the eye cannot say unto the hand, I have no need of thee: nor again the head to the feet, I have no need of you." Yet it very much feels like women are told, "we have no need of you in leadership."

When I talk to Latter-day Saint women who are happy with an all-male clergy, they advise me to listen to this certain talk, or that certain YouTube video, by this or that female church member. They suggest this book about priesthood, or that podcast by a woman who so eloquently explains how amazing and forward-thinking we are as a church towards our women—as if my disappointment is a matter of not knowing all the facts rather than disappointment in those facts. I have thought about the status of women in our church for decades, have they?

Flip the narrative and see how often we have Latter-day Saint men speak to other LDS men about their equality. Do men go on podcasts, write books, and give speeches about their equality? If that sounds silly, it should. A man's contributions to leadership in the church are obvious. We would never have to convince men through talks, conferences, and podcasts that they're as needed as women, yet that's exactly what we do when we try to convince women that they have full equality in the church. Spoiler: if you have to explain to a group of people that they are equal to another group then equality doesn't exist. Equality would be measurable, factual, and obvious.

Many other conservative Christian denominations refer to an all-male clergy as 'complementarianism.' Some Christians want to go back to calling it what it is called biblically: patriarchy.[2] I find it interesting that other Christian churches tried to soften the derogatory nature of a patriarchal system by calling it complementarianism whereas in The Church of Jesus Christ of Latter-day Saints, we have never had a problem with using derivatives of the word 'patriarchy.' The word is riddled throughout our ordinances, callings, and our organizational hierarchy. In *The Making of Biblical Womanhood*, Beth Allison Barr says:

> Instead of being a point of pride for Christians, shouldn't the historical continuity of a practice that has caused women to fare much worse than men for thousands of years cause concern? Shouldn't Christians, who are called to be different from the world, treat women *differently*? What if patriarchy isn't divinely ordained but is a result of human sin?[3]

Researcher and author Jana Riess wrote, "Research has determined that having women clergy makes a significant impact on the lives of girls. Girls who had direct examples of clergywomen in childhood grow up with higher self-esteem, better employment, and more education than girls who did not."[4]

If *history* shows that patriarchy is bad for women, and *data* shows that girls and women fare better when they can see themselves at every level of leadership in our churches, schools, and societies, why do

4

Latter-day Saint women and men continue to cling to old ideas that deny history and data?

In a famous speech defending the current status quo for women in the church, a female speaker asks: "What do we (LDS) women get? Answer: knowledge, power, revelation, endowment … We get everything our Father in Heaven has to offer."[5]

Yes, we get every blessing, but do we get every opportunity to use our talents, skills, and gifts? Do we get to use those talents equally leading alongside men in our wards and stakes? To quote the musical Hamilton, are we in the room where it happens? Where decisions are made? In our church, do women make even one decision that can't be overruled by a man? If the late Supreme Court Justice Ruth Bader Ginsburg was right—that women do belong in all places where decisions are made—then why do we uphold a system where women are most definitely not in those places?

Telling a woman what she does get at church is like telling a stay-at-home wife in the 1950s she got every blessing of a career through her husband. She was blessed with food, clothing and a home. Though we know not all women, particularly women of color, were provided monetary blessings through the men in their lives. Women had limited benefits and opportunities in professions that society allowed for them such as secretaries and teachers. Many women were happy with societal limitations for careers, but it wasn't wrong for *some* women to want other professions, to serve in politics, and to lead companies. Likewise, it is not wrong for *some* LDS women today to want a female bishop or for a young girl to want to pass the sacrament when she's old enough.

In that same question of asking what do women get, I would like to list what Latter-day Saint women *don't* get.

Let's start with the obvious list where women and girls are ineligible due to priesthood ordination: Women do not get to serve as a bishop, bishopric counselor, patriarch, stake president, stake counselor, high councilor, temple president, temple sealer, district president, area authority, general authority, apostle, or prophet.

The list of duties and callings that women don't get despite ordination *not* being requisite:

Girls do not get to prepare the sacrament, nor pass the sacrament, despite neither of these things being listed in Doctrine & Covenants

20 as Aaronic priesthood duties. For that matter, girls do not get a section in scripture at all detailing their church responsibilities.

Girls do not get any parallel responsibility at age eleven that boys get when they're ordained as deacons. That is a large and embarrassing blank for teenage girls in the organization.

Girls do not get to collect fast offerings.

Women do not get to extend any callings to anyone, not even girls or women within the stewardship of a Relief Society or Young Women position.

Women do not get to have stewardship over boys after age eleven.

Women do not get to issue temple recommends, even to young girls they may have stewardship over in their Young Women organizations.

Women do not get to help with ward boundary changes. Wards are always aligned by the number of Melchizedek priesthood holders. According to the Church Handbook, 180 full-tithe paying men are required to create a stake, and one full-tithe paying man per twenty other ward members to create a ward, with a minimum of twenty men. The handbook also states that four full-tithe paying men are needed to create a branch. Number of women required to form a branch, ward, or stake? Zero. If no women existed in a stake, all the units could still be formed.

Women do not get any control of church funds. A woman is not allowed to determine budgets, nor count tithing, nor reimburse other women for Relief Society, Young Women, or Primary expenses.

Women do not get to serve as a ward mission leader. Even though this calling has become optional, only men can serve if a bishop chooses to fill it. 'Optional' means it may or may not be needed, so why can't a woman be a ward mission leader? Most likely because women can't supervise men. The one exception is that a Primary president is allowed to supervise men (sort of) so maybe that's not the reason either?

Women do not get to serve as a ward temple and family history leader. Just as with the ward mission leader calling, this is also optional now, but even so, women are not allowed if a bishop chooses to fill it. It can be unfilled, or it can be filled by a man.

Women do not get to serve as clerks of any kind. Not as a ward clerk, stake clerk, membership clerk, financial clerk, executive secretary, etc., despite a clerk never being required to lay his hands on a person's head and exercise priesthood authority as part of that calling.

Women do not get to serve in Sunday School presidencies. (Yes, there are rare exceptions where women can be the secretary. Apparently a woman taking notes and handing out attendance rolls is female-appropriate in *some* wards.)

Women do not get to officiate nor pray in a temple endowment session.

Women do not get to decide if a person has access to saving ordinances.

Women do not get to determine a person's 'worthiness.'

Women are not allowed to hear, help, or discuss another person's sins with them, nor help her, nor counsel her through the repentance process, including and especially sexual sins, not even as a Relief Society leader counseling with a woman.

Women do not get to interview people, including children, youth, or other women within the stewardship of a leadership calling.

Women do not get to sit in any membership council. (Formerly called disciplinary councils.) A woman is *always* judged by *only* men.

Women do not get to add an annotation to a member's record nor can they remove one.

Women do not get to hold their babies during a baby blessing. (A few exceptions have occurred but these are anomalies and not the rule.)

Women do not get to choose their Relief Society president despite this being a women's organization that only serves women. In the early days of the church, the Relief Society president was elected by other women.

Women do not get final say as a Relief Society president to approve food orders or any other welfare expenditures.

Women do not get to approve the yearly Primary program. She can write it, teach it to the children, but only a man can approve, or disapprove, what she's written.

Women do not get to preside at meetings. If a male priesthood leader is present it will almost always be announced that he is the one presiding.

Women do not get to perform civil weddings in LDS Church buildings.

Women do not get to conduct funerals in LDS Church buildings.

Women do not get to conduct baptism services.

Women do not get to conduct sacrament meetings or stake conferences.

Women do not get to approve musical numbers for sacrament meeting.

Women do not get to be consulted as to who could be potential new bishops or stake presidents.

Women do not get to name church units. Every ward and stake name was chosen by a man.

Women do not get to choose the color and decor of new church buildings. (Usually the stake president makes the choice.)

Women did not get to help write *The Family: A Proclamation to the World* in 1995. It has had zero revisions since then, despite the exclusion of women in the writing process, yet it is still held up as the leading document on families over thirty years later.[6]

Women do not get to decide to cancel church for weather, natural disaster, viral outbreaks, etc.

Living women do not get to be sealed to more than one spouse. There is no limit to how many times a man, living or dead, can be sealed. Five times? Ten times? No limit.

Lastly, women do not get to fix any of these inequalities. Every change for the betterment of women has occurred because a man decided to change it. Quite literally, women are at the mercy of men wanting and instituting change. May the men who lead us want more for the women as well.

DANCING WITH THE PATRIARCHY

"Like racism, patriarchy is a shapeshifter—conforming to each new era, looking as if it has always belonged."
—Beth Allison Barr[7]

Susan:

My grandfather owned a dance hall in central Utah. Sometimes if I was lucky, I'd get to go with him to check on the Saturday night dance. I remember the thrill of eavesdropping as he exchanged quips with the ticket lady over my head, the blush when he told everyone I was his date, then made a show of asking me to foxtrot. I'd step onto his toes and into the crowd we'd go. He had all the moves, but I was the one who felt special.

Fast forward about fifty years. My daughter told me about filling out some paperwork that included the question, "What is something your mother hates?" She had to think for a long time. Really struggled with it. I could have helped her name several things easily, beginning with seafood, but an answer finally came to her: "My mother hates the patriarchy."

We had a good laugh about it, but I was left with questions. Why was that the one thing she thought of? How could she have forgotten seafood, and coconut, and not having an aisle seat, and bad grammar, and the Midwest in February, and all the other things I move through the world hating loudly?

And how had I managed to communicate that to her so convincingly? Because she's not wrong . . . but she's not exactly right either.

Hate is a strong word, for one thing. But so is patriarchy. In fact, if we have to call it that, let's go ahead and say I hate it. Because the 'p' word does make me itchy.

I think it's somehow tied up in the fact that I have a hard-wired negative response to authority, and the reality of a woman's life is that by the time she's an adult, she will have been subject to the authority of men in a lifetime of situations, both personal and institutional. It's hard to distinguish between chafing at authority and chafing at the authority exercised by men when they're so often the same thing.

No matter who's trying to exert control, my immediate reaction is likely to be: *You're not the boss of me.* But with men in the equation, there's an additional layer to that response: *If you're a man, you can't possibly understand what it's like to be a woman, and therefore you have no frame of reference, no relevance in this conversation.*

I understand that generality is not only unfair but unhelpful, and I offer it only in the interest of full disclosure. This is an emotional bias that has been with me since before the dawn of my own time. I can't explain its genesis.

Still, I'd like to frame my discussion with a few disclaimers, right up front. First of all, I like men. I really do. In fact, I've always enjoyed male friends as much or more than female ones. That was the case a million years ago in school, and it's still the case now. I also like it that men generally seem to like me. Maybe that's because I feel like I'm getting away with something because they like me, but they don't know how much I secretly hate the patriarchy, of which they're part even if they're only guilty by association. *Oh dear, I was trying to explain to you why the assertion that I hate the patriarchy is not necessarily true ...*

Which brings me to that other p-elephant to which our church's patriarchy is inextricably linked: priesthood. I've always said I don't care one whit about not having it, and that's still true. I've felt like I knew something the men in the room didn't, as if God and I knew the real score and some day they'd catch up. While I've believed the priesthood has the ability to call down God's power from heaven, my life has shown me that I do too. While the men in the temple were doing all the visible work, women laid their hands upon me in a separate room. While my husband was right there when the babies were born, I was the one who birthed them. I simply knew things he could not know as a result. So what I mean is that I haven't much minded not being in charge of an organization that is so lopsided, it was clearly invented by men. If I were making a club, I'd have likely put the girls in charge.

Secondly, the day my older sister asked me, decades ago now, "Why do you have a weird negative reaction to men?" I was able to offer a bunch of evidence that she had it wrong. But I was troubled by the fact that somehow I had come across that way. How had my love for men been mistaken as something quite opposite?

I've scoured my childhood for clues. Because for me, being partial to men goes way back. I was very close to my foxtrotting grandfather from a young age. I spent a lot of time hanging out with him by choice, even in the junior high years when I was supposed to be busy with my friends. He was a vaudeville musician who moved through life with an easy showmanship and ready sense of humor, and seemed to be recognized wherever we went. He was also the twenty-eighth child of a long-ago polygamist, his dad the iconic leader of the Utah State Penitentiary band, who served time rather than renouncing the young wife who bore eighteen of his thirty-one children. Gone decades before I was born, he was only a handsome legend sporting a silver coronet and striped jumpsuit, the curious centerpiece of ancient family photos and seemingly tall tales. My grandfather's stories fascinated but also deeply troubled me, introducing a conflict that raged in my Mormon-girl heart before most of my friends even knew what the word polygamy meant.

But more than anything, as a kid, I wanted to spend time with my dad. He wasn't home much because he worked like crazy, sometimes on the opposite side of the country. When he came home on weekends, it was to spend time with my mother, who needed him more than I did. That was the line of reasoning offered, or maybe just the explanation I developed for myself to ease my longing. Either way, I accepted it. My mother was ill for a chunk of my childhood, and the family made a lot of accommodations for that. It was a given. But oh, how I wished for attention from my crew-cut, horn-rimmed, important-executive Dad.

Instead, I spent most of my time with my older brother. Our childhood was a private clubhouse built by us, where we spoke our own language of movie lines and show tune lyrics, and the lonely difficulties of our small lives twisted into an ever-expanding catalog of inside jokes. We thought we were hilarious. When he got too old to want to spend time hanging around with his little sister, I quietly pulled a blanket and pillow to the hall outside his bedroom door at night and slept there, developing a love for Chicago and The Carpenters, Neil Sedaka and Barry Manilow, very quietly right along with him, as heard through his closed door. I needed to keep up or risk losing my membership in our club.

There were influential women too, of course. One of my biggest female influences was my Aunt Lillie—great-aunt technically—who was near seventy by the time I was born. She never married, but lived with my grandparents from the time they were newlyweds, a constant fixture in the back bedroom of their tiny house. More like my grandmother than her sister ever was, she was a frequent caregiver and best friend in my childhood, yet somehow managed to retain a bit of mystery. Lillie owned a store and went to work daily. She refused to wear a bra on principle, slept in men's pajamas, read *True Confessions* magazine, and loved gambling. At a young age, I could see these things set her apart from the Mormon women I knew. She also rolled her eyes at men behind their backs but lit up like a sparkler whenever one talked to her. With Aunt Lillie, I always felt I was in some kind of confused club where the main rule was, "No Boys Allowed," but the best thing that could happen was to have one drop by the clubhouse for a visit. One of my favorite things she ever said to me, clutching her chest with a conspiratorial whisper, was, "Never let 'em get your jewels." It still feels like good advice.

Lillie never joined the church, a freedom which I envied her. She lived wholly immersed in a Mormon family, but as she explained, "Someone had to stay home to cook Sunday dinner." Maybe she could see that her church life as a single, working woman in small town Utah would have been a fraught one. But even though she loomed very large in my young life, I can't say for sure how much influence she had in the formation of my reaction to the patriarchy. She never gave a church leader one second of control, even when she lived with one. But she also never dared drive a car for herself, and in some ways willingly deferred to any man in the room. Whether she yearned for a husband or felt grateful she dodged the bullet of marriage, I cannot say. I saw signs of each. Perhaps I can trace an inkling of my complicated feelings to her.

I had another grandmother too, of course, a force of nature in her own right. She took no nonsense from anyone, and the legend of the day she climbed on a kitchen chair and yanked a nest of yellow jackets off the porch where it menaced above the screen door, carrying it barehanded to dump in the river, is completely believable. It hardly matters whether it happened or not. If that story is not true, surely six more remarkable ones are. But she was very quiet. The only loud opinions in her house belonged to her husband, who was full of them and expressed them to anyone who would listen. She loved the church my grandpa devoted his life to complaining about, serving for many years as a Relief Society president and telling me about giving blessings of support and healing to the pregnant women in her small farming community as part of the job. It was a glimpse I never received anywhere else, since that practice was discontinued before I was born. So I'm not sure she felt any lack of power as a woman at church—on the contrary, it seems she experienced, or at least exercised, power more directly than I've ever had the opportunity to. I wish she were here to tell me more about that. I referred to it in a Relief Society lesson I was teaching once, and was called into the bishop's office directly after. I shouldn't have been surprised because I saw his wife march out the door and down the hall before "Amen" even got to the N.

But during my childhood, that stoic grandma spent most of her time in the kitchen, cooking three meals a day for working men, which amounted to full time, and she probably spent as much of that time biting her tongue as rolling out dough. She just didn't need to talk much, so my views weren't inherited from her.

Her husband, my grandfather with all the opinions, is probably a bigger factor. He weighed every word for its shock value, deftly loading his arguments with spiky weapons tailored to their intended audience. A conversation with him always teetered on the line between acceptable and cover-the-kids'-ears. He was an armchair philosopher who never had a good thing to say about the church, until he did an abrupt about-face at the end of his life and began showering us with a testimony I didn't know what to do with. By then, I loved the man I'd spent a lifetime tiptoeing around more than the new, softer version I didn't have time to get to know. His railing against the church surely had more impact on me than his last-minute testimony bearing ever could. I wonder if he'd wish it were the other way around, but I'm honestly not sure. For a future of religious dissatisfaction, growing up around his farm was a good place to pick up seeds.

Last in this circle of influences we come to my mother, who when she wasn't ill and confined to her bedroom, was a whirlwind of talents, giving her all to anything she was involved with. That includes service. She never waited for anyone to give her an assignment, believed in doing every job 110 percent, and also in never putting off until tomorrow anything you could possibly do today. The bounce between these two places—incapacitating mental illness and soaring accomplishment—made her a Ping-Pong ball in my childhood that could be hard to cozy up to. One thing remained constant though: her devotion to the church, and that she seemed completely unbothered by anything in it that might be described as patriarchy.

My mother feels tremendous respect for, and deference to, the priesthood. Also to the very real mantle she perceives to accompany its various offices and callings. It's not that her experiences have all been good. In fact, she's bumped up against the patriarchy as often as any Latter-day Saint woman—probably more than I have—as an employee of the church for many years, and a General Board member before that. Yet any man at the dinner table will always outrank the women when it comes time to call on someone to bless the food. It's just the way she sees the world and her place in it, but it's an idea that, even having grown up in her house, doesn't naturally occur to me. I'm as likely to call on someone or do it myself without thinking as I am to look to my husband.

When I think about influences, I should probably also consider my own three daughters. Raising girls in the church meant continually deconstructing the cultural messages they were receiving. I attempted to reframe those messages in a way I hoped would empower them to feel they could order off life's full menu. I didn't have any boys, or perhaps I would have found more value in things like scouting, more significance in things like priesthood advancement. As it was, I was mostly interested in communicating the message that despite what they saw and heard clearly each Sunday, it wasn't quite as bad as all that. Women were valued equally. Never mind that the Scouts were canoeing the Boundary Waters every summer while the Young Women were measuring the length of their shorts and swimming in tees at a dreary old Boy Scouts camp.

But I've never been very good at lying to my daughters. They claim my voice goes up a bit when I'm not being completely truthful, trying to convince them of anything I don't quite believe myself. I wonder sometimes whether I didn't go through their childhood speaking about their limitless potential as Mormon women with my voice pitched a bit too high.

No matter how your mom spins it, there is plenty to notice if you're paying attention while growing up a girl in a man's church. You might notice from a very young age that there are only men sitting on the stand, only men speaking, and only men praying, for instance. That if you ever get a chance to dance, it will only be because you're standing on someone else's wingtips. Some of this has changed now, of course, but I lived plenty of my life looking at and listening to men conducting all the meetings and speaking at them too.

Even with women sharing an equal part of the program in sacrament meeting, conferences still skew heavily toward men's voices, and the fact that women around the world celebrated finally hearing a woman pray in general conference speaks volumes.[8] We're willing to herald baby steps as real progress. I think that says more about the repression than about the progress. And our leaders seem to want credit for really doing Something Progressive with these kinds of changes. Shouldn't we all be a bit embarrassed by them? What's taken us so long? God was willing to put Eve in charge of a big part of getting the whole plan rolling to begin with, but in a spectacular power grab, Adam somehow managed to take control of everything that came next, and women have been punished for having stepped into the spotlight first ever since. No one ever had to explain this to me in words—the story continues to tell itself. Men have all the moves, but somehow expect the women to feel special.

You might also notice, as a young girl, that boys prepare and pass the sacrament. That boys go on better adventure trips than girls do. That boys step into the priesthood while they're still busy shooting spit wads at the other sixth or seventh graders and can hardly keep their pants long enough for two Sundays in a row. Not that there's anything wrong with giving young men responsibility, it surely can't hurt to encourage them to step up during a vulnerable time. But what about the other half of the room? Because believe me, they're watching, and they're getting the message.

While the boys are growing up and figuring out what they want to do with their lives, the girls are growing up and waiting to get married. I know, this is getting much better than it was when I was a kid, but it hasn't changed at the rate it should. So many girls are still taking the card they're handed in Young Women and sticking it in their lives as a placeholder where their Real Job will be. Then they go off to school, ready to surrender their dreams whenever they're asked to do so. There's no coercion involved, of course, but if you've ever been a young LDS woman, you know that your grandmother is going to start wondering loudly at family gatherings where the husband and children are, if you get much past about twenty-three years old. Again, change isn't coming fast enough.

If you receive a calling at church, it will be from a man. You can explain to him about your children or your exhaustion or a need for adult conversation that is a hole so deep, no amount of Sunday interaction could ever begin to fill it so you're hoping to bask in every second of Relief Society you can get. Yet he'll (after listening politely) still call you to serve in the Nursery. And there's very little you can do to refute revelation that comes from your bishop. You can turn it down, of course, but it isn't comfortable and it isn't appreciated. Many church members will tell you, "We don't turn down callings." Though some of us do, you will have heard that message enough times to shift in your seat uncomfortably while you do it.

I once had a stake president ask me how many children I had, and when I said I had my hands full (with three), he responded, "Your hands could be more full." So I smiled and tried again, adding, "Trust me, I've been amply blessed." And he said, "You could be more blessed." It didn't feel like an invitation to explain my lifelong struggle with anxiety and depression. Or how being a stay-at-home mom was something I was committed to but was also the hardest thing I'd ever done in my life. How I felt I deserved a real award of some kind every time Friday came around and I'd survived another string of identical weekdays in the lonely world of young motherhood, buried under a pile of limp snow-suits and damp mittens in the depth of a Midwest winter and before the invention of the internet. He obviously wasn't listening, so I just shoved his advice in my pocket with my newly signed temple recommend.

Then I applied the tight-lipped smile I've learned to always carry with me as a woman at church, in case I need to cover my gritted teeth.

I won't indulge in a catalog of individual offenses by my lifetime of priesthood leaders—we all have them, and the only reason to keep them around is as a reminder that we survived and hopefully learned to love anyway. But I offer that one to show that the power differential is real, and in such a conversation there's no way for the woman to come out on top.

Any time you have two groups of people and you put one in charge of the other in some way, you've set up a precarious existence for those on the bottom. A particularly bad mix of personalities or circumstances can inflict spiritual wounds with lasting scars. My stake president had personal opinions about my life and choices, felt entitled to offer them, and ranked higher on the official revelation totem pole than I ever could. In fact, many members (men and women) would probably encourage me to doubt what I knew to be right for myself before I doubted his direction. Why did he choose to open our interaction this way, other than to remind me of my place? I'll never know. But three decades later, it continues in my memory as a prime example of patriarchal abuse of power. As a young mother, I needed nothing more than encouragement, and I thought my responses might have made that clear. Instead, I was weighed and found wanting. Needless to say, he did not have the same conversation when he interviewed my husband.

So perhaps it's fair to say I hate the patriarchy. I'd like to clarify that I hate it wherever I see it: in government, in education, in history, in society at large. As an artist, I hate the fact that work by women makes up only about 13 percent of the art in major museums. I hated, when we lived in the American South, that men treated me as if I didn't know enough about automobiles to purchase my own car wash token. The church is not so much the inventor of patriarchy as it is another product of it. And yet it seems if we claim to have Truth—and we do—we would cast off things that are blatantly harmful.

But here's something that's surprising: it's possible to hate the patriarchy and love priesthood. Even if men are the only ones in the room that have it—the kind that allows you to run wards, sign recommends, and conduct meetings, anyway.

I have had experiences with blessings at the hands of priesthood holders that fed my spirit in a way nothing else has. I have felt known and loved, been comforted and strengthened. I have felt blessed, in real ways and in my times of most dire need. There is a specific weight to the feeling of a man's hands on my head that seems to automatically impart a connection to something bigger I don't know how to access any other way. It's as if a conduit is opened, and I am no longer alone. Whether that is the power of priesthood or something else, I cannot know.

I imagine I would feel something equally powerful under the weight of my sisters' hands. Perhaps I would feel something so miraculous and new, so ancient and true, it would change everything forever. A glimpse of what I've always believed but held silent in my heart. But because I have only experienced these peculiar and most personal messages of God's love via priesthood blessing, I feel a measure of genuine gratitude and respect for the messengers by whose hands they have been delivered. And those hands have belonged to men.

I remember sitting next to my dad on the bench during sacrament meeting as a small girl. I remember the subtle plaid of his suit, the smell of his aftershave, the unexpected fanciness of his cufflinks. I can still conjure the comforting weight of his jacket when I was cold. I felt nothing but awe and respect and love for the goodness of him, equally willing to tie a knotted mouse from his handkerchief and make it jump up his arm to entertain me as to sit on the stand and take charge of the meeting. I never felt he put one kind of responsibility above the other. I have a hard time reconciling my feelings for that beloved Mormon man, and the many others with whom I've lived my life inextricably connected, and the patriarchy they've received by birthright, whether they're willingly complicit in its injustices or not.

I will be the first to admit, I have loved the patriarchs. I will also allow that dancing goes more smoothly when someone leads. Still, the relationship between these steps and this music may simply be too complicated to ever fully reconcile, too intricate to ever perform with grace.

So to my daughter, I will concede that I do hate the patriarchy, so far as it has been weaponized and used against me, against her, and all of our sisters around the world. In the church, in societal institutions, and in many of our personal lives and families, patriarchy continues to keep us neatly under its thumb in subtle and not-so-subtle ways. I have never not noticed it, never known a single moment where I couldn't feel its weight pressing against me in some way. It is so pervasive, its influence such a given, I can't quite imagine life without it. Still, I dream of equality—for my daughters? or will it be their daughters?—in the church and out of it. Someday we will surely do more than just dream of dancing on our own feet. We will insist on it.

TO ORDAIN OR NOT TO ORDAIN?
THAT ISN'T THE ONLY QUESTION

"Women belong in all places where decisions are being made."
—Ruth Bader Ginsberg[9]

Cynthia:

I was in a Zoom meeting with mostly strangers, made up of everyday people who had signed up simply to learn better ways to navigate differences—respectfully—around various polarizing topics. At one point, one woman asked another woman how her faith or religious beliefs played into her perspective around the topic we were discussing. The woman being asked about her faith declined to answer. She said that her answer would say things about her that she didn't want to be assumed by the audience. I felt for her. In that moment I thought about what others could assume about me if they knew I was a Latter-day Saint. Would they assume they knew my political leanings? Would they assume I was a woman who is happy with an all-male clergy? I hoped that others would see me as an individual first, and as Latter-day Saint second. I don't assume a Catholic woman supports her church's stance on male-only clergy, so I hope others would give me that same courtesy.

When it comes to priesthood ordination, maybe the first question we need to consider is: do women need to be ordained? Do we need ordination to be equal partners in the organization? As it currently stands, yes. But does it have to be this way? Not necessarily. Policies could be rewritten to get us closer to parity, such as allowing women to serve on high councils or as bishopric counselors, since neither of those callings require priesthood keys. (More on priesthood keys in a minute!)

I care deeply about our lack of female clergy while at the same time I couldn't care less about priesthood ordination. Like Ruth Bader

Ginsburg, I believe that "women belong in all places where decisions are being made." So if a decision at church will affect my life, I want women in the "room where it happens." But not just in the room—women deserve to have decision-making power. As our structure currently stands, that is not the case. Ever. There is not one single decision a woman can make in this church that cannot be overruled by a man. In my opinion, and in my lived experience, that's a problem. So for a woman to have decision-making power within the current structure, ordination *is* required.

There's much to be said about the need for priesthood ordination for a woman in her personal and family life as well. But for the purposes of this conversation, we will focus on priesthood ordination within the context of the walls of our churches. My goodness, notice how the ordination topic quickly sends out tentacles that touch every facet of a woman's life? Yeah, it's complicated!

Ordination is *the* key card. We have to swipe it for entrance into certain rooms and access to certain callings, like bishop. Personally, I would love to have a female bishop and I see no reason why this shouldn't be already happening in the Roaring 2020s. But within our current structure, bishop is an office of the priesthood so the key card of ordination is necessary to open that door for women.

We have had a female vice president of the United States. We have female CEOs, soldiers, and firefighters—all jobs once limited to men. I don't think I realized how hungry I had been for female clergy until I visited my local Episcopal church where I saw women officiate in their sacred ordinances, like the sacrament. If seeing that gives me a pang deep in my heart, clearly I want this for women in my own faith tradition.

I realize by now plenty of you might be thinking, has she forgotten the R word—Revelation? As a lifelong member of the church, trust me, I completely understand that prophetic revelation is the means by which things change in our church. I also believe that good information leads to good inspiration and revelation. Utah State University professor Patrick Mason said in an interview, "People have already started to do the work to sketch out a theological rationale that would allow for the kind of revelation that allows for women's ordination ... with the passage of time, what was once possible then becomes probable."[10]

That's what we are trying to do in this discussion—sketch out the *possibility* which may lead to the *probability* someday.

Susan:

I listened to a podcast where Richard Rohr talked about why much of his work has been aimed at helping men find an access point to the spiritual journey. He explained:

> Here was the assumption that cultures came to, and at this point in history, I don't think it needs much proof: that unless the male was led on journeys of powerlessness, he would always abuse power. I know that seems damning, but the male can't handle power unless he has somehow touched on vulnerability/powerlessness.[11]

In response to Rohr's observation, I've wondered: Is there any place in the journey to adulthood for the Latter-day Saint male when he is made to touch on his own vulnerability or powerlessness? Many girls grow up wondering, "Will someone ask me to marry him? Will I be sealed to a worthy priesthood holder? Will I bear the children I am meant to bear and thereby live up to my divine, eternal potential?" But by bestowing the priesthood upon our males at age 11—literally gifting boys with special power as our cultural rite of passage—do we completely deprive them of ever knowing or understanding powerlessness within our culture? And if so, could there be any hope that patriarchy and/or priesthood would not exercise at least some degree of unrighteous dominion in the church? It is clear to me that when you put one group of people over another, you set up a dynamic that is bound to be problematic. That's Humans 101.

To me, that suggests that at least on the surface, ordination would be essential to women experiencing real equality in our church. But this question of women "needing" priesthood is steeped in muddy water for a few reasons. First, let's acknowledge recent progress—some callings that used to be solely men's responsibilities are now deemed appropriate for women. We know policy fluctuates over time, and has across the whole history of religion. Think of women named as priestesses or apostles in the Bible, for instance. There are female Rabbis now but it was not always so, and there's female ordination now in some Christian denominations but not in others.

My own grandmother told me of administering to women before childbirth as a Relief Society president. There have been times when women have assumed more responsibility around sacrament preparation. Women in the temple exercise priesthood authority in performing initiatory ordinances. So there's obviously some latitude in what can be done, not just in other churches but in ours too. As you said, we believe in continuing revelation and/or restoration. The idea that none of this can change, or that we already fully understand God's ultimate *plan* for women—even on this earth—flies right in the face of our history and our stated position of being open to further light and knowledge on all things at all times.

Of course, our leaders have to be willing to ask questions in order to receive answers. And I'll admit I'm distrustful of any system in which the main message I'm getting as a member is, "It's not okay for you to ask about that," or maybe even worse as a woman, "don't worry your pretty head about it." I don't know any faster track for a woman to become a pariah in our church than making noise about wanting ordination, do you?

Second, I think our leaders have blurred the lines and continue to do so. Elder Dallin H. Oaks comes to mind, especially this quote he left us from his 2014 general conference talk:

> We are not accustomed to speaking of women having the authority of the priesthood in their Church callings, but what other authority can it be? When a woman—young or old—is set apart to preach the gospel as a full-time missionary, she is given priesthood authority to perform a priesthood function. The same is true when a woman is set apart to function as an officer or teacher in a Church organization under the direction of one who holds the keys of the priesthood. Whoever functions in an office or calling received from one who holds priesthood keys exercises priesthood authority in performing her or his assigned duties.[12]

When I taught a Relief Society lesson based on this talk, I came up with what I thought was a good metaphor. The lesson happened to coincide with getting my first car with keyless ignition, one of my favorite technological advances ever! Keys are the bane of my existence—my tendency to obsess manifests in a ridiculous amount of checking to make sure I have them. Being freed from worry about keys actually improved my life. A keyless ignition means as long as the key is in the car, I can drive it. It can be in my purse or in a pocket—mine or someone else's; either way, I need only press the start button. I never have to touch a key let alone hold one in my hand. Doesn't that quote describe exactly the same relationship? When it comes to callings that require keys, shouldn't the keys being in a pocket some-where up the organizational ladder enable a woman who is set apart to do any calling that functions under the authority of that key? We should be able to drive the car.

What sounded clear on the surface turns out to feel more like mud when you dig down a bit, right? I'm also thinking of the social media kerfuffle in March 2024 when one of the general women's leaders pos-ited that women have more authority in our church than any other.[13] Thousands of women responded in the comment thread that 'author-ity' is not how they would describe their experience in the church. No social media post from a church leader had received that type of reaction before.

Frankly, I'm confused about how the terms 'priesthood power' and 'priesthood authority' are used these days in our narratives about women. It feels increasingly like trying to tell the story both ways—women don't have the priesthood, but they do operate with priesthood authority when they're serving in some callings, etc. Women don't have the priesthood, but they're entitled to every blessing of it. Huh? As a Latter-day Saint woman, I need our language around this to be more precise, to actually *mean* something specific rather than just sound like a verbal pat on my head.

Is it really that there are just some keys women are not allowed to have? Is that all we're talking about? If so, let's say it. Because I think of the priesthood as being the vehicle for divine power on the earth. Yet I don't feel I have less access to God's power than men do. For instance, I've never heard that *my* faith can move mountains, but *a man's* faith can move bigger ones.

Chieko Okazaki described it like this:

> Priesthood seems to have three forms in which it impacts our lives. First, it is an eternal principle, separate from any earthly function or individual; second, it is the organizational structure and ordering principle of Church government. And third, it is a personal power conferred upon worthy men which they can use to bless the lives of others, not only through formal callings but also as followers of the Savior.[14]

I know I don't have organizational power, but the way she lays it out makes it clear I also don't have the "personal power conferred upon worthy men" she's speaking about. I guess I don't see myself in any of

Chieko's three definitions, unless the "eternal principle" she describes is the power to which the endowment entitles me. See? Muddy water.

And if this is only about keys, let's open every calling that doesn't require any to women as well as men. We could do that starting next Sunday! I'm guessing a lot of members assume priesthood keys are required for more callings than is actually the case. The fact that we've been hampered by tradition and probably inertia—very resistant to change organizationally and culturally for most of my lifetime—makes me think there's probably more that can be done. Would a willingness to talk about it openly and more precisely help us see where and how changes could be made?

Cynthia:

It was such a gut punch to me the first time you said that—that the church could, if they wanted to, open every calling to women not requiring priesthood keys by this Sunday. It forced me to really sit with the idea that maybe the church leaders don't want to move us, even optically, toward parity and equality. I don't like making assumptions about the intent of others; however, now that we've seen a small handful of callings and responsibilities expanded to women in recent years, such as stake auditors and witnessing baptisms and sealings, I can only believe they are completely aware that a large number of callings and responsibilities do not require ordination (See What Women Don't Get for a full list of callings women could have *today or by Sunday*).

Were our male leaders persuaded by women leaders to make those changes? Was it just logical to have women be witnesses for sealings and baptisms because more women attend the temple than men? Either way, I want more changes for women, but especially for our young women and girls growing up in a society where church is the most sexist organization they belong to. I hope our leaders are aware that studies show that girls greatly benefit from having female clergy. Jana Riess has written:

> Research has determined that having women clergy makes a significant impact on the lives of girls. Girls who had direct examples of clergywomen in childhood grow up with higher self-esteem, better employment, and more education than girls who did not.[15]

I am sure it sounds like I am cheering big time for women's ordination. Before I answer that, let me explain a bit more where I am coming from. I once asked my husband if he thought he had something I didn't. He took a long pause and said, "I know I have the *right to do* certain things." He has authorization to do certain things within the current church organization—from passing the sacrament as a little boy to baptizing our children as an adult—but in essence, no, he didn't feel like he had some extra portion of God's power that I do not have. I'm veering off into my personal feelings about priesthood as access to God's power, and we did say we would focus on the organization. But my personal feeling about having access to God's power does affect my organizational views about ordination.

When I hear fellow Latter-day Saint women say they don't want the priesthood, I wonder: is it because, like me, they don't feel like they have less access to God's power in their life? However, would these same women want to see more callings and responsibilities available to them and to girls? Across all religions, over 75 percent of all men and women think women have too little influence in religious organizations.[16]

There are also men who are finally saying out loud that they too don't want ordination.[17] They just want to be fellow disciples of Christ. That's a tricky desire for Latter-day Saint boys and men because it essentially cuts them off from any participation in the church. After all, even eleven-year-old boys require ordination to participate in baptisms for the dead in our temples. Baptism isn't even an ordinance that requires ordination! Yet we force little boys and men toward ordination while banning the option for all girls and women. Will there ever be room for any and all Latter-day Saints to move forward with their participation in the church in ways that speak to their personality, temperament, and desires?

Susan:

I'm thinking about your husband describing it as having "a right to do certain things." One group having rights that another does not is something I can't put any kind of peaceful spin on for myself. It's a description of an inequitable system that is at its heart oppressive. I don't like the word 'rights,' because of those implications, and it's not fixed if I say 'entitlement.' Power? Same problem as rights for me, especially since I'm in the group without any. Responsibility? Maybe, but that makes it sound purely organizational while priesthood is that but also much more. I wish women felt free to throw our creative muscle behind this question—to really let our minds wander in search of answers that move us forward. As it stands, we can't talk about it at all, except for whispered conversations in the hall or parking lot with our most trusted friends.

How I wish the men who do have power to effect change were interested. If our leaders are actively asking, pondering, and seeking on the question of women's relationship to priesthood, we're not hearing about it. I don't mean to assume they're not, but also … why would they be? Power generally protects itself, doesn't it? I think that's also in the Humans 101 syllabus somewhere.

Something I'd never thought of until you suggested it is that there are men who don't necessarily want the priesthood. Here's another place we might benefit from changing the way we talk about this, because giving 'rights' to everyone within a specific subset—in this case men—while denying it to those outside the group just highlights the oppressiveness of the system. It might feel less so to me, however, if only men who wanted ordination pursued it. Those men would need to do something extra, besides just being born male, to gain a privilege others in the group don't have. This might move us one tiny notch closer to a path for female ordination.

Someone reading this might think I'm agitating for ordination when, like you, I don't care one whit about having the priesthood—or not having it—myself. What I do care about is equality of voice, influence, and representation for women within the organization, and I will argue that's impossible to achieve within the status quo. What keeps me up at night is what is mentioned above: I have granddaughters, and their experience of the world and their place in it is completely different from what they experience at church. I don't think that disparity is tenable.

Maybe it's a function of my age and the fact that my church experience was, for much of my life, closer to mirroring my life experience than it is for today's youth, but it never occurred to me to care about being ordained—I've spent exactly zero seconds of my life wishing I had the priesthood. I worked at a bank when I was young and had a boss (a woman, incidentally) explain to me, when I asked, why the brand-new male employee I was training was being paid more than I was. She said, "He'll be expected to support a family. You won't." I'm pretty sure I wouldn't get that answer in the same situation today; it made me angry enough at the time that I quit the job, but her reasoning wasn't unexpected. It matched so much of what I heard and experienced in the world around me.

But I've spent a lot of seconds of my life wishing I weren't marginalized in my church. I saw a graphic after a recent general conference with pictures of all the men who spoke on one side, and all the women on the other. There were thirty-five pictures of men, and four of women. I was floored when I realized that four meant we'd heard *double* the number of women's talks in that conference versus the previous few. Twice as many women's voices? I felt like it ought to be a cause for celebration. But I couldn't muster any enthusiasm at all, because visually it was nothing but demoralizing to me. I wouldn't have been surprised to see that graphic tacked up on the break room wall at the bank ca. 1979, but I couldn't believe I was being asked to accept it without complaint in today's social media feed.

I believe that as long as women are not ordained, our work in the church is not going to be valued at the same levels that men's work is. Our voices are not going to be listened to. Our ideas are not going to be privileged. No matter how much faith we might have, without the priesthood, some mountains in this church will never move for women.

Cynthia:

I'm with you, Susan! I have spent zero seconds pining for priesthood ordination, but I have spent a lot of time wishing I could have a female bishop. Or to have had a woman interview my teenage daughters for their temple recommends. Or have a woman place her hands on my head and bless me. Or to have had a woman be the one to give me my patriarchal blessing. (I guess that would make it a matriarchal blessing!)

For those dreams to have been reality, ordination would have to be an option for women, unless church leaders are willing to completely reimagine and thoroughly overhaul the organizational structure. In an ideal world, so many systems of government would start over from scratch with the underlying goal of egalitarianism. Writer and poet Kathryn Knight Sonntag once said on our podcast that we can't just plug women into patriarchy.[18] I agree. The current structure seems problematic. But I'm willing to accept that we don't live in a perfect world where power structures are remade from the ground up. I don't think any gender *needs* ordination, but as long as we're playing by the current organizational rules of the current structure, ordination needs to be an option for women.

Personally, I'm not sitting around waiting for the boys to invite me to be a member of their club. I picture a proverbial Ordination Clubhouse, high up in the trees, slapped together with uneven boards, sunflower seeds spit on the floor, smelling like dirty socks. That just doesn't look enticing. However, women belong in all places where decisions are being made, even less-than-ideal clubhouses.

We like to talk about an Imagination Committee that could think up new ways to do old things. I think part of an overhaul to the organization would be to require some type of theological and pastoral training to qualify men—and women—for ordination. A friend once told me that her dad, a real estate attorney, was called to be a bishop. The night he was set apart, he received a call from a family in the ward. Their daughter was suicidal so they asked the brand-new bishop to please come help. How was a real estate attorney with zero pastoral training supposed to help this family? Currently, the only requirement to serve as clergy in any ward is the male gender. I want qualified clergy—male or female—to be well trained in pastoral care, with background checks, to lead and serve our congregations.

Susan:

I've thought a lot about the assertion that you can't plug women into the patriarchy. I guess that's what the church has tried to do. We see women sitting on the stand at general conferences now, but if the church were ever to equalize the numbers and positions of men and women in the organizational structure, it would no longer be patriarchy, would it?

It's women who most often end up with the children in a ward, but why? Nursery and Primary callings felt crushing to me as a young mother looking for any break from my daily grind. Decades ago in a suburban Chicago ward, our Primary was entirely staffed with men. The president and her two counselors were women, but everyone else from the secretary on down was a man. My husband taught the five-year-olds and still describes it as his favorite calling. The children in that Primary room saw big men in small chairs, heard male voices singing children's songs, and never realized their brains were being imprinted with a different model of callings in our church—a blurring of which jobs belong to men and which to women—than they'd probably ever experience again. Why is that ward still the outlier among all the wards I've ever lived in? Why was that bishop the only one thinking outside the box?

Within the Relief Society, the women don't choose who leads. Not even the music. There's nothing I can think of that shows it more clearly: women are not in charge of even basic, pragmatic decisions at church. If we were, I feel sure our ward organizations would look different.

In fact, my cynical side can't help but notice that over time, male leadership managed to take over the church's women's organization. It was subsumed by the patriarchal org chart! I guess there was only so much autonomy women could be allowed within a patriarchal system. Anyone or anything that can't be plugged into the patriarchy can't exist in our church. It goes beyond a glass ceiling—the supervision of women is ongoing and absolute, and true equality cannot exist. So as was said, we'd probably have to knock it all down and reimagine it from the ground up. But why is that impossible? I don't think we should regard anything as impossible in a 'living church.' It's getting harder to define specific roles by gender; the world's old ideas about gender roles are not holding up in people's lived experiences. If we can't pin those roles down and make them stay put on earth, how could I believe we have a full understanding of gender in any kind of eternal context? The one thing I do know is that gender—and by extension in our church, priesthood—is all substantially less clear-cut than we continue to insist it must be.

Cynthia:

I will never forget when I realized that Relief Society is a man's organization for women. I was sitting in Relief Society, listening to the opening announcements, when the bishop hurried in for two minutes to extend some callings and ask us sisters to sustain those women to their new Relief Society positions. Due to handbook policy changes, until that day I had never seen women sustained in new callings in Relief Society instead of sacrament meeting. The optics of a man issuing a calling in an all-women's meeting stunned me. I immediately texted you, "Why couldn't the RS president herself have said the names of the new women called and asked for a sustaining vote? Where's the priesthood in that, in reading off women's names in a women's meeting?"

Women don't even get to choose who leads the music in a women's-only meeting. A Relief Society president can suggest the name of a woman to the bishop, but ultimately it is his decision to call that requested person as the chorister, or someone else. And maybe that's why a man has to show up to an all-women's meeting to issue callings—so we all know *he* and not *she* is in charge. I've never seen the Relief Society the same since that day. He staffs the organization. And so often women who supposedly are the presidents of organizations are left scratching their head at who the bishop chooses to call!

Personally, I love all the talk around gender in our society right now. How much is biology? How much is God-ordained? How much of what we think is God-ordained is just socialization? Like the title of this essay says, ordination isn't the only question, because like any organization, we've been affected by—and continue to be affected by—our sociology, biology, religiosity, anthropology, culture, and history. All those factors have led The Church of Jesus Christ of Latter-day Saints to where it is today. Like you said, pinning down rigid gender roles isn't working anywhere else in society. I'm eagerly watching to see how this all unfolds. Pass the popcorn.

FOR THE MEN IN THE ROOM

"But I ask no favors for my sex. I surrender not our claim to equality. All I ask of our brethren is, that they will take their feet from off our necks and permit us to stand upright on that ground which God designed us to occupy."
—Sarah Grimké[19]

Cynthia:

On our very first episode of *At Last She Said It*, we boldly proclaimed, "We are not interested in explaining ourselves to men!" But we never expected to have as many male listeners as we do, and we certainly never anticipated how many women would write to tell us that our podcast was helping them facilitate conversations with the men in their lives—their husbands, bishops, fathers, and sons. Facilitating conversations was always a big goal of the podcast, so occasionally we have tried to paint a picture for Latter-day Saint men about what it means to be a woman in a patriarchal church. And yes, I didn't get past the first paragraph of this essay before using one of the big p-words: patriarchy. If that's a tough word, I get it, set it aside and we can come back to it in a bit.

During the COVID lockdown, I watched a fireside on Zoom with Patrick Mason. Right up front, he gave a disclaimer. He said that the church was made for people like him: white, male, straight, American. I appreciated that he wanted his audience to know that the church structure is probably easier on his life than mine. Sometimes I think that's half the problem—that men do not realize their privilege in this church. Oops, second paragraph and I dropped *another* loaded p-word: privilege. Deep breaths, it will be okay.

I realize that the men in my life, who are just everyday men (no general authorities or apostles in my family tree), can't change much structurally in the church. But a better understanding of my experience as a woman could create empathy. I believe that's what Mason was trying to do in that fireside with his disclaimer. He modeled empathy by showing his audience that he had gotten curious about the churchy experiences of others and had determined that in many cases, his experiences were probably easier.

On the podcast we like to do what we call 'flipping the script.'[20] It's a pretty good framework for increasing understanding and building empathy. For example, a simple flip could be a typical Sunday at church: you walk into sacrament meeting and imagine all women on the stand to preside. A woman would conduct the meeting and make the announcements, issue any new callings, announce the meeting's agenda, etc. Imagine seeing young women bless the sacrament, and even younger girls passing it. Those young women would also make sure the presiding woman is given the sacrament first, emphasizing to the audience the matriarchal hierarchy. Imagine the visiting high councilor, a woman, is visiting your ward that day and extending stake callings. Later in this meeting, she will speak to your ward. She'll bring a companion speaker with her, and if she chooses to bring another woman that day, that will ensure that the meeting has an all-female lineup. Zero men will have participated. On some Sundays, you might also see a group of women bless the babies and confirm the children who have just been baptized. And this is all in just *one* meeting!

Men, how would imagining such a flipped script affect you? I can tell you as a woman what happens when I envision such a meeting: my eyes fill with tears and I wonder how my entire life could have been different had I regularly seen women lead one of our most sacred and systematic meetings. There are so many more examples where flipping the script could increase curiosity and empathy among men about women's church experiences: ward councils, membership councils, temple recommend interviews for teenage girls and women, etc. Would we all be less likely to see men as leaders if we never saw them lead? Would men feel equal if the tables were turned? And if women saw women lead, would we be more likely to see women as leaders?

Several years ago, my husband Paul was the stake clerk and would have to attend disciplinary councils (now called membership councils). As he left for the meeting, I would say, "Please just tell me if its for a woman, because if it is, I will pray for her all evening as I can't imagine being judged by a roomful of men." I needed to express my pain out loud for my husband, but I also wanted him to be curious and just a little bit embarrassed about policies and practices that can hurt women.

I also often say to him as he heads to all-male meetings, "Please keep this question in mind: Where are the women?" Paul is quiet by nature so I knew that Level One of this question would just be for his own awareness. But I hoped in time that he would begin to voice this question out loud to the men in the room,

"Where are the women?"

Can LDS Men acknowledge the Church is a patriarchy?

It might be uncomfortable, but let's talk about patriarchy! Yay! We should be soft on people and tough on systems. We're going to be tough on the *system* of patriarchy throughout this book, but that in no way should be interpreted as anti-men. I shouldn't have to say this, but I am just as much invested in the physical, spiritual, and emotional well-being of my son, grandson, and husband as I am in my daughters' well-being.

Patriarchy is a system of society or government in which men hold the power and women are largely excluded from it. But 'patriarchy' doesn't equal 'men' and talking about it shouldn't be seen as being anti-men. We mainly talk about the effects of patriarchy on women, but anyone can be hurt by patriarchy—women, children, and men as well. In fact, we hope more men will speak up about its effects on them. Many times over the years, we have been contacted by men who ask if we are aware of a podcast like ours, but for men. At Last He Said It!? Great ring!

Patriarchy is the water in which we *all* swim—a system where men make the rules, and also the culture that results from existing in such a system. Whether one agrees or disagrees that our current method of church governance is God-ordained, there's no argument to be had about what it literally is. The Church of Jesus Christ of Latter-day Saints is, by definition, a patriarchy.

Speaking of systems, it's worth noting that the problems of patriarchy are not unique to the church, as this is a worldwide system thousands of years old. There's a reason the *Barbie* movie, which tackled larger societal problems of patriarchy with campy humor, was the number one movie in the United States in 2023, grossing more than 600 million dollars. To be fair, I am not sure all those movie watchers who contributed to that 600+ million dollars knew that *Barbie* was a commentary on patriarchy. I sat in the theater with a girlfriend laughing hysterically the entire time while all the rest of the theater, albeit in conservative Provo, Utah, was completely silent. An exposé on patriarchy is definitely not PG—Provo Grin and bear it! We are all feeling the effects of patriarchy in America (and elsewhere) and finally we are willing to talk—*at last*—about those effects: in our country, government, businesses, churches, and movies too.

Susan talks about her experiences living in an area of the United States where misogyny was much more prevalent in the culture than anywhere else she had lived, and was a huge culture shock to her and her family. So it made sense that it was also deeply ingrained and problematic at church. It was blatant but also subtly different from plain-ol'-structural patriarchy. Seeing this difference helped her better identify what is misogynistic behavior and what is structural patriarchy. Sometimes people just behave badly—generally, that has not been our experience with the men we have dealt with in the church. But having the opportunity to experience that helped her more fully appreciate that there's a difference. Bad behavior is one thing, structural patriarchy is another. And we're talking about the latter.

Getting back to 'flipping the script,' our question for men is this: If roles were reversed and women were The Decision Makers at church, would that bother you? Susan even asked her husband once, during a general conference weekend, "If it were ten hours on a weekend of women speaking to you, would you stay home all weekend and tune in to watch that?" And he said, "Uh, no." She appreciated his honesty because she knew the answer to the question when she asked it, but it had never occurred to her that members are asked to tune in and listen to messages given by approximately 90 percent men. This is the reality that women have always been subject to in the church—to listen to scriptural interpretations, advice, and perspectives almost exclusively from men. Church leaders insist that men and women are equals, but would men feel equal if, year after year, decade after decade, 90 percent of general conference talks were by women?[21]

Can LDS men start seeing the pedestal?

One of the ways we continue to get away with the idea that women are equal to men in the church organization is due to the patronizing pedestal on which women are placed. The pedestal is a distraction because it obscures a lack of equality in favor of rhetoric that placates members of the church. Instead of giving women equal responsibility, we give them praise. Instead of decision-making power, we give them a crown.

Remember at the end of *The Wizard of Oz* when the dog Toto pulls back the curtain and reveals that the real Oz is just a man, and not the powerful superhuman projected in front of the curtain? That's what the pedestal does to women. We project women as angelic and spiritually magnificent, distracting all into thinking we're superhuman. In reality, we are just regular people like Oz who deserve to serve alongside our brothers in the church, at every table where decisions are made.

In fact, it's a common trope to say that women are inherently *more* spiritual and *more* 'in tune' than men. That raises the patronizing pedestal even higher! If that were true, it would mean God has entrusted their power on earth to a group of people—men—who aren't quite so naturally attuned to spiritual things. Are we seriously okay with that? We're fond of saying that "God qualifies whom He calls," and sadly, there is a belief that persists in our culture that men need the priesthood to be able to 'step up' and be equal to women. That's another way we raise women higher on the pedestal while simultaneously denigrating men. But why wouldn't God choose the people to lead who are already more qualified? Interesting thought exercise, don't you think?

We can all think of women and men in our lives that defy all kinds of gendered stereotypes. What's interesting about this pedestal is that it pacifies women through praise, raising them higher than men, but ironically it doesn't really succeed in denigrating men because it's hard to denigrate a group of people that holds all the power. The pedestal is brilliant as simply a way to preserve current power structures. So far, it has worked in our culture.

Can LDS Men Mourn with Women?

The church announced in 2021 that in Europe women had been called as Area Organization Advisors for the Relief Society and Young Women organizations.[22] What fascinated me was reading the press release from the church announcing the change, and highlighting what our general women leaders had to say about this change. Linda Burton, the Relief Society General President from 2012 to 2017, said: "It is the link that has been missing." Bonnie Cordon, Young Women General President at the time, said: "It truly feels like the missing piece of the puzzle."

What's difficult about their reactions is that we never would have heard these women utter these statements—that it felt like something was *missing*—prior to this change. How long had they thought something was missing? Years? Decades?

Statements like Burton's and Cordon's only come after men *decide* to make a change. Whether that change was suggested to the men leaders by the women leaders, we have no way of knowing. What we do know is that only men can make that kind of change, to call Area Organization Advisors. Can LDS men mourn that with us? That every change ever made for the betterment of women comes because a man thought it was a good idea? Can they sit with us, their sisters in the gospel, and mourn our lack of autonomy and decision-making power?

Getting back to Burton's and Cordon's comments, this is one reason why women who are so hungry for change feel so alone—because no one, not even the women at the top, can talk about any 'missing puzzle pieces.' Susan is fond of saying that there is nothing like having the feeling you can't talk about something to give it the wrong kind of power. It feels as if women are only allowed to talk about change, let alone celebrate change, once the men make that change. We can be happy in hindsight—that's okay. I would personally feel less alone and less crazy, if I knew that women at the top want change too. That's the number one comment we hear from women when they find our podcast. They tell us they now know it wasn't just them—thankfully, they weren't going crazy. They weren't the only ones who knew the emperor didn't, in fact, have any clothes. It should be obvious to women that of course there is no way they're the only ones desiring change, but our culture of silence can surely make someone feel that way.

I am also left wondering in what other ways our general leaders see missing puzzle pieces? It would set an example for all women if they could speak freely about what is and isn't working. It would lessen the repercussions on everyday women in wards and stakes who also feel the need to say 'something is missing.'

We once made a social media post about the church sending surveys to young single adults.[23] They were asked questions like, would you want alternate classes for the second hour, shorter general conferences, a variety of speakers, etc.? The comments on our social media were filled with women and men discussing their excitement at even the thought of change.

But then someone left this comment: "This is Jesus Christ's church, not even President Nelson can change things until the Lord tells him to. Things will change when and if the Lord commands. The testimony we need to gain is that Jesus is at the head of this church. I know he is and I will wait patiently until he decides what to do."

This is what happens when women speak up—others, usually women, are quick to testify as a means to pull outspoken women back into the proverbial crab bucket. (We have more to say on women up-holding patriarchy in another chapter.)

Policing women's speech is the worst kind of policing as it signals to the person wanting the change that they are less faithful and less patient, hence the virtue signaling through public testimony sharing in a social media comment. I can't even imagine the repercussions Burton and Cordon, public figures, would have faced had they made their comments years before the change. It simply isn't done.

Can LDS men be our allies?

So what can the everyday Latter-day Saint man do? Several ideas have already been mentioned: flipping the script and asking where the women are. Here are a few more:

Men, please consult the women in your lives and call out places for improvement.

A male podcast listener and friend of Susan's sent her an email upon hearing us talk about the 2020 church policy that women could now hold the calling of stake auditor. He holds a stake calling in the eastern United States and after hearing that episode, he decided to send an email to his stake president that said, "Here are specific suggestions for changes that I think we can make. And here are suggestions for who we can put in those callings ... Let's release some of the brethren and put the women in. We have an opportunity to do something here." The stake president agreed, and several women auditors were called.

Men, please default to believing women when they tell you their experiences.

And validate those experiences! Don't try to minimize, dismiss, or put a silver-lining on them. Acknowledge the problems that are pointed out to you.

Men, please research women's issues.

Read books, blogs, articles, and listen to podcasts where women's issues—especially those in other patriarchal religions—are highlighted.

Men, please take the time to understand how patriarchy has impacted you.

You may have an ingrained expectation that men are always in charge, or a mistrust of men around children, or a hesitancy to be emotional around other men, or an association of emotions with weakness, or a negative perception of strong women. Pay attention to these kinds of things—you may not even realize you've internalized them.

Men, please don't immediately deflect with the idea that you're 'one of the good ones.'

Again, we're talking about a system, not individuals. There are many good men, and many not so good men. We all do good things, and we all do unhelpful things without even thinking about it, especially when we've not yet recognized the harm in the system.

Men, please boost female voices in the workplace and especially in church meetings.

Be mindful in meetings and conversations, and be really careful about talking over women. When women do speak up, studies show they are often interrupted. When this happens, speak up and ask women to finish their thoughts. In a Brigham Young University Magazine article, entitled *When Women Don't Speak*, research found that it literally requires a supermajority of women in meetings for women to speak their proportionate talking time.[24] Ward councils and stake councils do not have a supermajority of women, so any help is greatly appreciated.

Men, please role model that women are not less-than, in life or at church.

Boys experience girls as being equal peers in other places in their lives. While none of us can fix the optics at church to be reflective of that equality, try to allow women at church to be whole rather than shallow stereotypes. Celebrate their individual accomplishments instead of exalting a predetermined gender role. Treat women like they are of equal worth, and our youth will believe it.

Section Notes

1. Brittany Karford Rogers, "When Women ~~Don't~~ Speak," *Brigham Young University Magazine*, Spring 2020, magazine.byu.edu.

2. Beth Allison Barr, *The Making of Biblical Womanhood: How the Subjugation of Women Became Gospel Truth* (Brazos Press, 2021), 12–13

3. Barr, *Making of Biblical Womanhood*, 186.

4. Jana Riess, "It's Good for Girls to Have Clergywomen, Study Shows," Flunking Sainthood column, *Religion News Service*, July 17, 2018, religionnews.com.

5. Sheri Dew, What Do LDS Women Get?, YouTube, youtube.com.

6. Gregory A. Prince, "There is Always a Struggle: An Interview with Chieko N. Okazaki," *Dialogue: A Journal of Mormon Thought* 45, no. 1 (Spring 2012): 112.

7. Barr, *Making of Biblical Womanhood*, 186.

8. Sister Jean A. Stevens, counselor in the Primary general presidency, gave the historic closing prayer in general conference, April 6, 2013.

9. "Ruth Bader Ginsburg in Pictures and Her Own Words," *BBC*, Sep. 19, 2020, bbc.com.

10. Emily Kaplan, "The Rise of the Liberal Latter-day Saints," *Washington Post Magazine*, September 27, 2021, washingtonpost.com.

11. Krista Tippet, host, *On Being* podcast, episode 738, "Growing Up Men," April 13, 2017, 52 minutes. Guest Richard Rohr.

12. Dallin H. Oaks, "The Keys and Authority of the Priesthood," April 2014 general conference.

13. J. Anette Dennis, "There is no other religious organization in the world that I know of that has so broadly given power and authority to women." Instagram @churchofjesuschrist, March 17, 2024.

14. Chieko N. Okazaki, "Boundaries: The Line of Yes and No," Association of Latter-day Saint Counselors & Psychotherapists (AMCAP) Journal, *Issues in Religion and Psychotherapy* 21, no. 1, Article 2, April 1, 1995.

15. Riess, "It's Good for Girls to Have Clergywomen, Study Shows."

16. Jessica Grose, "Young Women Are Fleeing Organized Religion. This Was Predictable," *New York Times*, June 12, 2024, nytimes.com.

17. Ian Thomson, "The All Male Draft," Sunstone Symposium, Sandy, Utah, July 28–31, 2021.

18. *At Last She Said It* podcast, episode 30, "The Mother Tree," November 10, 2020. Guest Kathryn Knight Sonntag.

19. Seneca Falls and Building a Movement, 1776–1890, Library of Congress, loc.gov, accessed Jan. 16, 2025.

20. The first time I saw an example of 'flipping the script' was when I read 'Dear Mormon Man' by Amy McPhie Allebest. While flipping the script is my phrase, I want readers to know this isn't my original thought. dearmormonman.com.

21. In the October 2023 general conference, there were thirty-three talks, only three by women.

22. Sydney Walker, "Area Organization Advisers: Women Leaders in International Areas to Provide Instruction, Mentoring," *Church News*, March 17, 2021, thechurchnews.com.

23. Jana Riess, "What the LDS Church Wants to Know from Young Adult Mormons," Flunking Sainthood column, *Religion News Service*, March 22, 2021, religionnews.com.

24. Rogers, "When Women ~~Don't~~ Speak."

OUTSIDE THE BOX

IN SEARCH OF A LARGER GOD

*"Our minds are constantly trying to bring God down to our level rather than
letting him lift us into levels of which we were not previously capable."*
—Christian Wiman[1]

Susan:

We should start at the beginning. Perhaps the problem began with Joseph Smith having seen God as a man. I imagine God would probably show up in the form most likely to be understood by the seeker, so I can't help but wonder whether we may have placed too much stock in that First Vision's details.

Was the wonder and mystery of the experience tempered by this specific form of God-as-man, almost to the point of being completely extinguished? And how has this influenced everything that has come since?

On my walk one evening, a beautiful moon hung just above the outline of the hills. I was gifted with that illusion where the moon appears to be huge at the horizon, then seems to shrink quickly as it moves into the sky overhead. It wasn't a full moon, rather my favorite moon—what I call a fingernail moon. Just a sliver, but quite bright. I wasn't even getting the full sliver, because two clouds partially obscured the bottom of the arc, and the whole thing was so picture perfect I wasn't sure I'd ever seen a moon in real life that looked quite so much like the moon of an artist's imagination.

As I watched, it occurred to me that part of what made it so wondrous had nothing to do with the moon itself. There was the fact that it appeared larger through a trick of my own eyes and mind—the way I was experiencing it had a lot to do with my perception of it. And those clouds that seemed impossibly perfect in their shape and placement made my experience of it even better. Without the clouds, without it being my favorite kind of moon—the kind of which I can only see a little—without it being near the horizon, and my human eyesight doing what it does, it would not have had the same beauty. What remained obscured, and what was skewed by my own faulty seeing, were what really gave it value for me. Those were the things that caught my notice, those were the things that made it a gift. Without that, it might have been any slim moon in any night sky—still beautiful, still shining, but not shining so personally for me.

As the moon climbed, the clouds parted to let it pass and I could see the rest of a faint circular outline. It became smaller, though still as bright, and it didn't stay lodged in my wonder. It passed through me on its rise, illuminating a dark place briefly, rewarding me for looking up, for pausing to watch, acknowledge, and feel gratitude. Then it went back to being just a moon, and I went about my walk. Perhaps larger myself, and a bit lighter.

I've been trained to look for a full-moon god while my heart has yearned for the god of that fingernail moon. The one that appears impossibly large, the one that remains partially hidden in ways that might actually create beauty and meaning for me. The one that doesn't manage to permanently lodge where I can see its fullness, but passes through me in glimpses, giving me just enough to keep me walking. This is the god that speaks in a language I can see ... or can't quite. Maybe the whisper of the parts I can't see are what my heart can hear. The still small voice to which I've been afraid to listen.

And that's the funny thing to me about a church that touts a living prophet, as well as an article of faith that says, *". . . and we believe that He will yet reveal many great and important things ..."* It's astounding how resistant we are to change, how distrustful of the parts we cannot see or know, how uninterested in asking Big Questions, how non-seeking in our lessons and discussions, how fixed in our prayers, how small in our imaginations—how utterly closed, for lack of a better word. We are closed. Not truly valuing the outer world or the inner spiritual connection, our eyes and ears are trained to page and pulpit. Our own adaptation, our own possible surprise or expanding vision do not figure into our collective worldview.

When I was a child, a copy of Rembrandt's *Night Watch* hung over my brother's bed in a gold-painted frame. It was there for so long, I almost stopped seeing it, once I had memorized every detail. It was fascinating to me, telling a story I did not know and so made up for myself. When I finally went to the Rijksmuseum as an adult and stood before it in wonder, I laughed—at fourteen feet by twelve feet, it bore no resemblance to the small image I'd known like the back of my childhood hand. I was completely overwhelmed at the way I had underestimated this painting—a story much bigger than any I could have told myself about it. I've never forgotten it coming into view and my realization that what I was seeing was something I had never come close to glimpsing in all my years of looking.

I know I'm in the presence of great art—what I call 'capital A' Art rather than run of the mill art—when I get a specific feeling. I started noticing this when I was very young. Sometimes when I would hear music, see a painting, or read a poem, I experienced an expansiveness. Something was calling me to be larger, better, or somehow *more*. A deep acknowledgment that I was part of something too big to fully grasp, and yet I had a place in it. I knew I wanted to be where that feeling lived. I loved experiencing the magnetic pull of its great secret, feeling there might be more revealed if I could only get to the source.

I sensed it in the wonders of nature sometimes too, in impossibly graceful moons or gasping cliffs. In things or places so beautiful, they completely transcended humans' creative abilities, and almost comprehension. Things that made even our best attempts at creation seem puny.

If I were going to bear my testimony about this feeling, I'd say that after a lifetime of pursuing a testimony in places like scriptures, prayers, and church pews, it turns out I know something is True when it makes me realize everything is bigger than I thought it was. It shouldn't have surprised me that spending all my formative years in a religion of such specific parameters eventually found me beating my head against the sky, begging to understand anything at all beyond the cage.

Probably what drives all creative people is this feeling that there's something big they can't quite put their finger on—can't quite capture—so they need to keep trying. I wasn't very old before I started to make and write things myself, always falling woefully short of getting anywhere near that feeling through my own efforts. I had tremendous reverence for it and a desire to possess it, to surround myself with it and keep it with me, but my own creativity didn't seem to have the code. When I looked at anything I made or did, it seemed what I could mostly see was my own small fingerprints all over it.

But great art reaches beyond the old toward something new. It clears space. It's only recently that I've begun to perceive that the inner expansion I'd been chasing all my life had nothing at all to do with art or the forces that create it. It had nothing to do with nature itself. The expansiveness I felt was the manifestation of God—the pull of deep wonder—and the yearning was my need for a larger one than the one I had been given as a child, the one with whom I'd been trying to have a relationship, but never quite succeeding.

I needed a bigger god.

I had to come to this big realization through a much smaller and more painful one though. I had to begin by understanding that, in addition to needing a bigger god, or maybe as a result of that need, I needed a bigger church. Something larger than the one I'd been raised in, and in which I'd raised my children, and that was the key—it was in raising my children in The Church of Jesus Christ of Latter-day Saints that my need for what I didn't find there was exposed, again and again. Until finally it expressed itself (or I guess I should say my beloved daughters expressed it for me) in their leaving it.

Of course from their very first day, my children bore the fingerprints of hands much larger and more mysterious than my own.

Though they have turned out to be imperfect people, just like the rest of us, from the moment they arrived I experienced them as a bright and perfect vision, a glimpse of God's great secret, teaching me in ways I'd never been taught before.

I could see clearly that the creative act brought me more personal connection with God, or with something I could perceive as God, than any other approach I had tried. I first sensed the seeds of divinity in myself by seeing those seeds clearly in them. I also realized that my love as a parent and my yearning for relationship with my children didn't feel like the relationship I'd grown up envisioning my Heavenly Father having with me. The things I'd been taught were most important to Heavenly Father weren't important enough to me to stand between my daughters and my love. So this heavenly vision that answered some of my deepest questions also revealed a gaping, personal lack of any real god-knowledge.

Joseph Campbell said, "The image of God is your final obstruction to a religious experience."[2] I was looking for messages from God, but these deep, painful love-lessons from my children kept presenting themselves to me instead, and somehow I didn't trust the messengers enough to easily open myself to learning them. There were things I had to unlearn first—I had to untangle my expectations from my reality, my faith from my belief, my relationships from my Mormonism.

I'm hardly the first person to raise children and then feel wounded when they walked away into their own lives in a direction different from the way I'd been pointing. We're meant to find our own way, and heaven knows I've made a lot of noise about my right to do as I please all my life. But knowing that going in didn't lessen my strange grief when they did it. Many children shed the traditions of their fathers, but I think we always hope that our own might pick it up again. After all, they can live with piles of dirty clothes on the floor as teenagers, dropping things casually on their way from the door to the bed and then stepping over them for days after. But a mother always trusts that, eventually, they'll become tired of living that way and decide to pick things up for themselves.

My daughters did the dropping part. But in this thing it doesn't appear likely that there will be any picking up. They shrugged off the blanket-god we'd spent decades wrapping them in so carefully, and left it on their childhood floor, closing the door behind them. This was something I didn't know how to reconcile—to address with them, with myself, or with the Heavenly Father I was supposed to know. It was a tear in the fabric of my mother-universe so violent, it felt irreparable and unfair, unexpected and deeply personal. Even as it was understandable on a logical level (knowing them as I did), it somehow felt inconceivable on a spiritual one. And these feelings their choice brought to my surface were shocking. I was as unprepared for my own emotional response to their leaving as I was for the leaving itself. I found myself unequipped to deal with it on just about every level.

They obviously needed something different from what I'd given them.

I needed something different from what I'd been given too, but I'd allowed the gnawing to grow inside myself rather than let my hunger out in pursuit of actually being filled. Not finding satisfaction from my spiritual life had, in a twisted way, become a hallmark of it—a sort of plausible deniability in which it didn't really matter whether I possessed any truth about God or not as long as God knew I'd spent my life working off the approved checklist. So my kids shrugging off my version of God probably wasn't an actual rejection of any specific spiritual relationship so much as my failure to really sell the importance of the list. I'd given them plenty of what I had, but how could I give them what I didn't possess, or even understand I wanted?

And now, what good was a church that was not big enough to hold my own beautiful children? Without my family, the box I'd expected to always contain our shared god felt hollow, echoing and suffocating all at once. Richard Rohr writes, "God is always bigger than the boxes we build for God, so we should not waste too much time protecting the boxes." It seemed I'd invested a lifetime in guarding the box only to find that what I assumed was inside maybe wasn't there at all. Once my children left the God Box we'd all lived in, they somehow took everything I recognized as God with them. The vacuum their departure created sucked all the God-ness out of my careful box and I found myself alone, unable to breathe there.

Did I never really know God, after all? What about my decades of careful observance, my willingness to swallow big questions rather than endanger myself, and everyone around me, by speaking them out loud? Suddenly I felt I'd been grasping at god-straws forever, knowing all along they probably couldn't save me. Had my own potential ability to experience the Divine in the way my spirit yearned to—as large and small and mysteriously both personal and universal—been hampered by the box that my religion built? A result of one man's very specific experience of God? A box I'd not only been willing to accept on faith, but had spent a lifetime trying to make my own?

What about the fact that I'm a woman, whose woman-god never quite materializes in our theology? She's nodded to but never revealed in any detail at all, a character veiled in reverent rumor, sought by many but existing in hush and shadow. The truest line in the Bible, for me, has always been that "... Mary kept all these things and pondered them in her heart." It speaks deeply to my own experience. I realized as a young girl that I might have to look harder, if only because I was not reflected in the god-mirror held up for me by religion. Yet I knew creativity was inseparable from God, knew that the world in all its diverse beauty was born even before the man, and that women continue God's sacred and powerful creative work, even if it—inexplicably, to me—never earns the label of a Priesthood. And what about the testimonies of truth the wonders and beauty of this world had borne to me from the time I was a child? What if I'd gotten God all wrong, pursuing an idea that could never satisfy because it was never really mine to begin with? What about the sacred truth of my own experience? Is it possible that in my entire spiritual life I'd never given myself permission to look—to see God in and for myself—afraid that what might be revealed could violate the agreed-upon blueprint with no hope of ever fitting in the box at all?

I had to go back to the beginning. I didn't know another place to start.

I was born of goodly parents—a mother who never doubted, and a father who I think perhaps did but kept his questions tucked carefully in a drawer, the exact contents of which his children were never allowed to see. Sometimes I heard it though, opening and closing quietly, as if in the next room. I'm comforted by the idea that there are things about my parents I don't know. It's a bit of truth that calls some of the things I think I do know into question—a dynamic I like when it comes to religion.

Going back further, into my personal preexistence, there are pioneers and polygamy, the gods that made me. People who gave everything to build the Kingdom, or at least Utah County. Devoted men who went to prison rather than renounce their plural wives. Relief Society presidents, hands-on women of legend who quilted in community, planned bazaars, and blessed the sick. From this stalwart Mormon stock descended my tribe of aunts and uncles and cousins who kept family group sheets, gathered for Sunday dinners and summer reunions, and across the generations, prayed to a common God.

In my childhood home, we did all the things a Mormon family might, living in the Salt Lake City of the 1970s. We went to church—morning and afternoon—and so kept our dresses on all day. We had Family Home Evening and family prayer. We read the Book of Mormon together, carefully underlined the important parts in red. We had robust discussions of principles like justice and mercy at the dinner table, gossiped about ward members in equal measure, sang our beloved hymns together in the car, participated in road shows and sacred ordinances with the same religious zeal. Our church, family, and community lives were all of a piece, seamlessly woven into the kind of durable fabric you'd be more likely to mend than throw out if it ever did happen to develop a hole.

As a natural questioner, I've wondered how I accepted my family's shared version of God without asking too many questions out loud. It's uncharacteristic behavior for me, so as a child I must have deeply needed or wanted the comfort that the sturdy, stable Mormonism of my heritage delivered. It's safe to say I never really considered building my life on any other template.

It was easy to be in that life though, without always remembering God was the point of it all. People were there for all kinds of reasons—probably still are, but some of the infrastructure that kept people coming whether they cared much about finding God or not doesn't really exist anymore. Things like church basketball tournaments, dance festivals, and mid-week homemaking workshops formed the framework of neighborhood life. Some people were having deeply spiritual experiences, I'm sure, but I was a kid and the other stuff kept me busy enough that I didn't stop to wonder whether or not the doctrine of my church could sustain me for a lifetime.

Without ever saying it out loud, at some point I realized our church members generally assumed God to be one of us. I have yet to say this to anyone without having them initially dismiss it as a ludicrous—if not blasphemous—simplification, but upon thinking about it, it's hard to make any other argument. If The Church of Jesus Christ of Latter-day Saints is regarded by its members as God's official church upon the earth, that makes God a Mormon.

But isn't our church life really only part of this *human* experience? And if God is a Mormon, and Mormonism could not hold my children in this life, would its God hold them in the next?

Thomas Merton wrote, "The life of the soul is not knowledge, it is love."[3] So what are we doing with our declared knowledge, our collective belief? Some Sundays I see glimmers of the God I yearn for, but many Sundays are what I've come to describe as "small-god" Sundays. A good example happened when a Relief Society teacher began a lesson by saying, "We all know love is important, BUT—" The rest of the lesson focused on everything that came after the 'but.' That was disappointing, since the part that spoke truth to my heart came before it. Looking around the room, I wondered whether I was alone in my discomfort—whether anyone else needed more, or—like me—significantly less. So often what is missing for me in our religion is everything that cannot be said, that peace-giving space where we need not know any more than this moment and the people with whom we are in it. In that immediate place, knowledge is replaced by hope, which I find to be much more reliable, and how I live becomes a decision made to improve things here and now, one made out of love and not with an eye always trained on gilding my eternity. My life can be an exercise in love, and my God can be allowed to love without a lot of additional rules and regulations that quantify a child's worthiness or God's willingness.

Cynthia is fond of saying that, for all she knows, God may actually end up being a talking rock. That would be okay with her … and with me. I think about that all the time—the truth that *not* knowing somehow suits me better than knowing would, and how ill-fitting my religion is for a woman who prefers the god question to the god answer. All I really do need, at this point, is for God to be bigger than anything I'm able to get my puny head around. A talking rock would be as good a surprise as any other, the joke being on us because we've made all kinds of silly human-based assumptions about a divinity that exists beyond our comprehension. That's what I hope for—that's what speaks promise to me. Please let God be bigger and more mysterious than a man.

So what do I need or want to know now? Going back to the beginning meant an assessment of what I do know of God, or would want to be true, anyway, if I could know the truth—the kinds of traits that are important to me but no one talks about on Sunday.

Having spent a lifetime in church, it turns out that most everything I believe about God, I didn't learn there at all. I learned it by doing things like walking at night and wondering at moons. Like getting my hands dirty in pursuit of ideas I can never quite express. I learned it from a love for my children so big, it came out of seemingly nowhere to fill parts of me I never knew existed, and yet, it came out of me— that must teach me something. They were my own first vision, the thing that continues to inform and enlarge everything that has come since. I know it is true. As surely as Joseph believed his own eyes, I trust my mother heart.

But it didn't teach me everything. I continue to learn from living in the world, being willing to look around while I do. So much is made plain in the seeing:

God likes diversity. *God made giraffes as well as ducks, intending them to live completely different lives, and didn't stop there.*

God enjoys a good joke. *What other explanation could there be?*

God is no respecter of persons. *Go ahead, try applying a merit-based system to human beings. See?*

God is patient. *God uses drops of water to carve canyons. Any artist willing to engage in that kind of process work isn't in a hurry.*

God is okay with imperfection. *There doesn't seem to be anything perfect on this earth, so it seems God was particularly obvious with this lesson.*

God is not a control freak. *Stuff happens. And so much of it.*

God intends to surprise us. *Is there anything in a life that goes exactly the way we thought it would?*

God is doing complex mathematics. *I had a grandfather who only went to 8th grade, but could see the answers to complicated math problems just by looking at them. This didn't make him at all helpful with homework. Knowing the answer didn't mean he could show us how to do it. God is doing math we just don't understand.*

God is interested in the human story. *Each of us is allowed our own, to be told in any language, or with no words at all. The whole point of God's Son coming to earth must be to assure us that our story is understood.*

These are a few of the simpler things I've noticed, and there is surely much more than meets my small eye. I've heard it said that we can only know God through an open mind, just like we can only see the sky through a clear window. We won't see the sky if we've covered the glass with blue paint.

The idea of painting the sky on a window before we look out so it appears exactly the way we want it to, or think it should, or hope it will, sounds silly. Yet sometimes, when I'm sitting in church surrounded by what feels and sounds like certainty about ideas that for me only point to larger questions, I have the vague feeling I'm looking at a painted sky. It's pretty, sunny, warm and reliable, but if I could somehow just scrape away the blue paint, I might get a glimpse of what the sky really looks like.

And if I were to open the window and lean out, I might see even further.

When I think of the God about which I've spent my life learning, and the church in which I've learned, I see human fingerprints all over both of them. That's okay, even the greatest, most inspiring art in the world is created using human hands. It isn't given to us by miracle, but requires patience, trial and error, the disappointment of false starts and the humility of beginning again. Like people building a tower to the sky—or a box meant to hold all the answers of eternity—I feel we have inevitably fallen short. How would we not? A god defined by commit-tee is an exercise bound to miss the mark. Forming a church from the ground up would inevitably require tempering of the individual imag-ination. It would become the product of agreement by compromise, marked by the fingerprints of politics, personal opinion and personality, social and cultural change. Practical considerations and questions would require specific answers. Things some might prefer to leave unexpressed would be written down. The small 't' truths of one might be given a capital 'T' in the testimony of another. An idea as big and unwieldy as God must be made more manageable if it is ever to be packaged.

And the result of all this truth-wrangling, of men's insistence on taking charge of and organizing the unknowable, is that those leading the church's way have somehow arrived at a god from which I some-times struggle to feel any expansive, godlike pull at all.

Yet no matter how often or how explicitly the official version is spelled out for me by someone else, my experience insists on a god that loves me as much as I love my own children. I need a church that is big enough for me, for them, and everyone else who might want to be here, a god large enough to hold us all. I want to be rid of boxes altogether, to be free to see what is made obvious to me, to learn from my own experiences, to honor my own vision, to follow the magnetic pull of a huge, overwhelming love wherever I feel it, to find peace in finally naming and knowing it for myself.

I want this god whose faint, full outline I've only now begun to see. The god of the fingernail moon, who doesn't take away the dark-ness but affords me a slit of bright hope against it, one graceful ray of promise shining from a crack in the next room. The glimpse is enough.

Life is nothing but mystery, as I have experienced it. At least the memorable parts—the encounters that urge us to grow, teach us about ourselves, about love and our own place in a universe too big to comprehend but of which we are somehow an important part. I am continually blindsided and bewildered, but also amazed beyond my capacity to hold my own wonder. If I don't have a god big enough to encompass all of the actual dimensions of my personal human expe-rience, with a lot left over so I can trust in something larger than my tiny understanding can grasp, where can my mind rest? It has been unable to find rest in a box so small it doesn't seem to hold everything I have right now.

So I turn away from the confines of what I have been taught, God re-created in the language and pictures of someone else's vision, and toward what I have seen and lived for myself.

Going back to the beginning required me to peer into my own darkness with a willingness to really see. I've had to learn new words, try new ways of listening. I've had to search new scriptures, say new prayers, dare to ask different questions than the ones I've asked before. I've had to clear space for myself. To stop pretending to knowledge I don't need or even want. To allow growth in the places I've kept small. The secret to being reached may reside in becoming reachable. The secret to finding a larger God may be looking everywhere, all the time. Seeing a sacrament in the ordinary, because the ordinary points to the universal truth. Accepting that the whole world is a holy place, and being ready to take off my shoes and stand, allowing God to exist in even the most mundane or imperfect moments. I have a poem that speaks to this:

Babel
God speaks to us in any language
we can understand
God in birds, in trees
in wind, tall grass, its whisper
and its bend
God in pie, if it's the kind my grandma made
God in the dishwater slipping through her hands
after we were filled, God in the suds
and in the song she hummed
Listen.

Can a new god be found when you're sitting in the same old church? I believe the answer is yes. We all conjure God for ourselves—we all "tell [God] slant," as Emily Dickinson might say—an amalgamation of our own hopes, beliefs, and experiences. Joseph Smith arrived with his version first—we accept that and then tweak it a little to make it feel more personal. So it wouldn't really require anything new except an acknowledgment that, by going back to the beginning, reimagining my personal slant from scratch, I'm at risk of being surprised by what comes ... and I'm willing to take that risk.

It's not unlike a blindfolded pin-the-tail-on-the-donkey. It could be, when the blindfold is removed, that we'll all have a good chuckle at the things we've been confused about or gotten wrong. The tail hung on the donkey's eye, or dangling from a hoof, or even stuck on the bathroom door, having missed the donkey altogether and wandered down the hall.

There's a scene at the end of the old movie *Little Big Man* in which an aged Native American chief, well known for his visions of things to come, is talking to God at the end of his life. His eyes have long failed him, yet he says, "Thank you for my vision … and the blindness in which I saw further."

Following our questions, walking with our doubt is probably more important than getting it right 100 percent of the time. Walking forward anyway reflects a larger, braver kind of vision than sight. It reflects hope. It does no good to have definitive answers, when the point of the test is to see how well you can do without them.

The older I get, the more sorry I feel that I've spent my life distrusting my spiritual instincts. I've been robbed, even if that is in large part by myself. Who wants to seek when they fear that what they find may be unacceptable? But I have a hunch (and a hope) if I were able to have a conversation with Joseph, I might find him to have exactly the ingredient—genuine spiritual curiosity—that I often, sitting in a small-god lesson that seems an endless loop of the same few ideas and approaches, find the religion he founded to lack. That hope is meaningful to me.

For Latter-day Saints, the big spiritual experience—conversion—is to receive knowledge that the church is True. Personal experience with the Divine is not celebrated nor necessarily even welcomed, unless it strengthens the existing box of accepted doctrine. The idea of legislating belief in one man's God fails me as often as I try to make sense of it. Taking a room full of people and laying out a list of acceptable beliefs, then asserting that if they ask sincerely, identical beliefs will distill upon each of their minds, seems precisely the same as assuring a group that they can believe in Santa Claus if only they will try hard enough.

Under the Santa Claus scenario, once that belief is gone, I find it difficult to imagine that it could ever be reclaimed, even by those with the most sincere and ardent desire to do so. However (and this is a big however), I have no problem imagining a room full of people who remain devoted to the idea of Santa Claus, find meaning and hope in his spirit of giving and strive to internalize it, and wish to raise their children with Santa as the centerpiece of a Christmas morning gifting tradition, remembering fondly the remarkable ways their belief informed their own experiences. The idea of Santa Claus is appealing, long after you've stopped believing. And a room full of people devoted to it could exist very peacefully, so long as no one stood up and announced that if you no longer held a literal belief in Santa, you didn't belong in the room.

If faith is a living thing, there will be many among us whose beliefs will shift.

Our pews should extend to welcome those who no longer believe in exactly the way they once did, but still find personal meaning in our traditions. Emphasis on an ongoing restoration would suggest the most open of windows, the most seeking of minds and hearts.

How can you define belief in the context of things you openly acknowledge not knowing? Is it enough to accept those things as your partner on this earthly journey, and walk forward anyway? We're here for the walking part, after all, to see how well we do it, how long we're willing to keep putting one spiritual foot in front of the other and go where it leads us.

To ask our big questions, and then move our feet in the direction we feel we ought to go if we ever wish to find the answers, demonstrates a belief in the value of the question itself. It's worth making the journey whether or not we get to an answer. In fact, it's worth making it our life pursuit. Finding a sure relationship with God, then passing it successfully to our children, must not be the main thing we're meant to accomplish on earth. The point must be what we do with our not knowing.

I seek a seat in the church where I can not only look out the open window, but also describe what I see. I intend to find one. I want to walk through the world open-eyed too, gathering God in all ways and places, ideas and faces, to bring with me when I come to worship. Even if I can't create a church big enough to hold my unique family, I can invite God to create in me a more expansive faith. A personal faith with room enough to hold all the things I know, and the things I don't know yet. The small part I see, the faint outline of something much bigger.

So much of my life has been given to control—trying to control myself, trying to control others, trying to control outcomes, trying to control God—trying to control it all through my own righteous actions and desires. But also chafing against the constraints of a religion that taught me, falsely, to think perhaps I could.

What I need from a relationship with God is someplace in my life where I can cede control. That would be rest to me, that would be the promised peace at last, the rock of my salvation. I have a deep spiritual longing for something so large and mysterious I can't possibly control it, so I don't need to worry about trying. It's just not within my small, white-knuckle grasp. It's not within my actions, nor even within the capabilities of my mind—math too complex for me to see the answers, even if I'm able to show a lifetime of my own work. This is what I want now, a set of questions with answers too endless to fit in any box, so our default answer is love. In re-envisioning my God, I am reinventing my faith.

Beginning again—searching for a larger god—meant searching for a larger self. God didn't need to change, my own heart and mind did. I needed to stop protecting the box to discover endless room for truth. Attentive as I walk, alert to the smallest glimpses, the faintest whisper and pull, I feel my anxious heart relaxing into a larger spiritual home. It's right here where I've always lived, yet I can see the outline of something much bigger, a vision at last my own, love truer and brighter than I have seen before. Hope enough to keep me walking.

GRACE ON A CHRISTMAS MORNING

"Sometimes grace works like water wings when you feel you are sinking."
—Anne Lamott[4]

Cynthia:

In 2022, I was asked to be the Christmas Day speaker for our upcoming sacrament meeting program. My ward had a lovely program planned—all musical numbers—and just *me* as the one speaker. The topic given to me? The atonement. Christmas fell on a Sunday that year, so I knew all my grown children, with varying levels of activity in the church, would most likely attend, along with my husband Paul. And if that was true for my family, it could be true for other families that day—lots of visitors all over the belief and participation spectrum. I had three weeks to prepare my talk—to prepare *the* Christmas Day sermon—no pressure, Cynthia! I decided to craft a talk that met three goals.

First, I wanted it to be a generic Christian message, rather than specific to Latter-day Saints, so all those in attendance felt as comfortable as possible. Second, even though I was asked to speak on the atonement of Jesus Christ, I decided to morph that message, which feels more Easter to me, into a message of grace. I am not even sure I understand atonement enough to give a sermon on it, let alone make it sound perfect for Christmas morning. But grace!? Grace seems more like a Christmas package to me, one with a big shiny bow just waiting to be ripped open by a person who least expects the greatest gift they'll ever get. Lastly, I wanted it to be uplifting and hope filled. After all, people were attending on Christmas morning and I wanted my message to be maybe only slightly less enjoyable than if they had stayed home in their jammies with cinnamon roll cream cheese frosting crusted to the corners of their mouths. I delivered the following message:

Being a follower of Jesus has always provided a moral compass for me, but now more than ever, I feel like the words of Jesus are really stretching me. That stretching can be really uncomfortable. Nobody really wants to go into that growth zone, but that growth zone is where we do our best learning. Some of that stretching and discomfort has come from studying the parables. One that I keep coming back to over and over, from all different angles of discomfort, is the parable of the laborers in the vineyard.

In the Christmas carol *Silent Night*, there's the line, "radiant beams from thy holy face with the dawn of redeeming grace." Christmas is when we celebrate the day that grace came into the world through the baby Jesus. Let me go ahead and quickly sum up this parable for those of you who maybe don't know or have forgotten what it's about. Basically, there's a land owner who needs workers for his farm and vineyard. So he goes into the marketplace and he grabs workers early in the morning, then he goes back at 9:00 a.m. to get more workers. He repeats this at noon, 3:00 p.m. and finally again at 5:00 p.m. Each time he enters the marketplace, he tells the prospective workers what he's willing to pay them and they all agree to the day's wage. Jesus crafts this story in such a way that the 5:00 p.m. folks are paid first and the early morning folks are paid last. The entire story hinges on that fact—that those early bird workers saw the late comers get paid the same.

In Matthew 20:11, the NRSV version, it reads:

> And when they received it, they grumbled against the landowner, saying, 'These last worked only one hour, and you have made them equal to us who have borne the burden of the day and the scorching heat.' But he replied to one of them, 'Friend, I am doing you no wrong; did you not agree with me for a denarius? Take what belongs to you and go; I choose to give to this last the same as I give to you. Am I not allowed to do what I choose with what belongs to me? Or are you envious because I am generous?' So the last will be first, and the first will be last.

What gives even more meaning to this parable is to understand that it's totally possible that Jesus knew what it was like to show up and wait to be offered a day of work. Paul Thornton wrote, "Modern references to Jesus' profession as a 'carpenter' abound, . . . but the Greek term used to describe his work—'tekton'—betrays a more hardscrabble existence, something more akin to a day laborer or a handyman."[5]

Knowing this about Jesus, that he crafted this parable possibly because he knew for himself what it was like to wait for daily work, reminds me of the people so many of us see outside hardware stores in America, also wondering if anyone will show up at 9 a.m. or 5 p.m. and offer them work.

I've heard that to read scripture correctly we have to be willing to put ourselves in the role of the least likable character. So in this story, that's the whiny workers who complain that others are being overpaid. If I am honest with myself and willing to enter that uncomfortable growth zone, how am I like them? Do I prefer fairness over grace and mercy? Or maybe you think the least likable persons in the story are the 5 p.m. workers. How dare they do a fraction of what I have done and get the same reward? In modern terms, as an active, participating Latter-day Saint, the grumblings could sound something like this, "Hey, she hasn't come to church in years. I sure haven't seen her! She doesn't deserve to be here in the temple." But here's the thing—even if this parable makes you uncomfortable, whether you see yourself as the 9:00 a.m. workers who hustled for their daily bread, or the lazy late comers, too bad! You can't dismiss the radical grace of this story. It's not a one-off. It's not an outlier. Most of Jesus's parables are about God's grace.

How about the parable of the two debtors in Matthew 18? Basically, one person owes a ton of money that they'll never be able to repay, and that debt is wiped clean. The parable of the prodigal son? He spends all of his inheritance, then his dad throws him a party and gives him a feast. What about the parable of the wedding banquet found in Matthew 22? The wedding was filled with, as the scriptures say, good guests and bad guests. All of these parables are stories of unearned abundance. In Isaiah 55:1, we read about that abundance, "Come, buy wine and milk without money and without price." That's what this parable highlights—that some people are buying their daily bread without much, if any, money that they earned.

This parable, mainly referred to as the parable of the laborers, really is not about how hard anyone has worked. It's about the abundant nature of an employer. A better name for this parable may actually be 'the parable of the generous employer.' When will we learn that Jesus is constantly involved in all this craziness about abundance? He takes a few loaves of bread and a few pieces of fish, and multiplies them to feed thousands. He talks about a mustard seed, that if you have even the tiniest faith of a mustard seed, that faith can move mountains. Abundance, abundance, abundance!

In earlier parts of my life, I used to be the person that showed up at 9 a.m. ready to work. I could hustle with the best of them. Susan once said to me about this parable, "I don't understand how once anyone gets a glimpse of grace, they would ever get back on that hustling hamster wheel." Agreed! So why do we do that? Why do we sometimes prefer the hustling hamster wheel rather than accept the free gift of grace? Lutheran pastor Nadia Bolz-Weber said:

> What makes this the kingdom of God is not the worthiness or piety or social justicey-ness or the hard work of the laborers . . . none of that matters. It's the fact that the trampy landowner couldn't manage to keep out of the marketplace. He goes back and back and back, interrupting lives . . . coming to get his people. Grace tapping us on the shoulder.[6]

It seems clear to me now that in this parable, Jesus wants us to believe in a God of grace, forgiveness, solace, and salvation. Richard Rohr said: "We in the Christian world have used the word salvation which is Latin for the word solace which means healing. Salvation is the ultimate realignment, the ultimate healing."[7]

At Christmas time, we celebrate the very moment in history when "the word was made flesh." (John 1:14) That's always been one of my favorite scriptures.

And on Easter the Christian community celebrates the day that salvation was created. Quoting Father Rohr again: "We finally have in the Risen Christ the perfect icon of a god who is safe and a universe that is safe. A god who doesn't blame. A god who is not punitive. A god who doesn't threaten. A god who does not dominate. A god who breathes forgiveness."[8]

I would add to that, "A god who overpays."

Elder Jeffrey R. Holland gave an entire general conference talk about this very parable.

> This parable—like all parables—is not really about laborers or wages any more than the others are about sheep and goats. This is a story about God's goodness, His patience and forgiveness, and the Atonement of the Lord Jesus Christ. It is a story about generosity and compassion. It is a story about grace. It underscores the thought I heard many years ago that surely

the thing God enjoys most about being God is the thrill of being merciful, especially to those who don't expect it and often feel they don't deserve it.[9]

My favorite line in this parable is when the landowner says to the workers in Matthew 20:4, "I will pay you whatever is right." Isn't that fascinating? Jesus gives us what is right, not what is fair. So to me, this is a Christmas story because Jesus's birth ushers in a new era, an era of being overpaid.

American Episcopal priest Robert Farrar Capon said, "If the world could have been saved by bookkeeping, it would have been saved by Moses, not Jesus. The law was just fine."[10]

I think about that a lot, that before Jesus, we lived by the law. But after Jesus, we live by grace.

Jesus, through this crazy story, is trying to teach us that our Heavenly Parents don't give us what we deserve—They reward and bless beyond that. Always. Author Rob Bell said:

> We're not doing the law here. We're doing grace. We're doing Gospel. And for so many people their understanding of Gospel was so shaped by law and transaction that when they hear actual Gospel it sounds wrong, it sounds heretical, it sounds too good to be true, because it's so alternative, and so different and counterintuitive.[11]

Because Jesus's free gift to us, giving us what is right, makes us holy and healed, we are now free to stop worrying about our own enough-ness, our own worthiness. We're not going to get on that hustling hamster wheel anymore! We're now free! Free to do what Jesus called us to do—feed his sheep. "If ye love me, feed my sheep." (John 21:15–17)

After delivering my talk, I was overwhelmed by ward members and visitors. So many people for months asked for a copy. One young adult said she'd like a copy for a friend who is struggling with church right now, "She doesn't need a list of things to do right now, she just needs a message about Jesus and his grace." Another woman, still sitting in the chapel, grabbed the sleeve of my satiny Christmas outfit as I walked by and said that after a lifetime, she still didn't understand grace. She began to cry and said, "Maybe I never will. But Cynthia does, so I'll believe her." I debated whether to share this feedback, because I don't think I said anything new or profound as I basically copied the thoughts of my favorite Christian thinkers and regurgitated their words. I'm including these comments because every time I speak about grace in formal settings like talks, I realize just how foreign messages of grace sound to Latter-day Saint ears. Foreign, but delicious. Like that good fruit Jesus speaks of.

DISCIPLING

"Peter was grieved because he said unto him the third time, Lovest thou me? And he said unto him, Lord, thou knowest all things; thou knowest that I love thee. Jesus saith unto him, Feed my sheep."
—John 21:17 KJV

Susan:

I think the word disciple deserves a bigger role. By using it as a verb, I can imply that a disciple isn't just the thing we strive to become, it's the becoming itself. That it isn't something you either 100 percent are or 100 percent aren't, more direction than destination. As members of Christ's church, 'discipling' describes everything we're supposed to be about.

Discipling is more than following. Jesus isn't just marking a path for us. He actually is The Way. We go *to* Him, we go *with* Him, we go *through* Him. We cannot go alone. We must be shown both the goal and the way to reach it, taken by one hand to be led while using our free hand to hold a light for others to find their way too.

It makes sense that God's plan for us would involve a path. That it would require a process whereby we work together to make of our lives something worthy of our true selves. God knows what we're capable of becoming, but that's bigger than our minds can fully comprehend. Operating from a limited perspective, we'd need a way to get there that was easier to grasp—a path that would take us off the edge of our human maps and deliver us to these larger selves if we'd just keep walking. Becoming is how we become.

I wrote down a snatch of dialogue from one of my favorite TV characters years ago in which I found a deeply valuable lesson, and have revisited it many times since. Speaking to someone for whom he has concern, he says: "I have a rabbi friend with a small gambling problem who, when he hears someone say they're fine, he always asks again until they say something other than fine. So . . . how are you doing?"

As an introvert, I'm good at noticing—overhearing and observing from a distance—but I'm not often willing to risk my own discomfort to look directly into people's eyes and ask the question that might help me also glimpse their heart.

Discipling asks me to notice people in ways Jesus might have. To stop, to really look, to truly listen, and hopefully see and understand something about them—and about myself in relation to them—as a result.

In Jesus's ministry, it was often those who were largely ignored or marginalized by others that drew his attention. And when He saw them, it was not as "less than," tainted by their association with some other tribe, nor as unclean, unworthy, or undeserving of his notice. He saw people as whole people—women seemed to receive the same quality of attention from him that men did. Lepers were not unapproachable. A poor widow was not insignificant. The multitude's willingness to pass by did not impact his own decision to stop and fully see the beggar. He noticed people's needs, their shortcomings, their flaws, but also their similarities and significance as God's children.

Of course, to disciple first requires desire, or more specifically, faith. We measure faith not by what we think or believe or even hope, but by what faith leads us to do. It is living only when it is a catalyst that moves us. I think of faith as our hope and desire given legs and taught to walk. Once we can stand on our own, we are ready to use our legs to take up the path. Our first official step on the path of discipling is baptism.

Our baptismal covenant as outlined in Mosiah 18 reads:

> And now, as ye are desirous to come into the fold of God, and to be called his people, and are willing to bear one another's burdens, that they may be light; Yea, and are willing to mourn with those that mourn; yea, and comfort those that stand in need of comfort, and to stand as witnesses of God at all times and in all things and in all places that ye may be in, even until death, that ye may be redeemed of God, and be numbered with those of the first resurrection, that ye may have eternal life—

Sometimes I wish I took the opportunity to read that covenant more often. It is a powerful accounting of what we are specifically called to do as Jesus's disciples. And the call is at once extremely simple and something that will require everything we have to give over a lifetime of messy interactions and relationships.

The key words are bear, mourn, comfort, and stand. How often do we think of our responsibilities as Latter-day Saints reduced to such one-word specifics?

Am I bearing? I find it hard to pick up more burdens than I already carry, most days. My arms feel quite full.

Am I mourning, but not wrapping myself so tightly in my own grief that I can't see anyone else's?

Am I comforting anyone but myself?

Am I witnessing—standing confidently on my own faith-legs in a way that provides something not only for me, but for someone else who might benefit from what I have?

When I walk through my neighborhood, I notice how many barriers people put up between themselves and others. Fences. No Soliciting signs. Beware of Dog signs. Bars on doors. There's even a mailbox on my street with a sign that says, "Don't let your dog stop here." All of these are meant to create distance between people. In an increasingly crowded and busy world, it's understandable to want a little breathing room.

Sometimes when I go out to eat alone, I bring reading material, but as interested as I am in reading, I'm more interested in establishing a perimeter around myself. Being very shy, "leave me alone" may be my most consistent broadcast message to the world.

Contrast this with Christ's message: *Come unto me.* The next word in the phrase is, "All . . ." So first thing, if I really intend to *disciple,* I'm going to need to change my broadcast. Jesus was a gatherer. Gathering is a different thing from sorting or sifting. Gathering casts a wide net to bring things in. Gathering invites. Gathering adds. Sorting and sifting subtract by determining whether or not what has been gathered is good and should be kept. It's not part of our job description as disciples to make that determination. For the most part, the things we can see about people do not provide reliable criteria for sorting them. We are all sympathetic characters, and also not so sympathetic. So it makes sense that we are instructed to bring everyone unto Christ.

Of course, most days I'm pretty wrapped up in my own suffering. And how can I carry anyone else's burden when I'm struggling to hold up even my own small end of things?

Having lived with anxiety and depression since my childhood, even regular things sometimes feel overwhelming for me. I have days where the best description I've been able to come up with is that I have bricks piled on my head. The psychic weight feels like physical weight, and it makes it hard to move, let alone accomplish much, because even the most normal activities are more difficult when you are carrying a pile of bricks.

But I've come to be thankful for my bricks. I can recognize signs that another woman is carrying them, and know what that means and how it feels. Even if it's different for everyone, I have an insight that people who've never had to carry psychic bricks don't have. It could be that our burdens are meant to teach us how to do exactly this: how to glimpse others' unseen bricks so our own pain becomes the pathway by which we find true empathy for others. How else would we learn to mourn with those that mourn?

I heard Latter-day Saint scholar and writer Melissa Inouye say, "Suffering's value is fellowship with others and unity with Christ." I wrote it down, because this insight gives me a handle to grab my own suffering with a more useful grip. Holding my pain a bit less tightly, in union with the suffering of others and of Jesus, I can learn empathy. To mourn *with* someone requires that we ourselves must mourn. Sitting side by side with others, each under our unique piles of difficulty and struggle, seems a good start to discipling.

I recently discovered that in the accounts we have of His life, Jesus asked literally three hundred times more questions than He answered. I've thought a lot about why that might be. I think Jesus asked questions of the people around Him because it was the shortest route to making disciples. His questions exposed their biases, their motivations, their personal and collective values. His questions encouraged people to actually see and know themselves, with the implication that they might need to adjust their perception of others, too. By exposing the gaps between their words and actions, Jesus tried to help people see how they might close those gaps.

Even when He healed people, He didn't just wave a magic wand. Instead, Jesus put the healing back on them, suggesting that it was through their own actions—their own faith, desire, willingness, or seeking—that the healing occurred. I think He was trying to teach that we must see and understand ourselves in preparation for reaching out more effectively to others.

The lessons Jesus left for us were not preached in synagogues. He showed us things in His daily walk and interactions. Imitating Jesus's life and teachings does not happen in church, but in our lives. With all

His questions, I believe He was asking us: Who do we want to be to each other? And who do we want to be to God?

The reality is, Latter-day Saints are exactly like everyone else in the world, in my experience, except maybe a tiny bit worse because we won't admit that even to ourselves. Our kids go to jail or flunk ninth grade, our spouses have affairs or can't seem to keep a job, and maybe they hate our mothers. Speaking of our parents, sometimes they are addicts or bigots or in the worst cases abusive or withholding of love. Many of us yell and swear and some even drink both hot and strong drinks when no one is around, which is also when we eat whole buckets of ice cream and sleeves of Oreo cookies because we feel so bad about the swearing.

Our men like to be in charge, including of the women, but our women are a little controlly themselves, which they take out on the people around them by trying to do everything perfectly so they can then photograph the proof and put it on Pinterest.

Our pews on Sunday are full of all these problems plus about 150 more—enough, coincidentally, to fill a sacrament meeting with a few left over to sit in the overflow.

So we grow up swimming in the same human soup as everyone else, worthy-dogpaddling like crazy and pretending we've solved our humanness by being very very good and having so many answers that, if we're all doing it exactly right, no one will ever need to ask a question again.

If this sounds overly cynical, it's because I haven't talked about our goodness. The neighbor who shoveled your snow for a whole winter, pretending he just liked shoveling (which no one does that much), or the woman who brought you actual homemade lasagna and cleaned out your fridge when you couldn't face it during the overwhelming exhaustion of a move. Or the amazing leader who took your surly daughter to girls' camp and loved her so well and with such deep magic that when she came home she didn't pick a fight with anyone for almost a week. These good works are glimpses of discipling—remarkably from the same people who are self-flagellating with desserts to atone for their secret swearing and everything else. Experiencing such goodness can help us feel for ourselves the spark of divinity we sometimes struggle to find because we are unwilling to see and embrace one another as true siblings, inextricably linked in our sameness, wholly and fully human by divine design.

The only real differences between us are the spaces we manufacture and carefully maintain. The kind of love Jesus taught is the filler of spaces, expanding to close both tiny cracks and enormous gaps that may seem impossible to bridge on our own. When we finally allow ourselves to move, willing to meet others where they are, we find the gaps between us are erased.

In the story of the woman who struggled with an issue of blood and came to Jesus to be healed, there's a phrase that I feel provides a key insight. You'll recall that He was in a crowd, and the woman had faith to be healed but didn't want to bother Him. So she reached out just to touch His hem. In two of the accounts, we understand that Jesus knew, despite being surrounded, that someone had touched Him.

> And Jesus said, Who touched me? When all denied, Peter and they that were with him said, Master, the multitude throng thee and press thee, and sayest thou, Who touched me? And Jesus said, Somebody hath touched me: for I perceive that virtue is gone out of me. (Luke 8:45–46)

I love that description. I imagine an almost tangible current of power—a very real goodness flowing from one person to another. Perhaps that is the marker of discipleship. In our interactions with others, could we perceive virtue going out of us?

My daughter told me of an experience she had coming out of a drive-thru in downtown Phoenix. I remembered glancing at the temperature reading on my own dashboard that day, and it said 108 degrees. It was a hot day, by any standard. The people in front of her had ordered ice cream cones, and she watched them being handed through the window and probably wished she'd ordered one for herself. The car pulled away. When it got to the corner, there was a homeless man. She saw the car stop, the window roll down, and then a hand. An ice cream cone.

Can you imagine how indescribably wonderful that must have been? What unexpected balm ice cream might be on a hot day for someone who carries such staggering bricks of persistent need and longing, hunger and want? She told me the gratitude on the face of the receiver spoke volumes. But then she said what she really wanted was to have been the giver. She wanted to drive through her life in the desert handing out ice cream cones.

She wanted to feel virtue going out of her.

Jesus invites us to walk with—and through—Him on a path that changes hearts and minds. In knowing and serving others, we learn to love and that we ourselves are loved. Richard Rohr wrote:

> Any good idea that does not engage the body, the heart, the physical world, and the people around us will tend to be more theological problem solving and theory than any real healing of people and institutions—which ironically is about all Jesus does! ... Jesus offered the world a living example of fully embodied Love that emerged out of our ordinary, limited life situations.[12]

This makes real sense to me, because so much of what I know about God, I've learned from the relationships in my life. One day I was watching a seven-month-old grandson revel in the simple joy of being able to sit up. He picked up one toy at a time, bringing it clumsily to his mouth before trading it for another. His sparse blond hair was bathed in the halo of a late-afternoon sunbeam. He was doing nothing remarkable—just doing what babies do. But in that quiet moment, I was filled with a different kind of love for him than I'd felt for my own kids. I was so busy as a parent, trying to care for and teach them, and feeling the weight of responsibility for every moment and aspect of their development and well-being. This was a freer love, without the same weight of responsibility. I had a flash of regret that sometimes I'd experienced my children's actions and choices as a reflection on me, and as a result of my own pride, struggled to respond with love and grace. As we rode the bumps to their adulthood, I grew to understand I loved them unconditionally no matter what they chose.

But there was a love learning curve I could suddenly see didn't exist with my grandson at all. My love for him just *IS*. It is not reliant on me, not reflective of me, not because of anything either one of us did or could do, but comes from some deeper place, larger than the myopic lens of self through which I measured every parenting moment.

I realized that a grandparent had probably once looked at me and felt the same wonder—a deep love completely untethered by any strings. A godly love. The realization felt like a personal revelation meant to comfort, but more importantly, to teach.

Discipling calls me to 'body out'—a phrase I love from writer Adam Miller—to body out God's love into the world.[13] In lifting others, my own burden is lightened. In providing sanctuary for someone, I somehow experience peace and holiness for myself. In mourning *with*, my lonely sorrow fades.

Bear, mourn, and comfort all speak of acting in love, but what about that last of our four covenant words, standing? I used to think that 'standing as a witness' required me to be willing to testify at all times, a phrase that has always made me uncomfortable. I'm not much for speaking up. But my understanding of what it means to witness has also changed in the direction of love.

One Saturday not long ago, I'd just finished my walk in the park and was standing near a group from a local church that had set up a table of water and snacks, with a sign asking, "Do you need a prayer?" Their matching t-shirts said, "The Church has Left the Building." I had a few minutes to wait, and as I stood a woman approached the group and said, "I need a prayer. Will you pray for me? I had a biopsy on Friday to find out whether I have cancer, and now I have to wait for the result. I'm having a hard weekend." The group gathered around her—this woman none of them had seen before that moment—it was like they just absorbed her, and one of them began to pray. It was a woman's voice that rose in prayer—a woman, praying over this other woman, this stranger-no-more. I'm not sure I've ever cried so much in a public place as I did then, seeing and hearing a group of disciples bodying out their religion in a park. Witnessing in a way that made one woman's life feel more bearable for just a moment. As the prayer ended, someone walked by and said, "What do your shirts mean?" And one of them answered, "It means we're coming to you. What good is the church in a building?"

They were not members of our church, but they definitely knew something about Jesus's path. They were living their love out loud in the world—creating a church with no roof or walls, but where strangers might feel safe to lay down whatever they're carrying for a moment of rest. They were witnesses for love. In such a church, there are no strangers.

I've received a witness of God's love from others too, who may or may not go to church at all, but move through the world with respect and kindness and outreached hands. Like the people in the beat-up pickup truck who bought my breakfast at the McDonald's drive-thru just because I happened to be in line behind them. Their truck had seen better days, but their religion was in full bloom. It reminded me that church is supposed to be, first: who I am, not just where I go or how I pray. That my witness is not so much about where I stand or what I say, but rather what the people around me hear and feel as a result of my actions. Witnessing doesn't mean we have to stand on street corners and preach or pray. It does mean that we need to move through the world in a way that we welcome people to come unto us, and then in our interaction with them, we feel virtue go out from us.

I am a better witness by loving than I am by testifying. My actions speak louder than my words. If I wish to bring others to Jesus Christ, I'll need to love them there. With my baptism I made a covenant to do that. Now I'm learning I will spend the rest of my life figuring out how to keep that promise.

There is a hunched-over old man—a ninety-plus-year-old widower—who walks every evening at the same park I do. For a while we smiled politely at each other as we passed. Then one night, he reached out his hand and slapped mine as I walked by. This continued for months. Eventually, the slaps became a squeeze. He began to stand up straighter, looking me in the eye as he smiled. After a while, he asked my name. I hoped we could leave it at slapping hands, but he persisted and somehow, in spite of myself, a friendship began. Now, he plants himself on the path with his arms outstretched, wanting a hug and to hear about my day and tell me of his. His shoulders seem to have permanently—almost magically—uncurled.

One night I walked later than usual, and found him waiting on a bench. He told me of his particularly hard and lonely day. He had come to the park hoping I'd be there. He said, "I think you're an angel—the Lord sent you to me."

But I am a fickle and grumpy angel. An unreliable disciple at best. This relationship requires more of me than I want to give—being asked to interrupt my walks is an irritation. Devotion to achieving my daily step-count is basically my other religion. So now, for these few moments each night, I find myself trying hard to be something slightly better than I am. I'm continually disappointed by my lack of progress and ongoing selfishness. Two steps forward, one step back. But as one of my friends sometimes reminds me, forward is forward.

I am learning to be thankful for my own imperfection, my stops and starts on the discipling path. My failures are what equip me to better understand and accept others in theirs. Each step I manage to take in the direction of love reminds me that my willingness to do what I can in faith has power to heal. So I get up and try again tomorrow, and the day after, stumbling the path marked by, with, and through Jesus, toward wholeness.

ARE YOU THERE, GOD? IT'S US, CYNTHIA AND SUSAN

"God is always bigger than the boxes we build for God, so we should not waste too much time protecting the boxes."
—Richard Rohr[14]

Susan:

That quote from Richard Rohr was one of the biggest lightbulbs that's ever gone off in my religious life. It's not an overstatement to say it knocked me flat, and once I had struggled back to my feet, those words became the turning point in how I think about and relate to God. There's a before-I-read-that-quote, and an after. As a Latter-day Saint, I never realized exploring the nature of God was anywhere in my purview. Those questions had been asked by Joseph Smith and answered by the experience he recorded for us and later founded our religion based on.

The realization that I had very small, narrow ideas about God felt so big I couldn't really stand up under the weight of it until I'd wrestled with it awhile. The word 'box' never occurred to me until I saw Richard Rohr use it. For some reason, applying the mental image of such a space-defining shape suddenly illuminated the truth: I'd struggled my whole life to have a relationship, not necessarily with God, but with the narrow definition I'd been given.

It never occurred to me that we all create God for ourselves; we don't know what God looks like, no one does. Joseph Smith had a mental image, but I can't fully understand the nature of his experience; though he has described it to us in words, that's not the same as seeing for ourselves. So we each conjure something.

In our church we also apply the label Father, which influences our individual thinking based on the associations we have with that word. Our image gets cemented by depictions we've seen in the temple. Other people have imagined what God looks like and have produced church materials that portray Him, which most of us accept the way we accept everything that comes from Headquarters. So if you don't really relate to the father-figure in the beard and shiny white robe, but you have to keep the whole thing in a tightly defined box, you're limited in what you can draw on for creating and experiencing your own vision of God. In the same way dictated language limited my prayer life, working with only someone else's imagery limited my whole God experience.

Taking the lid off that box was like opening the biggest, scariest present I'd ever been given. I suddenly had space to find God for myself: to toss out what I'd conjured, gather my own ingredients—others' ideas and those born of my personal experiences—and find a new version of divinity for myself. I would never have realized I could take off the lid if Richard Rohr hadn't spelled out the fact so plainly that I was dealing with a box to begin with.

If we blow the idea of God out beyond Heavenly Father to include a Heavenly Mother, I think the box is part of what keeps Her under wraps in our religion too. Most of us don't feel at liberty to actively use our imaginations in this area, and there's no space for a female god in the current box.

Desmond Tutu tells of talking to a group of older women about God.[15] He described them to themselves as "God carriers. God's partners. Created in the image of God." He saw them stand up straighter when they left the church than when they came in. If Bishop Tutu's description is true—and in our church we're told it is—and if I fail to relate to the god that's been described or explained to me, it means I need to use a little more imagination. And probably a mirror. I need to be able to visualize myself fitting in my own God-description and understanding.

A woman told us that her young daughter had talked about Heavenly Mother when she bore her testimony one Sunday, and she and her husband were immediately summoned to the bishop's office after the meeting. He was troubled by the testimony and wanted to know what they'd been teaching their daughter. Children are very literal thinkers. I think we create a barrier to helping our daughters understand and internalize their own divine nature when we can't openly draw a word-picture of God in which they can easily and clearly locate themselves. I believe any girl who has been taught about God in our church should naturally think and speak about Heavenly Mother. It is, after all, her own part in the larger story.

If I could wish one thing for everyone in their spiritual life, it would be permission to imagine widely in the process of our own God-creation. We're equipped to understand truth when we experience it, so we need not fear being led too far astray. But our starting box needs to be big enough to encompass all the ways and places God's children experience God, a box big enough to hold all the world's people, approaches and ideas. It would be difficult to call that scope of imagination a box at all.

Cynthia:

Opening up that God Box has been pivotal for me as well. For me, the 'Mormon God' was always a difficult one to feel close to. God always felt very transactional to me. If I do this, then God sends me blessings. If I don't do this, then God punishes me. One thing that helped me move away from the transactional view was studying and reading from all the great contemporary thinkers, writers, and theologians *outside* of our faith. I think that's because they're free to color outside the lines that Mormonism draws quite heavily. I am not saying that everyone in our church thinks of God in the same way. I am sure there is plenty of variety, but we're not really allowed to talk about those different perspectives in our church meetings.

In many instances, these smart thinkers also came from strict religious backgrounds so it felt incredibly calming to me to see other Christians who needed to rethink the nature of God that had been handed to them in their own faith traditions. Writers like Nadia Bolz-Weber, Rachel Held Evans, Peter Enns, and Brian McLaren have all greatly influenced my changing view of God. I've heard it said from many church leaders that I am simply creating God in my own image. Maybe, maybe not. More on that in a minute. I do think it's a healthy and normal quest for all adults to think about the nature of God.

I didn't invest anything prior to age forty in thinking about the nature of God. The thinking had been done by men in our church and I took their ideas at face value. My previous ideas came from the LDS ideas about God and that mostly worked, until it didn't. I say 'mostly' because hustling for God's approval was always easy for me, yet the idea of having a 'relationship' with God always eluded me. I was better at box checking than communing and 'being' with the Divine.

What initially led me to opening the 'God box' was that I finally started questioning whether all of my life events came from God. Is God the ultimate chess player in the sky, moving us around a game-board? Is God zapping one person with a trial while blessing another, all in the name of growth and well-being? Thinking about a God that sends me devastating trials makes it hard for me to want that kind of God in my life! No parent worth her salt willingly inflicts pain on her child. Whether or not God actually gives their kids 'whoopings' in the form of cancer or poverty, I have no real way of knowing. But if I am going to be a woman of faith, a woman who chooses to talk to and acknowledge a Divine Creator, the Ultimate Loving Parent, I choose not to believe that.

When I was a young newlywed, we faced the devastating news of infertility. Eventually, we decided to adopt. During this time, a family member, who had herself adopted all of her children, said to me, "Just remember that you chose this trial in heaven. You and Heavenly Father counseled together and you chose this." I recoiled and was furious at such a baseless and callous belief. One that I might add isn't doctrinal, per se, but the idea of being assigned trials still persists among many. It was then that I began to realize that my idea of God wasn't always going to align with my LDS culture.

It wasn't until middle age that I finally decided if something makes God look like a jerk, I don't have to believe it. Maybe that really is creating God in my own image, but I don't care. I need to feel loved by God, and a vengeful, wrathful god who teaches through punishments and trials isn't a god I want anything to do with. I align more now with this idea by Father Gregory Boyle, "I believe in a God that protects me from nothing but sustains me in everything."[16]

Susan:

You raise the age-old question. Without being completely swallowed by the theodicy rabbit hole, I'll say that in my observation, a lot of church members seem to find a kind of comfort in the idea that they agreed to the circumstances of their lives before they came to earth—they chose this, knowing it was going to be hard. This gives rise to ideas I also find unhelpful, like, "God doesn't give us anything we can't handle." I would say most members of our church believe God has a hand in what happens to us, and a lot of what happens is directly tied to our own choices. I'm never going to tell anyone else how they're allowed to draw meaning from their own experiences (or not), but it can be really gnarly when you start untangling this stuff. Where does God get credit, and where not?

I also know many people who take a non-interventionist view of God, believing God did set things in motion by creating the world, but doesn't have much to do with its day-to-day workings now. My personal tent is a little closer to this camp. I believe God is both invested and interested in us, and is available to help us personally. Not by arranging the physical details of our lives or situations, but by aiding us in responding to them in ways that help us grow and progress. I think it's natural that everyone will have their own views on this based on their experiences. There are plenty of things in my life I can't explain—places I've felt supported and connected, known and loved—and I'm okay with being unsettled on what exactly I experienced and what, if anything, that experience means. I'm more interested in what my experiences have done for me, and that's where I hope to partner with God.

Anne Lamott wrote, "Help is a prayer that is always answered."[17] Whether you believe receiving divine help means God will literally reach down and arrange the pieces, or just patiently bear you up while you're tossed around by this world of circumstances and consequences you so often can't control, in my experience, asking God to fix things is probably the fastest way to realize the truth that God's ways are not our ways. But I do believe in a god who is interested in the project—and a willing participant in the process—of our becoming.

There are pitfalls when we let our picture of God get too close to anything we see in the mirror, aren't there? It's too easy to, along with our body, project traits like our fragile human ego. Opening the box for me has meant giving lots of space for a god who does not act, think, judge, value, or behave like I do. For instance, I no longer believe in a god who needs worship for the sake of being worshipped. That doesn't mean I'm throwing out the value of worship, it means I believe it is for us, not for God. I think of it as me turning toward God, affirming my desire, setting my faith in a specific direction. It's a reminder for me, because I'm the one who needs reminders, my god doesn't. In my own spiritual life and practice, worship is whatever prepares me to enter into relationship by getting my heart right. Whenever I'm feeling and/or expressing love for God, I'm worshipping. In the NIV, Romans 12:1 says to "offer your bodies as a living sacrifice, holy and pleasing to God—this is your true and proper worship." That sounds to me like, more than any specific action, worship is meant to be who we are and how we live.

Cynthia:

I love that you brought up worship because it's something I have spent lots of time really pondering. Sometimes when I think about the nature of God I can't help picturing the most evolved humans ever—persons who are full of compassion, patience, wisdom, and a total lack of ego. Yet when I think about someone who requires worship, it feels like the ultimate egotistic need. Bow down! Kiss my feet! *Ewww* from a germy point of view to that type of prostrating posture. So I love your idea that worship is to center *us*. Jesus said, "The sabbath was made for humankind, and not humankind for the sabbath." (Mark 2:27 NRSV) I think that's what you're getting at—that worship is for us, not for God, as it helps soften my heart to enter a more teachable space. A space of expansion where I recognize there is someone out there bigger than myself who loves me and has my best interests at heart.

How many times do you see charities that say, "This was made possible by an anonymous donor." No ego! The giver doesn't need or want credit! Worship is egotistic, but if I slightly tilt it another way, it can become gratitude. For me, the greatest way I enter this worshipful space is through gratitude. I don't know if God needs credit for the good things They create in this world, but I do know that I need to show gratitude for all that surrounds me. Gratitude centers me, humbles me, and helps me focus on today's daily bread.

Maybe you've noticed that I keep referring to God not only in non-gendered pronouns, but I also toggle back and forth between singular and plural pronouns. This is intentional on my part. At this point in my middle-aged life, it's hard for me to think about God without my feminist-LDS glasses on. Those glasses have been tinged with all the harms that patriarchy has piled onto me throughout my life. For example, while I love our doctrine of a Heavenly Mother, the idea of a Mother God presents itself with some baggage. I am not so sure my wounds can picture a Goddess tied to being a mother or a wife. Motherhood is such a complicated title for me that I prefer seeing Her as sovereign and not attached to a man.

While we do have a doctrine of a Heavenly Mother in our church, she is also completely silent in our faith tradition. What is there to love and revere about silent women? A few years ago in my own ward there was a big kerfuffle that took place between men and women leaders about Heavenly Mother. A man in a leadership role, wanting to silence the talk around Her, tossed out that tired cultural line that 'She is too sacred to talk about.' Why would any woman want Mormon exaltation if that's the role we look forward to? A silent supporter? A quiet wife and mother who simply stands by her man?

I want to leave plenty of room for women and men who are parents or have amazing parents to see God as our Ultimate Parents, as a Divine Mother and Father. Our life experience with loving parents can be a great foundation for thought experiments about the nature of God. However, for those who have less-than-ideal relationships with their parents, or who have struggled seeing a spark of divinity in being a parent, this can also be a minus. As with anything, even thought experiments about Gods' character and nature, your mileage will vary!

Susan:

We're absolutely on the same page that the title Heavenly Mother has some itchiness attached. I've realized we don't really have any— *any!*—model of a divine role for women outside that title. I mean, we don't even know what She specifically does in this whole plan, do we? Tying God to the word Mother disappoints me in the same ways tying it to Father does. Those are titles that describe human relationships, and human relationships often disappoint in some way.

Also, I don't want to think of myself as only being a mother. I want to think of myself as being a Self. So please let my own becoming—my reach toward something greater—be about Selfhood, not Motherhood.

When we try to connect with God, and we're thinking of only a Heavenly Father—and I'm willing to guess this is most church members, most of the time—how can we expect to find the wholeness of relationship we seek?

That being said, now I'm going to turn around and immediately muddy my own water by reminding us how often I've said that everything I know about God, I've learned from being a parent. What I mean is, I've learned about the relationship part of God—about what love requires (hint: not always easy) and how it can nurture and grow us—from having my own children. I'm sure everyone learns about this in their own way, that's just how God has taught me about it. I don't think these lessons tell me everything about the nature of God though, because I'm definitely not a god to my children, nor would I want that dynamic to exist in our relationship. So while being a parent has helped me frame an approach to understanding the kind of love I identify with the God I have experienced myself, I consider it only a glimpse. It doesn't feel like any kind of comprehensive knowledge. This makes me think the title Heavenly Parents is a key to only one aspect of God's nature, not the whole of it.

Imagine living in a house with a mother and father, but only being allowed to talk to the father. I actually got a taste of that growing up with a mother who was profoundly ill for several years of my childhood. We lived in a very large house—she remained in her suite of rooms, and the kids were mostly kept elsewhere. Other grownups assumed our care, and we were not allowed to see her much at all. The deep loneliness I experienced in those years has stayed with me as a kind of vague longing that won't be filled. Childhood wounds do that sometimes. I think many women in the LDS Church find themselves carrying just such a wound now. How can we heal it?

When our Young Women repeat their theme on Sundays, beginning with "I am a beloved daughter of heavenly parents, with a divine nature and eternal destiny," where are they supposed to get additional info about their female parent? Where's any church-sanctioned narrative that might help them to better understand Her—and by extension their own—nature and destiny?

I'll admit I'm not that hopeful, because you can tell a lot about people by the choices they make. How they allocate time and resources, what they prioritize in their personal lives, what kind of public image they're invested in projecting—these things give us a much clearer picture of someone than their words do, right? Our children know we love them because of the things we do for them more than because we say so. So here's where it gets icky for me: I don't have to go very far out on a limb to conclude that The Church of Jesus Christ of Latter-day Saints does not care much about our doctrine of Heavenly Mother.

It gets worse, because I'm afraid ignoring Her is really just an extension of our attitude toward women generally. So what is it? Do we not believe our own stuff about women, or do we not believe our own stuff about Heavenly Mother? If we were to elevate the status of one—either women or Heavenly Mother—I believe the change would spill over onto the other. We talk about revering both but the choices we make tell a different story. Watch any session of general conference, overwhelmingly dominated by male voices, and you have a loud example of the kind of choice I'm talking about. I don't care how many talks I hear about the value of women, I believe our pedestalization in the church is designed to distract, and so far it's done a pretty good job. Many people who don't look closely at it are fooled, and that definitely includes women.

Yet many members find our professed belief in a Heavenly Mother to be a missing piece in their understanding of God. The idea speaks to some place of deep knowing for them, but don't those who have been yearning for that specific connection and believe they find it in our doctrine deserve more than just a female god-title we keep on a pedestal . . . hidden behind a closed door?

I think Kathryn Knight Sonntag spelled out this piece we're missing as Latter-day Saints trying to gain insight into the nature of God—and why it matters—so well:

> As children of Heavenly Parents, we embody traits from each parent. Because we have come to understand God as He, the majority of our discussion about divine attributes we seek to emulate originate from a male deity. We have had little experience thinking of God as feminine and masculine, let alone considering Mother God as an autonomous, whole being with unique traits that we, as Her spirit children, have also inherited. We are less experienced at seeking out the Mother's attributes. I believe that a knowledge of Her character, power, and purpose creates wholeness in ourselves, in our relationships, and in our theology. Harmonizing their divinely feminine and divinely masculine principles inside our souls leads to unity with Them.[18]

Cynthia:

Like you, I am also afraid that ignoring our doctrine of a Heavenly Mother, or a feminine divine, is emblematic of a greater problem in our church, and by extension, in larger society. Do LDS male leaders, like former church president Gordon B. Hinckley who instructed us not to pray to her, do so because that really could cause a feminist awakening in other areas? Not all women identify as feminists, but a hunger for a Heavenly Mother often begins the awakenings of feminism. For some women, it's the lack of a role model of a female deity that leads to a feminist awakening. For other women, their feminist leanings lead them to curiosity about a feminine divine. Whichever comes first, I am not sure this is a message that leaders can control anymore. Author Meggan Watterson wrote:

> It's not that an idea of God the Father was so upsetting to me, it was that it was so incomplete. God as the father and Jesus as His only son made zero sense. It just felt like one side of a far more inclusive and radical love story.[19]

Women are feeling that incompleteness and they're doing something about it personally and publicly. There is a wave spreading throughout our culture—books, art, and social media—that is filling that hunger. But many male leaders in our church are actively trying to dampen this wave of desire women are publicly displaying for Her. Is Watterson right? Are leaders in The Church of Jesus Christ of Latter-day Saints afraid of greater inclusivity? Elder Dale G. Renlund, in a speech given to the worldwide church in general conference, said about this topic that "speculation will not lead to greater spiritual knowledge, but it can lead us to deception or divert our focus from what has been revealed."[20] I can't help but contrast some of the words Watterson used versus Renlund. 'Inclusive' and 'radical,' which feel expansive and exciting, versus 'deception' and 'divert,' which feel blamey and contracting.

In one of the darkest moments of my life at age forty, I was folding laundry in my bedroom and I felt someone not of the world brush by me and bring love into the room. I don't know how to describe it other than it was a love that felt feminine. Was it divinity? Some people think the Holy Spirit is female, possibly Heavenly Mother. So is that what it was, a female Holy Spirit? Was it my grandmother Beverley Baguley? Was it my other grandmother, Ernestina Vega? I will never know. But in the dark, light was sent. I was hungry to be loved and the hunger was filled. I felt like I now knew 'the other side,' as Meggan Watterson wrote.

Susan:

I love that story! I wish I had a similar one. I had a profound encounter with God's love, but I never felt a connection to the feminine in it. It's been hard for me to feel personally invested in our doctrine of Heavenly Mother, and I've thought a lot about why that is. Knowing the contours of my own experience as an LDS woman, maybe I haven't felt that a female deity defined by our church would likely have an expansive role. That being the case, I've preferred to not think about Her. And there's always the pall polygamy casts over things. Here it's the question of whether Heavenly Mother is one, or one of many? This is something I've never heard any leader address, but I'm glad because I'd prefer to not get my information on this subject through men. Unfortunately, in our church women don't receive the official answers to questions, so it will have to come that way. Still, I believe there is no limit to the questions we could ask out of a sincere desire for more light and knowledge, personally and through our prophet. There is no good reason I can think of why questions about Heavenly Mother should be limited or discouraged. Four-year-olds drive you crazy with questions too, but they're trying to figure out the shape of their world. Questions prepare us to grow. As Thomas Merton says, "God makes us ask ourselves questions most often when He intends to resolve them."[21]

Thinking about each of our experiences with the divine, they both seem to come down to one thing: Love. It's the only thing I know about all this for sure, and has made so many other things make sense. It has given me space to make my own way along my individual path of faith. In helping me realize that I'm known and loved as-is, God sanctioned this journey. I can't stress enough how foundational my *experience* of that love has been. It colored my understanding of the atonement, of my self-ness, of what I'm meant to be doing in relationship to everyone else in this world.

As a very young child, one of my first church memories is of being on my grandmother's lap and hearing her sing, *God is Love*. I had kind of a hard time feeling and *believing* love—it didn't seem trustworthy to me as a kid. But this grandmother was one of the foundational pillars in my life. I believed the deeply familiar safety of her off-key voice. I felt the truth of it—one of my first witnesses of truth—because I knew and felt known by her.

I've often struggled to hear or believe God's love in my church life, but that childhood experience came to my mind many decades later as I began to find and understand God's love for me through my personal life experiences. The memory and the feelings that accompanied it helped me begin to trust that God *IS* love, and that I'd misunderstood the relationship I thought we were supposed to have. Standing at the threshold of old age, I now know what to listen for. If something doesn't speak love, it doesn't come from God.

Cynthia:

I think it's interesting how often you and I have used the word love in an essay about God. That doesn't seem like a very Mormon-y verb or noun. In fact, in the Topical Guide of our LDS scriptures under 'God,' you do find 'Love,' but you also find: Creator; Foreknowledge, Glory, Indignation, Intelligence, Justice, Knowledge, Law, Mercy, Omniscience, Perfection, Power, Wisdom, Father. I don't have anything particularly against those descriptors (well okay, 'indignation' gets a huge thumbs down from me). I just find it fascinating that when two women who have spent a lifetime in the church write an essay on God, we focus almost exclusively on Love. It seems to be the driving force behind everything we 'know' about God.

We're very different women, but we're also very much the same. Both of us finally experiencing the love of God is what has healed us in all our wounded ways. I've said a thousand times that I have never really felt like God has guided me or told me what to do. I can count those experiences on one hand. But expand that to how often I have felt completely loved, and that list just grows and grows. The common denominator is almost every godlike moment in my life has been one of overwhelming love. They've become my anchors. Nadia Bolz-Weber said: "God isn't waiting for you to become thinner or heterosexual or married or celibate or more ladylike or less crazy or more spiritual or less of an alcoholic in order to love you. Also, I would argue that since your ideal self doesn't actually exist, it would follow that the 'you' everyone in your life loves is your actual self, too."[22]

Yes! I don't feel qualified in any way to speak about most of that list in the Topical Guide, but I do feel qualified to say that throughout my life I have always felt that God loved my *actual self*.

Now I'm going to contradict something I said earlier—that I don't believe that I am creating God in my image, in choosing to define God as Love. It's possible I am. And here's an even crazier idea: maybe that's okay. I am not trying to make excuses for my excessive TV-watching with a large bag of Cheetos, while simultaneously thinking that in the end God will just "smite me with a few stripes." (2 Nephi 28:8) I am just not sure it's possible to *not* see God as the sum total of my life experiences. I am an imperfect human with a finite and flawed mind who is trying to understand God from a very mortal and very limited perspective. And God has manifested to us as Love.

In the essay, *In Search of a Larger God*, you said in the very second sentence, "Perhaps the problem began with Joseph Smith having seen God as a man." Whether Joseph Smith experienced God as he describes him in the First Vision, as a grandfatherly version of Joseph himself (male, white, English speaking) or whether God chose to appear to Joseph as someone Joseph could relate to, I don't much care anymore. To a certain extent, we all experience God in whatever ways our mind and life circumstances can handle. If that's creating God in our image, then I think a merciful God will understand.

Susan:

The way I've come to feel comfortable with the idea that I'm creating my own image of God is actually through the scriptures. Consider all the different versions we find there—Old Testament God is a specific flavor, for instance, and that tells us the men writing these stories were recording their own ideas of God, a portrait born of their personal experiences filtered through the lens of what they had been taught and understood. We see the results of their seeking for divine relationship. It was no different for Joseph, in my opinion, and therefore needn't be different for me. We're each entitled—even expected, if you believe Jesus—to seek and find for ourselves.

"Each man is a half-open door / leading to a room for everyone." These words from a Tomas Transtromer poem are a beautiful description of how I believe the process of finding God is meant to work in our lives.[23] We don't ever get a full view of the next room; instead, seeing others teaches us something about ourselves, and understanding ourselves within the context of all teaches us something about God.

At this point in my life, the mystery is what gives me peace. I know that is not the case for everyone. There was searching and suffering involved in learning it about myself. When I first stepped toward mystery thinking my own questions might be the resting place I hadn't found yet, it was the first real peace I'd ever experienced in my faith life. That's when I knew I was onto something not only *big*, but deeply okay.

Some people are attracted to religion because it provides answers;

I'm attracted to it because I believe it asks unanswerable questions and gives us a framework for living well in the face of them. Religion asks us to practice what Anne Lamott calls "Radical hope—hope in the face of not having a clue."[24] Actually, religion gives us a few clues and asks us to follow them. But personally, I don't ever want to mistake the clues for being the solved mystery itself. Questions and answers can remain happily separate for me while I'm on this earth. G.K. Chesterton describes it perfectly for me:

> The whole secret of mysticism is this: that man can understand everything by the help of what he does not understand. The morbid logician seeks to make everything lucid, and succeeds in making everything mysterious. The mystic allows one thing to be mysterious, and everything else becomes lucid.[25]

These words leave space for me to feel a bit baffled by all the answers I hear at church, but fed by the search for my own, even if it never yields anything but the next question.

I've decided even a fairly definitive phrase like "God is Love" will require us to spend our whole lives trying to live our way to the truth of it. It's a useless platitude unless we grab it and do our own experiments. We will attempt to prove it again and again, but I don't think we're meant to ever fully get it, only to get something from our experimentation that pulls us forward, always moving toward that larger thing just beyond our sight.

Cynthia:

Like you, I don't need institutional God Answers anymore. I started this essay saying that the LDS version of God worked great for me, until it didn't. Peter Enns says, "doubt enters when certainty has run its course."[26] That version of God had run its course. For forty years I loved my surety and my certainty about who God is. And now? I love the mystery. Moving from certainty to mystery happened virtually overnight for me. I woke up one day with all kinds of questions and realized my once-certain answers didn't suffice anymore. As those wrestle-filled years passed, I realized I didn't want to move from one certainty to another. And like you, I settled on mystery. And that mystery is where I have found my peace with the God question.

The comedian Pete Holmes loves to toss around the idea that God is the name of the blanket we throw over the mystery to give it shape.[27] I think that's exactly what I have been doing in this past decade of my evolving faith: giving shape to my life experiences that can't be named, calculated, or quantified. Again, I turn to Nadia Bolz-Weber who describes her need for 'god mystery' this way:

> I can't imagine that the God of the universe is limited to our ideas of God. I can't imagine that God doesn't reveal God's self in countless ways outside of the symbol system of Christianity. In a way, I need a God who is bigger and more nimble and mysterious than what I could understand and contrive.[28]

Section Notes

1. Christian Wiman, *My Bright Abyss: Meditation of a Modern Believer* (FSG Adult, 2014), 54.

2. Joseph Campbell, Bill Moyers collaborator, *The Power of Myth* (Anchor, 1991), 209.

3. Thomas Merton, *The Seven Storey Mountain* (HarperOne, 1999), 209.

4. Anne Lamott, *Grace (Eventually): Thoughts on Faith* (Riverhead Books, 2007), page.

5. Paul Thornton, "Christmas History: Was Jesus a Day Laborer?" *Los Angeles Times*, December 23, 2017, latimes.com.

6. Nadia Bolz-Weber, *Pastrix: The Cranky, Beautiful Faith of a Sinner & Saint* (Jericho Books, 2013), 58.

7. Richard Rohr, "True Self/False Self" (Franciscan Media, 2003), audio speech.

8. Richard Rohr, "New Great Themes of Scripture" (Franciscan Media, 1999), audio speech.

9. Jeffrey R. Holland, "The Laborers in the Vineyard," April 2012 general conference.

10. Robert Farrar Capon, *Kingdom, Grace, Judgment: Paradox, Outrage, and Vindication in the Parables of Jesus* (Eerdmans, 2002), 395.

11. Rob Bell, *The Robcast* podcast, episode 146, "Alternative Wisdom, Part 1," June 12, 2017.

12. Richard Rohr, *The Universal Christ: How a Forgotten Reality Can Change Everything We See, Hope for, and Believe* (Convergent Books, 2019), 106.

13. Adam S. Miller, *Letters to a Young Mormon* (Deseret Book, 2018), 10.

14. Richard Rohr, *Everything Belongs: The Gift of Contemplative Prayer* (Crossroad, 2003), 25.

15. Krista Tippet, host, *On Being* podcast, episode 1000, "Remembering Desmond Tutu," January 6, 2022, 51 minutes.

16. Gregory Boyle, *Barking to the Choir: The Power of Radical Kinship* (Simon & Schuster, 2017), 22

17. Anne Lamott, *Plan B: Further Thoughts on Faith* (Riverhead Books, 2006), 37.

18. Kathryn Knight Sonntag, *The Mother Tree: Discovering the Love and Wisdom of Our Divine Mother* (Faith Matters, 2022), ix–x.

19. Meggan Watterson, *Mary Magdalene Revealed: The First Apostle, Her Feminist Gospel, & the Christianity We Haven't Tried Yet* (Hay House Inc, 2019), 47.

20. Dale G. Renlund, "Your Divine Nature and Eternal Destiny," April 2022 general conference.

21. Richard Rohr, *Dancing Standing Still: Healing the World from a Place of Prayer* (Paulist Press, 2014), 6.

22. Nadia Bolz-Weber, *Shameless: A Case for Not Feeling Bad About Feeling Good* (Convergent Books, 2020), 180.

23. Tomas Transtromer, *The Half-Finished Heaven*, The Nobel Prize in Literature 2011, nobelprize.org, accessed Jan. 17, 2025.

24. Lamott, *Plan B*, 39.

25. G. K. Chesterton, *Orthodoxy* (The Bodley Head and Methuen & Co, 1908), 49.

26. Peter Enns, *The Sin of Certainty: Why God Desires our Trust More Than Our "Correct" Beliefs* (HarperOne, 2016), 157.

27. Pete Holmes. *Comedy Sex God* (HarperCollins, 2018), 149.

28. Bolz-Weber, *Pastrix*, 15.

WHAT ABOUT . . . ?

OBEDIENCE

"I run in the path of your commands, for you have broadened my understanding."
—Psalm 119:32 (NRSV)

Cynthia:

I've been perplexed by a unique phrase that has emerged in our LDS lexicon: exact obedience. It seems to have emerged in the last decade. One of the first uses of the phrase 'exact obedience' was in a talk to young missionaries in the Missionary Training Center. I think there is a lot of wisdom in encouraging young missionaries, many of whom have never lived away from home before, to be obedient to mission rules.

My uncertainty about this phrase has arisen out of my complete distaste for any talk, speech, or advice around perfectionism. I have spent my entire life happily living within the mantra, "it's good enough." I don't excel at any *one* thing but rather I have tried to experience and try my hand at *many* things. The phrase "Jack of all trades and a master of none" could be used to describe my efforts. So asking me to do anything *exactly* leaves me scratching my head and wondering, "How?" How am I supposed to be *exactly* obedient? And how is exact obedience different from regular obedience?

"Obedience brings success, exact obedience brings miracles" is the phrase President Russell M. Nelson coined that has gone viral in speeches among the other leaders.[1] I wish I could sit down with our leaders and ask them to give me a specific example of what 'obedience' versus 'exact obedience' looks like. It can be problematic, in my experience, to teach someone that their efforts bring about success, blessings, or miracles.

Perhaps I just have a different definition of success or miracles than President Nelson? Maybe this is an issue of semantics and nothing more, I really don't know. Maybe if we could sit down together and discuss this over donuts, we would find that we actually agree on the meaning of that phrase. But the way in which I have seen the phrase 'exact obedience' used in sacrament meeting talks, general conference talks, and Sunday lessons has left me confused.

First, I don't think I have that much control in my life. I am able-bodied, of a reasonably sound mind, not having suffered from mental illness, abuse, nor debilitating physical illness. Yet given all the privilege I have enjoyed in life thus far, I still struggle to do anything 'exactly,' let alone to bring about miracles. Advice and talks around exact obedience often leave me feeling like something heavy is resting on my head, weighing me down needlessly, like a mile long 'to do' list that never gets completed. Sadly, I have often heard friends and family say that they must not have been obedient enough to deserve a miracle from God. Exactly *how much* of a miracle came about because of my obedience? Where is the line I cross from exact obedience to an arrival at miracles? How much is due to chance, to God's intervention, and to my efforts?

When my son was getting ready to serve a mission, I told him that his job was to share messages of Jesus Christ with anyone who would listen, but he had zero control over whether they joined our church. Maybe they would listen to his message and become a better Catholic. He said, "Mom, isn't the goal to get them to join our church?" I explained to my 18-year old son that setting goals for another person isn't possible. His investigators would always have agency, no matter how exactly obedient he was to the mission rules or what goals he set for the number of discussions to give in a week. I wanted him to go out as a missionary with realistic expectations and goals. I wanted to spare him the disappointment I heard from so many returned missionaries—a disappointment born of unrealistic goals around their obedience that led to shame with phrases like, "I must not have done enough." We set up our young people for unnecessary discouragement when we teach them their actions control outcomes.

In my experience, the blessings of obeying the teachings of Jesus Christ are the blessing itself. I have a strong belief of 'internal' blessings; the success or miracle comes from within. However, I struggle with the idea of 'external' blessings, or what we might also call 'prosperity gospel,' as a direct result of my actions. (More on that in the blessings chapter!)

Eugene England wrote that in dealing with 'exasperating saints lies salvation.'[2] We think the *doing* will result in a subsequent blessing from God when in actuality I have found that the blessing, consecration, salvation, or holiness is in the *process of the doing*. Maybe the results of obedience should just be called 'consequences?' For good or for ill, consequences, results, and blessings are simply a result of the laws of nature. For my left-brained, analytical personality, this actually gives me a lot of peace. As a naturally obedient person, it has served me well as it has always been in my nature to listen to authority and comply. Nevertheless, I am grateful I mostly understood the difference between consequences of my obedience versus obedience bringing about success or miracles. I believe this understanding has saved me from a lot of shame and self-loathing.

I feel much more hopeful and encouraged by the words of our sacrament prayer admonishing us to be "willing." Or by the words of Jesus Christ inviting us to "Come follow me." Or "If you love me, keep my commandments." Quite the opposite of that weight pressing down on my head.

Willing. Follow. Come. These are all invitations to walk in the shoes of Jesus, whose yoke is easy and whose burden is light.

Susan:

I'm not a born obeyer. That doesn't mean I haven't spent the vast majority of my time on earth being obedient, it just means I chafe a lot while I do it. So there probably aren't many people who bristle at a phrase like 'exact obedience' more than I do. It reminds me of wool—I HATE wearing wool. It's scratchy and irritates my skin. Even with a layer of something else between a wool sweater and me, I feel itchy all day when I have it on.

But wool has a lot of value as a material. It's extremely warm and a great natural insulator. It's naturally water resistant. It contains lanolin which is good for skin. On a cold damp day, there's hardly a thing better than wool clothing or accessories. Still, it makes me feel so prickly, I won't wear it.

Strangely, however, I spent my career as a fiber artist creating with wool ... by choice! Once I started working with it, I couldn't imagine how I ever worked with anything else. I love the feel of it in my hands. I look at wool and see endless artistic possibilities. It takes dye beautifully. It can be spun into yarn, molded into felt, and knitted into fabric. Because of its unique structural characteristics as a fiber, wool responds in amazing ways to water and heat and pressure. It is versatile and forgiving and a tactile pleasure to work with.

I can make wool do just about anything I want it to do. Did I mention I hate to wear it? Hate it! But when I work with it, beautiful things happen. The point is, I had to get wool off my back and into my hands before I started to see its possibilities and realize that I could not only learn to love it but even choose to devote a great deal of my time and energy to touching it. I had to create the reward for myself. It wasn't there for me when I was just carrying it around.

I think obedience is the same way for me—hardly an itchier word I can think of. I have a natural aversion to it. But I've found value in it as I've created my life—I've been able to use it in positive ways. As a result, I believe understanding obedience is central to really putting agency to work for us.

There's a lot in the language surrounding obedience that might influence whether or not we choose it, and how we feel about that choice. The phrase 'exact obedience' may come from Alma 57:21: "Yea, and they did obey and observe to perform every word of command with exactness; yea, and even according to their faith it was done unto them; and I did remember the words which they said unto me that their mothers had taught them."

I don't know what the difference between 'obedience' and 'exact obedience' would be as President Nelson makes the distinction in his quote. I like to think he's talking about a difference in our hearts, and the miracle he promises is just his way of describing a true transformation of the same. But as you pointed out, Jesus taught us to obey in simple language that is easier to understand: "If ye love me, keep my commandments," and "Come, follow me." Somehow it doesn't sound so much like a military drill when he says it. It sounds like an invitation. I feel differently about invitations than about commands, and for me, being invited to personal transformation feels more accessible than being commanded to it. Christ's simple invitation calls me into my own work. It doesn't promise a result so much as show me how to participate.

Are there different kinds of obedience? Are some more likely to yield personal transformation than others? I think so. I find changing the way I think about obedience changes the way I feel about it.

Blind obedience is when we think laws should be obeyed just because the law exists. Such indiscriminate failure to really think about our actions 'because we've always done it this way,' 'because my boss said so,' 'because it's the law,' or 'because I was only following orders' causes us to abdicate responsibility for our choices and fail to take ownership of consequences. Things can go very wrong, but we believe we've done nothing wrong because we were following the law.

Obeying the letter of the law is a way in which loving the law itself can get in the way of ideal, spiritually mature obedience. Keeping all the commandments perfectly does not necessarily result in perfection, does it? A focus on exactness puts the execution on an equal footing with, if not above, the principle itself, a suggestion that the outward is at least as important as the inward. What about healing on the Sabbath day . . . was Jesus 'exactly obedient?' The Pharisees sought to demonstrate perfect adherence to the rule, but we know Jesus did not perceive them to be perfect. The real question is how to live the letter of the law *and* remain in the spirit of the law. As Latter-day Saints, we are expected to live the letter of the law but it's hard to do that without focusing too much on the law itself. Principles, not rules, are our ideal motivation.

Thoughtful obedience squares agency with obedience, in my mind. This means when I hear counsel from the prophet, I have a responsibility to engage with that counsel. I have a responsibility to pray about it, and when I have received a witness that it is God's will and personal direction as to how I should implement it, then it becomes binding upon me. I have a choice to make. Is it possible that, outside our core doctrines, one person receives different personal revelation and therefore obeys differently from their neighbor? I believe it is possible. Consider Eve—did she display thoughtful obedience, or maybe thoughtful disobedience?

Spiritually mature obedience is when we put down the map so we can fully engage in the process of self-navigation, of using our agency; when we have chosen where we want to go, our faith is realized by our feet on the ground. Such active engagement with agency has to do with authenticity, with our motivations and our experiences, and with what we want to create for ourselves. Personally, I believe our obedience will be judged the same way as our disobedience—individually. I don't see that all obedience is equal. What's easy for me may be hard or even impossible for you, and vice versa.

Rules are a path that can lead us to a life governed by principles—rules may become irrelevant if we have truly absorbed and adopted the principles behind them. The balance between rules and principles is 100 percent individual. Perfection is not realistic in mortality, no matter how 'exactly' we try to live, but obedience is an effective method for coming to understand principles, which can help us live better lives.

But you're right: personal 'perfection' in adherence to rules—or even to the principles behind them—does not grant us *any* additional control over all the things that are outside our control.

To hear Jesus tell it, all commandments can be reduced to the two most basic: "Thou shalt love the Lord thy God with all thy heart, and with all thy soul and with all thy mind. This is the first and great commandment. And the second is like unto it, Thou shalt love thy neighbor as thyself. On these two commandments hang all the laws and the prophets." (Matthew 22:35)

In my mind, that sets up the most reliable test when we're making a choice: "Am I showing love?" When I think of it this way, obedience becomes love, and exact obedience becomes perfect love. I am not yet perfect in my love. If that happens, it will indeed be miraculous, a transformation of self I yearn to experience. That invitation is more motivating to me than rules will ever be.

BLESSINGS

"Things falling apart is a kind of testing and also a kind of healing. We think that the point is to pass the test or to overcome the problem, but the truth is that things don't really get solved. They come together and they fall apart. Then they come together again and fall apart again. It's just like that. The healing comes from letting there be room for all of this to happen: room for grief, for relief, for misery, for joy."
—Pema Chodron[3]

Susan:

If we're going to talk about blessings, I want to start the conversation with an acknowledgment that it's as itchy for me as anybody, and my ideas about it are just that. I don't presume to have solved what I think is probably one of the oldest questions we're all swimming in on this planet: *If God is so great, why is there evil in the world ... and how can I keep the awfulness away from me and the people I love?*

You know I love a good wrestle, so let's dive right into the deep end with a quote from a general conference talk that I think highlights some of the specific Latter-day Saint brand complexity around this:

> Blessings from heaven are neither earned by frenetically accruing 'good deed coupons' nor by helplessly waiting to see if we win the blessing lottery. No, the truth is much more nuanced but more appropriate for the relationship between a loving Heavenly Father and His potential heirs—us. Restored truth reveals that blessings are never earned, but faith-inspired actions on our part, both initial and ongoing, are essential. —Elder Dale G. Renlund[4]

So blessings are not earned, but actions are required ... have I got that right? Clear as mud. No wonder this stuff causes so much confusion and pain, not just in our church but everywhere. Many people understandably don't know what to do with a God who apparently finds lost car keys, but also allows children to die of cancer. How can we make sense of it? How can we find peace?

Let's discuss that quote in tension with one of my favorite Kate Bowler ideas: "Our lives are not problems to be solved. We can have meaning and beauty and love, but nothing even close to resolution."[5] The reason I want to put those words right up front is I think blessings (as many people think and talk about them) are so often considered *resolution*—they are 'ends' of stories, morals tacked onto the other side of life experiences to tie them up in neat bows. We love the tidiness of connected dots. That's human, I think—the promise of a neat 'end' can be very motivating. It's so comforting to think things always turn out well, and that we can gain control over outcomes if we just [fill in the blank]. I can't even blame churches when they lean on that appeal, because it works!

But everything in our lives touches everything else; our stories are not isolated incidents with clear beginnings and ends. We can't see or understand the full consequences of anything at the time it happens, so how can we pair up 'blessings' with isolated actions or events with any kind of reliability?

Cynthia:

Nothing is clear when it comes to a discussion of blessings. Speaking of mud, perhaps our problem starts with even defining what we mean when we speak of blessings. In the LDS context, there's a lot to cover. We could mean receiving a priesthood blessing through the laying on of hands. We could mean the bestowal of God's favor that is earned through those 'actions on our part' (like that general conference quote above), like our 'good works' or our 'exact obedience.' We could also simply mean God's favors that are unearned, such as when we talk about grace.

Like you said, everything in our lives touches everything else, so trying to quantify that which can't be quantified or defined with any kind of formula that works with regularity is a losing battle. As Latter-day Saints, I wish we were content to say, "We just don't know how blessings work!" But in The Answer Church, we sure give it our all in trying to provide answers to all of life's questions, including defining what a blessing is and how to get it. I get it, ambiguity doesn't sell, but answers do.

In my own personal experience, the uncomfortable idea of just accepting the mystery of it all is less painful and problematic than the disappointing answers that have left me with my hands empty but my heart pain-filled. Hands open and outstretched to receive what I so desperately needed. Especially when I knew I had checked all the boxes.

For example, the definition of prayer in the LDS resource Bible Dictionary says:

> The object of prayer is not to change the will of God but to secure for ourselves and for others blessings that God is already willing to grant but that are made conditional on our asking for them. Blessings require some work or effort on our part before we can obtain them. Prayer is a form of work and is an appointed means for obtaining the highest of all blessings.

That explanation of prayer satisfied me for many, many years. I found myself using that definition in numerous comments and lessons that I taught. It eventually became less satisfying to me simply because life experience taught me otherwise. Prayer seems like less of a reliable qualifier to me now for several reasons. First of all, plenty of people appear to receive blessings for which they never prayed. And for those who do pray, sometimes the desperately needed blessing is never given. So the giant question mark still persists to the question as to why God helps one person find their keys yet another person's child dies of cancer. It's a heavy question.

Susan:

Prayer sits right in the middle of the mud, doesn't it? But the mud itself might be the word 'blessed.' As in, "I'm so—" I think for people of faith, the blessed life equates to the good life but that description implies there's more to it than just luck or hard work. Whether fortune has smiled or God has, "I'm so blessed" can read as one part gratitude, two parts self-satisfaction. Too cynical? I'm talking about the kind of bragging where someone's children all grew up to be perfectly obedient, their marriage never disappoints, their body never fails them, their career is one success after another, they're surrounded by gobs of loving friends, they don't have to worry about money—whether it's one of these things or all of the above, pointing to any of them as proof of blessed-ness is saying, "I'm so lucky!" with the subtext, "and I also did something to deserve this." Where do people get this idea? Well, I'm looking at you, Religion, and not just ours. So many churchy people (ours and others) are in the habit of looking for external manifestations of their blessedness.

Yet in Jesus's famous promise in John 14:27, there's that phrase, "not as the world giveth, give I unto you." The world rewards us in all kinds of ways, but so many of the things we might associate with being blessed come to us exactly "as the world giveth." Connecting our actions to tangible rewards is a sort of anti-grace, as I think about it. It trains us to trust mostly in ourselves, because our hard work yields so much good fruit! Unfortunately, sometimes in the blink of an eye what the world giveth it can also taketh away. When that happens, it's no wonder we find ourselves wondering what we did wrong. Equations done correctly are always supposed to yield the same answer.

Cynthia:

When I read the list of what constitutes a blessed life, I see a lot of overlap between what our church calls blessed, what evangelical Christians call 'prosperity gospel,' and also what society or 'the world' calls the blessed or abundant life. So that's a great point, that we might be missing the mark. Or maybe we just don't understand what Jesus is talking about when He 'giveth' to us.

Susan:

My big a-ha moment came around the whole idea of blessings when I decided to look up the word 'blessed' to see what precisely it might mean to declare, "I'm so blessed." Well, the word 'blessed' actually means: *made holy; consecrated*. Who knew? I mean, I guess I did—we bless the water and the bread, for instance, and I get that, so this definition makes perfect sense to me. But if to be 'blessed' means to be 'made holy,' that's entirely different from popular usage talking about things like good fortune, a desired outcome, or comfort.

That simple little definition opened a crack of light for me into this whole complicated conversation. I could suddenly see that a blessing is not an event, nor something we receive in exchange for what we do. It's independent of external circumstance, *because blessing is an internal state.*

Cynthia:

Dr. Kate Bowler actually wrote her doctoral thesis on the prosperity gospel. I don't find it hard to believe that in our American Christianity, living a 'blessed life' is enough of a phenomenon that she had enough material to make it her thesis! In America at least, how many of us see the blessed life—the prosperous life—as something we can control in our capitalist society? However, Dr. Bowler seems to align with what you're getting at, that being blessed is internal. She said:

> What would it mean for Christians to give up that little piece of the American Dream that says, "You are limitless?" Everything is not possible... What if rich did not have to mean wealthy, and whole did not have to mean healed? What if being people of the gospel meant that we are simply people with good news? God is here. We are loved. It is enough."[6]

As religious folks, I believe we should be the best at recognizing that to be blessed is simply to recognize that internal state of knowing that we are loved. But I think you're right—we definitely rely too much on 'anti-grace,' too much on our own works. The gospel of Jesus Christ isn't a meritocracy, but I believe it's far too easy for many of us to succumb to the allure of the prosperity gospel, the idea that effort always brings success. Or perhaps that's just me? All I know is that I can look back on my life, all the 'blessings,' all the abundance, and I took credit for most. I *made* this happen. But when we know better, we do better. And life eventually gave me a giant helping of humble pie, and for that I will be forever grateful. Living in a grace-soaked world leaves me wanting less, ironically, than living in my former world of hustle culture.

Susan:

Same here! I'm just not sure why it took me so long to figure out. But I'm going to say I didn't get much help from my religious life. Maybe some people have always been talking about something internal when they talk about their blessings, but that's not the way I've heard it, and I'm pretty sure I'm not alone. I can't tell you how much relief it brings me to shift to the idea that where blessings actually exist is within the mind and heart of the receiver. We are blessed when we create meaning from our experiences and gain strength from them. The events or things in our lives—good and bad—give us an opportunity to come into relationship with God through love and gratitude, and with other people through what we choose to do in the circumstances we're presented with.

If blessing is the realization or manifestation of a relationship with God, which also puts us in relationship with others, then I believe that must be the whole point. How else are we made holy than through the enlargement of our egoistic focus and the transformation of our self-centered hearts? How else are our experiences made holy than by helping us feel connected to God's love, directly or by the actions of others?

This also means blessings have roots in gratitude, rather than expectation. It's how we see and what we do with what actually happens, and that's an important shift from the approach of trying to *guarantee* what happens through our righteous desires or strict obedience. Blessings can't be neatly listed or quantified, because we can't draw lines around them. If you were to try, I think you'd find every blessing is linked to something—maybe even everything?—else.

Anne Lamott writes, "Small is how blessings, healing, progress, and increase occur."[7] If I don't feel 'blessed' in all the mundane minutiae of my life, but just focus on big events, I'm setting myself up for disappointment when blessings don't come the way I think they should. But more importantly, I've missed a big opportunity for ongoing relationship and the change of heart that accompanies it.

Cynthia:

I think most of us live small, mundane lives, interspersed here and there with fleeting moments of grandeur. So I absolutely agree with Anne Lamott that 'small' is how blessings occur. For me, blessings have roots in gratitude. Perhaps it's why we say blessings over food, even when that food might be a box of donuts. There might not be much nutrient-wise in a donut, but if it's the little mundane things that constitute a blessed life, then I am going to keep saying "thank you" to God for a maple cake donut. Like most practices in a spiritual life, saying a blessing over my food changes me, not God. I focus on what is literally before me, sustaining my body, allowing me to live another day.

A few years ago, I realized that the fresh pineapples at big warehouse stores never seemed to change price, even with inflation. For approximately three dollars, I could buy a whole pineapple. So for months and months during winter, when not much else is fresh, I decided to buy a fresh pineapple every week. Ritually cutting it up and serving it to my family and to myself was a sweet spot, a blessing, in a mundane winter. Indeed, I have felt blessed as I create meaning from my everyday experiences, and gain strength from them.

Focusing on gratitude for the mundane and the everyday has helped me to combat my American inclination for a life made prosperous by pulling myself up by my bootstraps. A focus on gratitude to a God for "lending me breath" (Mosiah 2:21) helps me to stomp on the flames of a transactional view of blessings that can often burn out of control.

A full-time missionary assigned to my ward once said he had taught an investigator that one blessing of paying tithing was that he would be able to pay his mortgage more easily. I winced. I can give grace to a young 18-year-old boy who lacks the life experience to know that isn't always the case, or maybe ever the case. Falsely connecting the dots of tithe paying and a life of financial ease should cause us, at the least, to reexamine our motive for charitable giving and at the most, to tear apart that kind of transactional theology.

Susan:

Can you start with a transactional view and somehow, through life experience, make a smooth transition to a relationship-based view of blessings? I'm not sure—I can't say my own views have evolved without navigating some big bumps. I know how I would connect the dots now between that young missionary, his tithing, and his mortgage, and it's different from how I used to think about it. But that pesky quote I used at the beginning of this is still sitting up there muddying the conversational water. Elder Renlund used the word 'qualify,' as in: "You do not earn a blessing—that notion is false—but you do have to qualify for it." So what's the difference between earning something and qualifying for it?

There's a phrase at the end of my patriarchal blessing that says, "These blessings are yours if you live for them." I've spent my entire adult life chewing on those words. They mean something my heart understands, even if my head can't really explain it. So if blessings cannot be earned, do we—can we—position ourselves to receive them? And if I accomplish that by living for them, what does that look like?

Maybe it means continuing to walk in hope, exercising my faith. Perhaps the relationship with God that lies at the heart of being blessed is something I develop through seeking and asking, trying to love God and my fellow men, trusting there can be forgiveness for the many ways I fall short, and allowing gifts of grace and atonement to work in my life. Maybe we grow the relationship by turning toward the source, and how that changes us is how we become blessed.

Could qualifying mean being willing to enter into that relationship— more to do with our hearts than with specific actions? Am I willing to show up in my desperation and ask for help, but then cede control of what happens next? And then let whatever it is turn me back to God?

Cynthia:

As I sit here mulling over your words, that perhaps another way to look at a 'blessed life' is simply by turning towards the source of all that is good, I think, can it be that simple? An acknowledgment that the very air we breathe is a tremendous gift. I used to think that was a bit hyperbolic of a phrase—*the air we breathe*. But it turns out to be scientifically true. As the threat of climate change continues, we've all heard many scientists talk about the possibility of colonizing Mars or even Jupiter's moon Europa. But never being able to breathe on my own again, to feel the rush of fresh air going into my lungs on a warm day outside, doesn't feel like any life I would want. So yes, King Benjamin had it right in suggesting that we show gratitude, awe, and wonder for even the air we breathe. (Mosiah 2:21)

I believe that gratitude, awe, and wonder can be real forms of worship. Can my willingness to turn toward the source mark that change from an ordinary life to a blessed one? That word—*willing*, or willingness—has become my favorite word in our religion. To be willing to do something is to do it ungrudgingly. To gladly give, to be disposed, or inclined. We hear it every week in the sacrament prayer: "*willing* to take upon them the name of thy Son." Or the scripture: "the spirit is *willing* but the flesh is weak." Being willing is the mustard seed of my life. It means I am leaning towards something bigger than myself. It shows my desire coupled with the tiniest bit of mustard-seed effort.

The older I get, the more often I find myself willing to exercise a bit of mustard-seed effort. Here's the tiniest example that will illustrate just how basic and small I need to begin to see the blessings in every moment. I live near two sets of railroad tracks so I decided to do a mini experiment on myself. Is it possible to be grateful even while stuck in traffic? After years of grumbling when I inevitably get stuck at those darn tracks while heading into town, I decided something needs to change, if for no other reason than to keep my cortisol levels down! After all, I have a warm (or cool) car with comfortable seats and there's always a protein bar in my purse.

Waiting for a train to pass gives me extra minutes to listen to a favorite podcast, audiobook, or make a phone call to a friend. So I've stopped the debating in my head—should I turn around, find an alternate route?—and have decided to lean into the moment that I have no control over anyway. My frivolous experiment of gratitude for traffic has yielded lots of mini results in learning patience over this last year, the greatest of which is now I am asking myself—can these lessons in patience be applied elsewhere in my life? Neighbors that fly political flags I find offensive? Probably. Adult children making less-than-ideal choices? Definitely. Who knew that gratitude for traffic and railroad tracks would start to help me let go of control in very Big Real Ways?

Susan:

There's that word: control. Sometimes I wonder how our conversations so often circle back to it, yet I believe so much of our inability to recognize blessing in our lives comes down to control. We don't control God, consequences, other people, their choices, or their responses. Our spiritual lives are one long exercise in giving away control, acknowledging we're not in charge, and living with hope in the somewhat terrifying face of that. Having hope *anyway* is the essence of faith, isn't it? That 'anyway' contains a lot: all the things we don't know, the things we wouldn't have chosen, and the things we're not sure how to live with when they arrive. I often say if I got a tattoo, it'd probably say *anyway*; it feels like the right word to sum up a lot of my life experience.

The quote from Buddhist teacher Pema Chodron at the beginning of this essay is one of my favorites because she reminds me the way to personal peace—all I really have any shot of controlling—is to hand God all the details. Keeping on in hope means being willing to receive with an open heart any blessing that comes, even if I don't feel blessed at the time. But my default tendency is dogged pursuit of the version of events I'm convinced I want.

I think praying and asking is for us, not for our Heavenly Parents. Turning to Them influences me more than it influences the outcome. I don't know any other way to think about it in a world where some children are healed of cancer while others are not. The real blessing must be the way I'm transformed by my experiences, good and not so. I can't deny I've had bad stuff in my life that has made me better. Was the bad stuff a blessing?! I don't think I have to accept that idea. Instead, I think the blessing is what I make of it, and how it changes what I do next, and next after that. Because in developing a relationship with God, I'm changed. I'm made holy. I'm consecrated. I become blessed. But there are zero guarantees things aren't going to just keep falling apart—I have to let there be room in my life for all of it.

I didn't learn this from my lifetime at church though. Latter-day Saints seem particularly prone to slipping into a transactional view of blessings, don't we? I think our emphasis on doing, on covenants and obedience—coupled with our lack of emphasis on being and on grace—can lead us to think we can put God in our debt, if we try hard enough.

Cynthia:

When does connecting the dots between specific events or circumstances in our lives and our own righteousness become sign-seeking? At some point, are we looking for validation or proof of our 'worthiness' in our 'blessings?' I have to admit that when I hear about organized fasts or a telethon of priesthood blessings for a sick person, or even putting names on temple prayer rolls, I think, "Well this could go badly."

The fasting, priesthood blessings, and temple roll prayers may not heal the sick person but may crush the faith of the participants. We could blame ourselves for not having had enough faith to get the miracle needed, or maybe we were not worthy enough, thus impeding God's power. Or maybe the miracle does come and then we say, "See? We are favored of God. We have the healing power. Our covenants and our righteousness made this happen."

Sometimes the miracle doesn't happen and faith isn't harmed. In addition to believing that we can sometimes affect change through fasting, prayer, and blessings, we also can believe that healing simply wasn't God's will. This might personally be the toughest justification for me to understand why some get miracles and some don't. In trying to understand more about the whole 'God's will' angle, I read the book *God Can't* by Thomas Jay Oord. I finally had the words to express why 'God's will' is such an itchy concept:

> A loving God who could heal singlehandedly would do what's best whether we prayed or not. Another question is related: if it's not God's will to heal, why ask? If God doesn't want some ailment cured, our prayer seems futile. We're wasting our time. If God doesn't want to do something

because it's not loving, why twist God's arm? Over time, I came to believe "if it's your will" is a cover-your-ass phrase uttered to avoid the tough questions we all ask when healing prayer fails. "If it's your will" makes no sense. We need a plausible explanation for why healing sometimes happens but often does not."[8]

This describes how I have always felt about petitioning God for a miracle, whether that be a physical healing, or spiritual healing. It feels like I am trying to twist God's arm into getting what I want, either for myself or someone else. In our scriptures, we would never use that phrase—twisting God's arm—but we do use a similar word, 'bind.' We believe that the Lord is bound when we do what He says.[9] And that's what makes this subject so impossible for me to grasp. Although that scripture seems to be focusing on repentance, in my experience we have taken it beyond repentance and applied it to, well, almost anything we need or want. We think we can paint God into a corner with our good works and covenant keeping.

I was explicitly taught that God blesses His 'covenant people' in all ways—spiritually, financially (think of that young missionary and his mortgage example), physically, and temporally. It would be easy for some Latter-day Saints to say I have been given so many blessings in all of those categories because I have bound God by keeping my covenants. But the suffering of those around the world haunts me so I push back *hard* against that kind of prosperity gospel cause-and-effect thinking.

So like you, if I want to maintain any kind of belief in blessings, I have to shift towards what we've been talking about in this chapter— that blessings can only be defined as an inner change. That to be *blessed* is to be *made holy*. But I do believe that we are swimming up-current in LDS culture with that definition of 'a blessed life.'

Susan:

I can't disagree, and the current is strong. But when it comes to some big questions, I simply have to prioritize my own peace of mind over alignment with any theology. When I started to really chew on this idea, I began to see the transactional view of blessings as looking for proof of God versus looking for relationship. In my own experiences, things like family fasts, temple rolls, and priesthood blessings have been a comforting signifier of relationship. I love the idea that we're unified—we come together in community—in trying to lift someone, and petitioning God on their behalf is a concrete way to show unity. There have been all kinds of studies trying to prove any scientific connection between prayer and healing. There's data that shows improved outcomes associated with prayer, and data that shows none. I would guess that, in general, feeling supported is beneficial to health outcomes. But—and this is a *HUGE* but—when it comes to healing, I think we have to be willing to give away all power over God's side of it. We can't think we're going to some-how control the outcome just because we want what we want. Where else does life work that way, no matter how sincerely we want it? We can't ever be so *SO* good that God—even just life?—won't surprise us with alternate plans. The most maddening part of the whole thing may be that our idea of the best possible outcome isn't always the best idea. We can't see around corners, for ourselves or others. We can offer our love, our support, our words, our desires, our faith, our hope, our hearts, and our presence—in whatever happens—and there's real good for both people involved in the relationship created. The act itself is teaching us and transforming us. But it doesn't bind God ... because we can't.

A "vending-machine god" breaks down when the vending machine does, which absolutely will happen to everyone at some point. I be-lieve being a 'covenant people' is about transformation for us—how we think and act, what we desire. To me, a god that can be 'bound' by man according to earthly circumstances is a pretty small one. We are inherently imperfect. None of us will ever do everything God says. Not a single one of us. Zero.

I can't believe the things I have on this earth are a result of my goodness—they are a result of a combination of factors, many of which are completely outside my control. If I had to believe in a god who gave me everything in my life according to some kind of worthiness math, I could not believe in that god. Full stop. Instead, I believe in a god who gave me my life, which is not the same thing. "Not as the world giveth," right?

I don't think I'm meant to understand how it all works, but to live from a position of faith. What's important to me is that I remain in awe of the blessings I feel and find in my world, that I keep gratitude in my heart, and hope in my daily walk. That I recognize God's hand in my life even when my prayers seem to bounce back on me, and nothing happens the way I think it should, and nothing is changed by praying but me. That I'm willing to receive. That in receiving, I keep my focus on the relationship rather than on any specific gift. I want to always remember that "the blessings are mine if I live for them," and keep trying to figure out how to do that, which I have a hunch will turn out to be as much about being as it is about doing.

FEAR

"Fear is a resistance to the unknown."
—Terry Tempest Williams[10]

Susan:

Of all the things that have confused me in our religion throughout my life, one of the most perplexing has been our relationship to fear. In my experience we often demonize it, then we weaponize it, reaching for it almost automatically when we need to bully ourselves or others back into line.

We also attempt to motivate people—ourselves and others—with fear. I say attempt, because while it is a tactic that may appear to work on the surface, this success fails to hold up for a lifetime, since fear isn't an effective tool when it comes to accomplishing the real goals of religion. Fear won't lead us to deep or lasting personal growth. It won't enlarge our hearts by introducing us to real love. Fear recoils. Fear contracts. We might keep rules or do what we're told out of fear, but fear will never transform us into disciples. Fear simply fails to work on the heart.

It could be that we turn to fear as a tool in our resistance to the unknown, as Terry Tempest Williams suggests. We like feeling certainty in our beliefs, in our actions and approaches. We like feeling that we know the best ways to access the things people rely on religion to do for them. Like other Christians, we pray, we attend meetings, we take the sacrament, we repent, we serve our brothers and sisters in community, we teach our families at home. As members of The Church of Jesus Christ of Latter-day Saints, we do all these things in the way we believe they ought to be done for maximum effectiveness. But what happens when *you're* doing all these right things, yet life continues to do what *it* does? What happens when, again and again, you're reminded that no matter how good you are, no matter how right, you're really not in charge of anything in this world except yourself? Our desire to control outcomes—to control God, even—is an invitation to disappointment and disillusionment every time we bump up against the bottom-line uncertainty of life. It only makes sense that we show resistance to our inability to control things, no matter how well we play by the rules, by reaching for fear.

I'm a naturally fearful person. If you asked my family for one word to describe me, they would likely say "fraidy cat." It was a defining characteristic as a kid that unfortunately persisted into adulthood. Though it's sad to admit, fear has kept me from living fully in some ways, preventing me from doing things I've wanted to do in life. But being so well acquainted with it has meant you can't fool me with it. With so much in my regular life, I want nothing to do with fear in my spiritual life. In fact, I want the absence of fear. That's the thing that keeps me in the pews. That's the reason I've chosen to pursue a life of faith.

But I haven't found respite from fear at church, quite the opposite. Thankfully, as I've gotten older, I've grown so tired of feeling it that fear has begun to lose its power over me. Being afraid requires a lot of energy. One must continually stoke the anxiety fire, but no matter how carefully and diligently I've tended mine, all my anxious fear hasn't brought me any additional control at all.

So now when I see fear being dressed up as something else at church—righteousness or worthiness, for example—and weaponized against me, I'm unmoved. I've grown deaf to messages grounded in fear. I want religion to help me embrace what is uncertain and unknown in my life, not resist it. I want my heart to grow beyond the limits of a small, fearful box of self.

In her essay *When Fear Arises*, Sharon Salzberg says:

> Fear isn't an easy feeling to allow, to take some time with, to face with clarity and compassion. I wonder sometimes how much destructive action takes place because we find we can't easily just sit and know we feel afraid. To avoid the feeling, we reach for anything that will give us a sense of power, however fleeting the sense of power—and however destructive the act. This has great implications not just for our personal lives, but for the societies we create and maintain.[11]

We haven't known how to allow fear to sit with us at church. Salzburg's words explain to me why, as a person who has struggled with fear and anxiety for many years, church has failed to be the balm I seek. Well-meaning leaders and fellow saints have reached for power by delivering words that have felt, to me, destructive and careless as salt poured directly into my spirit's wounds.

I come to church seeking sanctuary from those wounds, a place to relax my controlly grip and walk in life's darkness and uncertainty with others who are also afraid, but are more interested in loving than fearing. I want John 14:27: "Peace I leave with you, my peace I give unto you: not as the world giveth, give I unto you. Let not your heart be troubled, neither let it be afraid." That scripture sounds like church to me, but church has rarely felt like that scripture. How can we move away from fear and in the direction of peace? I don't think we'll do it by becoming so completely allergic to unpleasant feelings that we label them Satan and refuse to sit with them. It's those uncomfortable things and feelings we carry that we are seeking relief *from* ... where will we go to find it if we can't acknowledge they belong to us—an integral part of our human experience—and find a safe place to set them down?

Our messages around fear at church can be a complex rhetorical dance. At the same time we're told that if we're doing it all right, we won't feel afraid, we're painted a picture of an evil world dominated by an adversary we must fear.

This may explain why metaphorically "circling the wagons" is such a popular response in our culture and teachings. Although it seems to resonate for many, it's not a helpful idea for me. And as a parent, it flies in the face of everything I wanted to teach and give my children. Building walls between the world and my kids seemed entirely counterproductive to me. I wanted to build bridges TO the world for them, not walls to keep them separate from it. I wanted them to feel comfortable and fearless in ways and places I haven't.

In an *On Being* podcast interview, author Elizabeth Gilbert said:

> Terrified people make terrible decisions. Terror and fear make you irresponsible. They make you not think very clearly, and they make you willing to do almost anything to get rid of that awful feeling. And we've seen people do that on the individual level, and we've seen cultures do that. And we've seen politicians who find ways to exploit terror and fear in order to get short-term power—or, sometimes, long-term power, because if you can figure out how to hold the reins of other people's fear, then you can control them for a while.[12]

So all our collective talk and teachings that advocate circling church and family wagons in response to the world must be rooted in a desire for control, and fear that keeps us from acknowledging our lack of it. Church can become people wanting to control us, and us wanting the illusion of someone being in control and therefore willingly leaning into that narrative.

In addition to feeling like it's sometimes been used against me, as a Latter-day Saint I've felt bullied by my own fear. I've felt shame about it. One of the most painful recurring ideas in my church experience has been that if we have faith, or are prepared, or have the spirit, or are truly converted, or *whatever* the topic du jour may be ... we will not fear. I saw someone on social media use this against a woman who expressed her concern about returning to church during the 2020 pandemic. In response, she was told plainly, "Fear comes from Satan."

Well, I don't see it that way. I think fear is just a naturally occurring part of life as a human being. It occurs naturally in my life, anyway. And as a woman who has always dealt with a surplus of it, but has also tried to live my life in accordance with the teachings of Jesus, I can't figure out how or why Satan would have such a large hold on me. From the time I was a young kid! Such a suggestion does not bring peace, the antidote to fear I've wanted from my religion. Instead it feels like an indictment of my faith and personal worthiness.

The idea of Satan gives us a scapegoat to save us from having to look at what's really happening. We may also deal with discomfort about our lack of control—our fear—by willingly handing the control to someone else. But why would we want to assign Satan power rather than take it for ourselves? Maybe it gives us a way to explain things we can't fix or don't understand, or for which we don't want to take responsibility, like the actions of other people, or society's problems. It's a kind of denial—we don't have to look at the complexity or messiness of a thing squarely if we can just label it and move on. Satan's a handy fall-guy. "The devil made me do it" might be easier to live with than, "I weighed my options and still made that bad choice." Or, "A lot of the time, I'm just plain terrified."

We can't completely eliminate fear from our lives, no matter how good we are, but we may cause a lot of grief by insisting we can. When I was a kid, my mom used to encourage me to engage with my difficulties. "Make friends with it," she'd say, when I'd complain about whatever it was. This was completely maddening to a kid, in large part because it actually worked. For instance, when my anxiety would bubble up, she'd encourage me to see it for what it is and name it too. To look at those uncomfortable feelings and actually say the words, "Hello there—I know you." She believed calling hard things by their names helped bring them down to size, and might help me feel just a little more power over them. For such a simple thing, it's been an amazingly effective tool I've continued to use throughout my life. But that tactic feels like the opposite of the outsized way we allow—even encourage—fear to function in our church lives.

I've heard a helpful distinction made between fear and anxiety where fear is destructive in the ways resistance can paralyze us, but anxiety may be useful when harnessed as a tool to propel us forward. Performers of all kinds talk about anxiety fueling their performance. In my own life, writing and creating art have been a positive anxiety response, an attempt to project hope into a universe that doesn't always seem friendly. I can't make life bend to my will, but I can take some materials or words and exert a little control over them to achieve a desired outcome, whether it yields an essay or a piece of art for the wall. But those things are self-motivated, a reflection of personal hope and faith. I'd be unlikely to feel inspired to create based on a conviction that I must fear an evil world.

Meanwhile, I am a great lover of this world and its gifts, and am unapologetic about that. I wanted my children to have the same love affair with it I have. Why would a God who loves us give evil gifts? 2 Timothy 1:7 reads: "For God hath not given us the spirit of fear; but of power, and of love, and of a sound mind." I'm astonished at the things people create and what they give of themselves to others, a loving human antidote to all that is uncertain and unknown. In the same podcast, Elizabeth Gilbert also said, "Creative living is choosing the path of curiosity over the path of fear."[13] That has great resonance for me, and has manifested as truth in my life. I think a lot of my creative output has been a direct and intentional volley into the darkness—an offering to my own fear to prove to myself I'm not powerless against it.

Goodness that is motivated by fear will never throw off much real light. But if my anxiety in the face of life's uncertainties leads me to continually seek strength and comfort in a relationship with God, that's useful. And if it can also lead me to create beauty, to build bridges where I can, and to always privilege love over fear in this world, it may even be transformational.

Cynthia:

In 2017 Elder Dieter F. Uchtdorf delivered the talk *Perfect Love Casteth out Fear*.[14] Upon hearing this talk, I thought there would be a complete and total shift within the church. I felt like it was a real and honest attempt to start a dialogue about fear. It felt like a 'mic drop' moment for me. Like you said above, fear rarely has the power to change us. Elder Uchtdorf echoed this same sentiment:

> It is true that fear can have a powerful influence over our actions and behavior. But that influence tends to be temporary and shallow. Fear rarely has the power to change our hearts, and it will never transform us....
>
> There may be moments when we are tempted to justify our actions by believing that the end justifies the means. We might even think that to be controlling, manipulative, and harsh will be for the good of others. Not so, for the Lord has made it clear that 'the fruit of the Spirit is love, joy, peace, longsuffering, gentleness, goodness, faith, meekness, [and] temperance.'

Parenting might be the biggest way we often use fear. I have a friend who has five children. Several years ago, over tacos in a crowded restaurant, she lamented to me that her youngest child was making lots of poor decisions, some of which seemed to be leading her away from the church. In exasperation she said to me, "I just hope that the pressure of having all of her older siblings in the Church would scare her too badly to ever leave the Church." As a parent I understand that we have these moments we aren't proud of, that we often later regret. Maybe my friend regretted her choice of words, but in that moment fear is what she hoped would motivate her child to stay in the church. According to Elder Uchtdorf, that is not true conversion.

A guest on our podcast once said that the opposite of fear is curiosity.[15] She used that idea to parent her adult children who chose to leave the church by asking them thoughtful and curious questions instead of taking the easy route of fear and lecturing them. It was a very powerful lesson for me that if our goal is to increase peace and understanding, we have to find a way to reach and teach others that doesn't employ fear.

You said that fear is a bully. You're right! We are taught to stand up to bullies and I believe that is what Elder Uchtdorf was asking us to do: to stand up to the bully of fear. Once we can see that bullies use fear to disempower and control their victims, we are better able to resist such tactics. Maybe naming it like your mom taught you would be helpful: "Hello there, Fear. I see you!"

It is sad that I often hear more at church about Satan than I do about Jesus. There are only a few words Jesus is on record as saying. Perhaps we don't feel at liberty to put words in the Savior's mouth, but we feel less so with Satan? I have noticed for years that we love attributing anything we struggle with to Satan. In my cynical moments at church, I call it Scripts for Satan. We've all heard these scripts: Satan makes you yell at your kids; Satan makes you materialistic; Satan tempts you to waste time on social media, etc. It's ironic that at church I sometimes hear more about avoiding evil than I do about finding the good in the world.

There's this great comic by David Hayward, also known as The Naked Pastor, that shows God saying to a group of people that He has not given us the spirit of fear, and the church says, "Leave that part up to me." Ewwww. And also, ouch! I know we don't mean to focus so much on fear, but I have developed a pretty big 'Fear-dar' and I can spot it a mile away at church. Perhaps, like you said, we use that blame as a scapegoat to avoid confronting our own emotional reactions to unwanted distractions.

In those moments when our Fear-dar is picking up strong signals, I think it is beneficial to dig a little deeper and get super curious about our desires and choices. I'm not saying I never recognize unwanted desires as 'temptations,' but I am saying I find it more helpful to be curious about the temptation—to really look inward—rather than just attributing all negative feelings, emotions, and desires to Satan. No growth happens with blame.

What is it in our LDS narrative that makes us constantly echo how evil the world is? Does it give our religious life more importance if we can somehow set ourselves apart from the 'wicked world'? Elder Uchtdorf said,

> I wouldn't trade living in this time with any other time in the history of the world. We are blessed beyond measure to live in a day of unparalleled prosperity, enlightenment, and advantage. Most of all, we are blessed to have the fullness of the gospel of Jesus Christ, which gives us a unique perspective on the world's dangers and shows us how to either avoid these dangers or deal with them.[16]

A friend told me once she was buying garments at the Church Distribution Center, and the salesclerk helping her talked about how horrible the world is and how afraid she was seeing all the turmoil. My friend quickly replied that she thinks this is the best time to live: medical science, opportunities for women, violent crime is going down, etc. I agree with her and Elder Uchtdorf, what a time to be alive! Of course there is evil in the world—there always has been and there always will be. I am not saying we don't confront the tough stuff, on the contrary, I am saying just labeling stuff as 'evil' and being afraid of the bogeyman isn't helpful.

Speaking of the tough stuff, several years ago I made an appointment with my bishop to specifically tell him we need to talk more about the tough stuff. I said I wanted to discuss racism, LGBTQ+ issues, faith crisis, and more in our church lessons. He tried to explain to me that it's a difficult balance between having 'softball and hardball' lessons at church. He didn't want to make ward members fearful and uncomfortable but at the same time he acknowledged speaking about the tough stuff is indeed important. I can sympathize that a bishop wants to make church a good experience for all who attend, but I'm not so sure comfort should be our number one focus in our Sunday meetings.

As Rachel Held Evans said in *Searching for Sunday*, "Imagine if every church became a place where everyone is safe, but no one is comfortable. Imagine if every church became a place where we told one another the truth. You might just create sanctuary."[17]

FAITH

"When we grapple with the truth of our experience in relationship to our beliefs, we have the chance to deepen our faith. Does our experience match the belief system or not? If not, we can let the belief go. If it does, we can trust it as our own."
—Sharon Salzberg[18]

Susan:

One of the biggest challenges, when things in my faith life suddenly started to *rearrange* themselves, was untangling faith from belief. It started because I got into a discussion with someone about the phrase 'choose to believe,' a concept I hear people talk about but have never understood. I haven't ever been able to figure out how people could simply decide to believe something—could I wake up one day and suddenly believe the earth is flat simply because I choose to? I don't see how. I might wonder if it's flat. I could say it is flat. I could look for evidence that it's flat. But something would have to happen in my mind to make the shift to actually *believing* it, and I don't feel like that's within my control.

The person I was discussing this with had no problem with the phrase at all, and after going back and forth for some time it occurred to me there was a discrepancy in how we think about belief. As a child, my beliefs were mostly things I was given by others. I trusted what I was told from just about anyone who seemed to know more than I did. As an adult, belief has become a conviction I hold as a result of what I've learned and experienced for myself.

How my friend described 'belief' sounded more like how I would define 'faith.' I realized during our conversation that as a Latter-day Saint, I'd been encouraged to think of those things as being one and the same. Having faith was commonly understood to mean believing, and at church it usually went a step further: members express both those concepts—faith and belief—using the word *know.* "I know the Church is true," we say, or "I know Joseph Smith was a prophet." We're really saying we believe those things—something has convinced us.

But I don't think faith necessarily requires belief or knowledge. I think it springs from some combination of hope and willingness. We hope something is true, and we're willing to act as if it is.

It's curious to me that we insist on knowledge when Jesus made it clear in the scriptures that faith is enough.

Cynthia:

I agree! Jesus said faith is enough so why do we lean heavily on "I know" language? If I had a magic wand, I would wave it and banish the phrase, *"I know ..."* from our testimonies and talks. I don't think it has any place in our places of worship. Church is where we discuss things that are precisely *not* knowable. Something probably convinced a person to use 'I know' language, so tell me all about that instead. Imagine how differently our meetings would feel if we said, "I am convinced the Church is true because I feel God's love when I study the scriptures." I want to hear about everything that comes after the 'because.' Please, tell me all about this convincing process!

Knowing is rigid, but having faith is malleable. Faith is a willingness to accept the unknown, like the father of the ill child who approached Jesus and said, "Lord I believe, help thou mine unbelief." (Mark 9:23–25 KJV) That 'help' we seek is what faith is to me. It's the space between not knowing and knowing. As Latter-day Saints we don't hold that space very well. Is it because we see faith as fragile, but we view knowing as rock solid? Is it because faith is *more* mental work than knowing? For me, being part of Team Faith instead of Team Knowing has been much more work. Back in the days when I proclaimed that I 'knew' certain things in testimony meetings, I was simply using the verbiage of our religion without much thought. I can show compassion to my former self that proclaimed I 'knew' things that truthfully I didn't. Words are important! There is a huge difference between the definition of knowledge versus faith.

It's not that hard in our culture to understand why we want to quickly move through faith and get to the knowing part. It's part of being in a church that claims to have all the answers. Having the answers means the thinking is done. All that's left now is to endure. But

Susan, Jesus never commanded us to know. Instead, He talks about tiny things like mustard seeds and yeast. Maybe it's not a coincidence that those two parables are the shortest parables–just three verses total. Jesus said that a mustard seed is the "smallest of all the seeds, but when it has grown it is the greatest of shrubs and becomes a tree, so that the birds of the air come and make nests in its branches." (Matthew 13:31–33, NRSV)

The idea that my tiny seed-like faith is sufficient to provide refuge for myself and for other tiny creatures fills me with a specific kind of hope that now powers my faith life. Elsewhere in the scriptures Jesus talks about not having a home—that "foxes have holes, and birds of the air have nests; but the Son of man hath not where to lay his head." (Luke 9:58, KJV) Maybe my mustard-seed-sized faith is enough to give rest to *me* and those around me who struggle. And according to Jesus, if it helps the 'least of these,' it's pretty strong evidence we are one with Him. So is knowing really preferable to faith? I don't think so, not anymore. That kind of faith, driven by a desire to give rest to myself and others, is anything but fragile. In my experience, it's been enough to power my discipleship.

Susan:

I like thinking of faith, rather than belief, powering discipleship. For one thing, I think faith is more reliable. Something might come along to rock our beliefs or change the period to a question mark on our knowledge, but even so we can get up the next day and continue moving in faith. Faith is a verb in both Hebrew and Latin. We *faith*—just like we love, hope, or believe. In her book *Faith: Trusting Your Own Deepest Experience*, Sharon Salzberg writes:

> It is a common assumption that faith deepens as we are taught more about what to believe; in Buddhism, on the contrary, faith grows only as we question what we are told, as we try teachings out by putting them into practice to see if they really make a difference in our own lives. The Buddha himself insisted, "Don't believe anything just because I have said it. Don't believe anything just because an elder or someone you respect has said it. Put it into practice. See for yourself if it is true."[19]

That quote gives me some holy envy for the Buddhists! And yet, when you drill down, I'm not sure Buddhism and Mormonism are really that far apart in our characterization of faith. Though many members seem to link faith to specific tenets of belief, putting into practice things we don't know or can't quite believe, but continue to hope for, is how I think of faith.

I love that story where the father begs Jesus, "help thou mine unbelief." By healing the boy, Jesus makes it clear that even as the father confesses to struggling with belief, his faith is a perfectly acceptable offering. Seeking the blessing was enough.

The Buddha and Alma were on the same page, I think. Alma compares the word to a seed in his well-known sermon about the magic of planting, nurturing, and most importantly paying attention. Seeds are particles of promise, pulling us toward something greater if given even the slightest encouragement—careless or halfhearted dirt, water, and sunlight can bring results. (Alma 32:21–43) I've seen enough flowers blooming in the cracks of sidewalks to know it doesn't take much. Our tiniest glimmer of desire can be rewarded. And once it starts, we don't control the growing. Things happen, and then more things, and our experience carries us forward.

Lowell Bennion described it like this:

> Faith is adventurous and creative. It not only is the sphere of the possible, but is also the power which often makes the possible come into being. Faith is that remarkable quality of the human spirit which first envisages the possibilities of life, then lives as though these possibilities were realities, and by this action often makes them real. In the realm of knowledge, one conforms to what is; in the realm of faith, one creates life after the image carried in his heart. Faith adds another dimension to life. Recognizing the borders of knowledge, it transcends them.[20]

I'm pretty sure transcending the borders of our own—or especially a church leader's—knowledge or belief would be the opposite of how many Latter-day Saints think about faith. In our minds, 'Truth' often has as much to do with the authority of the person who pronounces it as it does personal experience. We tuck these things we 'know' in our pocket because we received them from authority we trust, and don't subject them to a lot of questions. After they've been there a while, untested, unquestioned, we simply take them for granted.

Knowledge looks back, faith moves forward, an infinitely adaptable companion for our growth. I'm with you about wanting to strike the phrase 'I know' from our meetings. I'm much more interested in words like change, process, and journey! Tracing the origins of faith in other people's personal stories can help me identify its seeds in my own. I want them to show me what's in their pockets, but I also want to hear how and where they picked each thing up. In the Alma sermon, I think "experiment" must be his most intentional word choice.

> Faith, in contrast to belief, is not a definition of reality, not a received answer, but an active, open state that makes us willing to explore. While beliefs come to us from outside—from another person or a tradition or heritage—faith comes from within, from our alive participation in the process of discovery. —Sharon Salzberg[21]

Sharon Salzberg uses the word 'discovery,' and I think she's talking about the same thing: faith as process rather than product. Scientists add to their knowledge by navigating a maze that is mostly wrong turns. They learn as much—and sometimes probably more—from what doesn't work as from what does. The point of an experiment is that the outcome isn't guaranteed; sometimes trial leads to error, but error is a seed too and we know what to do with those. They can lead us to something useful or nourishing or beautiful.

So I think of faith as more a description of how to approach our lives than a thing we attain. You could bring a bushel of perfect tomatoes to a testimony meeting and plunk them down on the podium, but that kind of show-and-tell won't do a single thing to help someone in the audience grow their own.

Alan Watts differentiates faith from belief in such a simple but profound way for me in this quote:

> We must here make a clear distinction between belief and faith, because, in general practice, belief has come to mean a state of mind which is almost the opposite of faith. Belief, as I use the word here, is the insistence that the truth is what one would 'lief' or wish it to be. The believer will open his mind to the truth on the condition that it fits in with his preconceived ideas and wishes. Faith, on the other hand, is an unreserved opening of the mind to the truth, whatever it may turn out to be. Faith has no preconceptions; it is a plunge into the unknown. Belief clings, but faith lets go.[22]

Belief clings, but faith lets go? Yes! How had I never noticed that belief wants to dictate outcomes, while faith lives through and adapts to them ... whatever they may be? As with so many things, this comes back to control! Belief warns us to hold on tighter, but faith allows us to loosen our grip and fully inhabit our experience. If I have to choose, I know which one I want.

Cynthia:

"Faith has no preconceptions"? This is too hard for Mormons, Susan!

Susan:

You might be right—giving up preconceptions in favor of possibilities may feel precarious for most Latter-day Saints. But would you rather have a pocket full of seeds, or a pocket full of preconceptions? Which one is more likely to help you grow?

I spend a lot of time these days thinking about young parents in our church; we have heard from so many wondering how—and also whether they want—to raise their children in an environment where they are likely to be subjected to black-and-white thinking and non-nuanced approaches to questions. But I think many other parents are afraid that if we teach our children to question well, with a willingness to accept nuance in areas where perfect knowledge or only one possible answer simply doesn't exist, their kids won't know what *(maybe even how?)* to believe. As if demonstrating nuance will necessarily sow confusion or doubt rather than faith!

To the latter group, I would say two things: 1) Truth can withstand our deepest doubt and confusion and inquiry—all human advancements have come from someone willing to question deeply, poke, prod, experiment, and make mistakes to eventually get to an understanding of the truth, and 2) Kids are going to experience confusion and doubt throughout their lives, so I would want mine to be equipped with tools to work through those things. I would want to give them skills to approach their seeking with confidence and then grow through it, rather than relying on brittle, rigid thinking—someone else's thinking at that!—leaving them vulnerable and unprepared to navigate change. You might pass a test by convincing another kid to give you the answers, but you won't learn the material. An A earned using someone else's knowledge is a useless measure, not a reflection of anything real, durable, or useful when life gets hard and suddenly demands we 'show our work' on the big questions.

About four decades ago, I tore a comic out of a Chicago newspaper that I kept on my bulletin board for years and still have in a box somewhere. The caption read, "A good mother teaches her children how to think, not what to think." When I first saw it, I had to chew on it a bit. I knew the idea seemed important, but I wasn't sure why. I had a new baby, my first, and what it meant to be a *good* mother was something I didn't quite feel sure of. At age nineteen, I hadn't ever thought to examine whether I'd been taught how, or merely what, to think. I guess I assumed all my thoughts were my own, without paying attention to the process by which they'd arrived in my head. Maybe I figured if I believed something, I must have a good reason for it.

I've revisited that idea many times throughout my life as I've encountered—sometimes with dismay—both kinds of thinking in myself: the ideas and beliefs I earned through personal experience, interrogation, and investigation, and the ones planted by others that I just accepted without much thought. I hope that well-timed comic falling in my lap, alerting me to what should have been obvious but somehow wasn't, helped me better guide my own children in their development of critical thinking skills when approaching religion and every other area of their lives.

Nuance happens in my head, but truth happens in my heart. I have found no downside to letting my head off its leash as often as it begs to go. The more information my head brings back for my heart to consider, the more my capacity for understanding grows.

Faith begins in the same place hope does: a place my head can't rule no matter how much it tries to assert its own importance. Faith supplies me dirt, water, and sunlight to plant my seeds and give them a chance to grow. By never asking the hard questions, never following any of my constant what-if thoughts to see where they lead, I would avoid ever coming into the kind of inner conversation where I might experience the spiritual clarity and recognition that signals truth. Why would I want to deny myself that interaction? "Ask, and it shall be given you; . . . knock, and it shall be opened unto you." (Matthew 7:7) It's an invitation to just this process! It's an invitation to faith, because the door won't knock on itself. And it's very different from, "Here's your answer. Good girl. Now we never need to have this conversation again."

REPENTANCE

"As we enter the path of transformation, the most valuable thing we have working in our favor is our yearning. Some spiritual teachers will even say that the yearning you feel for God is actually coming from the opposite direction; it is in fact God's yearning for you."
—Cynthia Bourgeault[23]

Susan:

A few years ago, my husband was teaching a lesson about repentance in Sunday School. A man raised his hand and started in on the idea that if you pound nails in a board, and then remove the nails ... the holes are still there. My husband didn't respond very well—he still feels bad about that—but we can't have this stuff floating around our Gospel Doctrine classes unchallenged, can we? It was a reminder to me that problematic ideas really do persist among members, even though our leaders have moved away from some of the damaging messaging of days past.

For fun, I once looked at Goodreads reviews of the notorious old book so many of us were given to read as wayward—or even *considering* becoming wayward—youths, *The Miracle of Forgiveness*. My favorite review line was: "A better title for this book might be, 'It's a Miracle Jesus Even Likes You.'" I admit, that made me laugh! But a theology of repentance that leaves the holes in the board no matter what we do feels just about as demoralizing to me.

We've heard difficult stories from people about repenting of past transgressions, only to continue to bump up against them later in their church lives. For instance, if someone had an affair that was resolved through proper channels but later wants to get sealed to another spouse, they're going to be required to jump through some hoops. Why? I once heard the cynical aside, "Sure, the Lord will remember sins no more ... but the church never forgets!" Funny, but maybe truer than we like to admit?

We're also living through a time when there are a lot of members who wish to hear an apology from "The Church" on any one of several difficult topics, but apologies are not forthcoming. So maybe it's time to have a conversation about repentance. How does it work? What does it mean? And what do members really believe about it?

Cynthia:

Belonging to a church that has gone on record as saying the church does not seek apologies or give them is a hard pill to swallow when they encourage us, the members, to be a repentance-seeking people.[24] As a child, I heard that I should repent every day. "At night before we go to sleep, we should review our acts and words of the day and ask the Lord to help us recognize the things for which we need to repent."[25] How can a church teach me to repent and apologize only to turn around and say but they do not?

In recent years, we have seen the Catholic church apologize to Indigenous people in Canada for the physical and sexual abuse of their children in the country's Catholic-run residential schools.[26] In 2024, President Joe Biden also apologized to Native Americans for abuse, neglect, and the eradication of their tribal identities in U.S. boarding schools.[27] I hope someday this practice of 'no apologies' can change for our church. Apologies go a long way in the healing process for victims.

An organization hurting its members is one thing, but to do it in the name of God is another level of hurt heaped on the victims. Joseph Smith said:

> Wherefore let all men beware how they take my name in their lips: for behold verily I say, that many there be who are under this condemnation; who useth the name of the Lord, and useth it in vain, having not authority. Wherefore let the church repent of their sins, and I the Lord will own them, otherwise they shall be cut off.—Doctrine and Covenants 63:61–63

I think Joseph was onto something there. For a church to hurt people in the name of God is to use His name in vain. One example of this is the temple prohibition on women of African descent prior to 1978. The 1978 revelation allowing all men to have the priesthood also finally allowed Black women to go to the temple. But why were women of African descent prohibited from temple ordinances in the first place?

As women, we are told over and over that's actually an awesome part about being a woman—that we don't need ordination to go to the temple.[28] So why were Black women banned from saving ordinances when women are not ordained? Are Black women owed an apology when there was never any doctrine prohibiting them from temple attendance?

And speaking of the temple, in 2019 many changes were made to temple scripts to remove unequal and painful language for women. I was sitting in an endowment session excited to experience the changes for myself, when a pre-recorded announcement was made about the changes. In essence, the announcement prefacing the sacred ceremony was that we were not to talk about the changes. For years, I cried over some of the unequal covenants women made compared to men. Several bishops had to endure my tears and questions about some of the wording. Those painful and problematic parts were suddenly gone without so much as an acknowledgment or apology to women. It was difficult to be happy for those changes I had been waiting decades for when I was officially told in the House of the Lord not to discuss those changes.

Even without an apology, much could have been done in the repentance process of the organization to the women of the church. I heard no remorse in the statement that day. Something as simple as this would have been enough: "We are sorry, sisters, that you endured this hurt for so long. We heard your cries and we took it to the Lord." Or better yet, what if a member of the First Presidency or an apostle had taken that opportunity to give a talk about honoring women? That our feelings mattered to them and brought about the change. Such statements could begin the healing process, emphasizing prophetic revelation and the beauty of a living church. Nothing of the sort happened at the highest levels. Luckily in my stake, we had a stake president who came to my ward's Relief Society a few months after the changes and asked us all how we were feeling about the temple changes. I raised my hand and thanked him profusely for giving us women an official outlet to discuss our feelings. Healing happened that day in my ward.

Susan:

That's an amazing story! I don't think I've ever had any kind of leader ask how something at church made me feel. I like to think I would welcome apologies from church leadership, and that I would extend much grace. But I once heard Philip Yancey describe someone who was unable to extend forgiveness like this: "You can't possibly be sorry. If you were really sorry, you wouldn't have done it in the first place."[29]

If I'm completely honest with myself, I'm afraid that might be my response to some church apologies, because it's hard for me to get my head around a church acting in Jesus's name, doing some things we have done.

I feel my resistance to graceful acceptance rise when I think of a few specific examples. I've thought a lot about what an effective apology from the church could look like, and what I might need to hear in order for it to feel helpful. Speaking for myself, I think I'd want to hear the four Rs of repentance: responsibility, remorse, resolve, and repair. Responsibility would be an acknowledgment of the problem, or if that's too much to hope for, even acknowledgment of the feelings people are experiencing as a result of it. There's healing validation in having our pain acknowledged. Remorse would simply be saying, "We're sorry we did this. Please forgive us." Resolve would involve a plan for how the organization can do better going forward. And repair would be doing whatever they can to mitigate the damage that has been caused. But I feel like as it stands now, we don't get any of those four.

I don't have any control over apologies from other people though, and that certainly includes organizations. One of the most helpful things I ever got from a therapist was when he told me I must stop waiting for the apology that was never going to come. It was painful to hear at the time, but internalizing that wisdom changed my life. It didn't mean I wasn't entitled to an apology to take away my hurt. It didn't mean my wounds weren't real. But it gave me a kind of release, allowing me to change my own orientation to the situation and move forward. As I think about it now, the decision to allow myself to grow was always going to belong to me. Even when I have felt imprisoned by past wrongs—my own and others'—it turns out I had power to change some things for myself. I could heal.

Richard Rohr talks about repentance as changing our minds: transforming our outlook, orientation, and as a result, direction. Looking for and taking opportunities in our lives for that kind of pivot sounds like it might position us for what we're really trying to get to: a change of heart. But as a Latter-day Saint, I think I've mainly been taught to think of repentance as a process of renouncing my sins to become more perfect. And I don't mean perfect as in whole, unfortunately, I mean perfect as in unspotted. But healed is not the same as spotless. My body bears all kinds of scars from things I've done and things done to me. But my body has healed from those wounds. I don't mind carrying the reminders: *Don't go screaming down that big hill on the back of your brother's bike when your mom told you not to leave the house. Avoid cancer if you can. Women make big sacrifices to conjure new life. Chicken pox is miserable, but you're going to be okay.*

I don't mind the holes left in my board—they reflect where I've been and inform where I want to go next. They remind me of the grace I've been given and the grace I will yet receive.

Some church members I've talked to struggle with the idea of grace because if we downplay justice or punishment, what will motivate us to become better? For me, being devoted to the idea of punishment for sins makes the meaning of this whole earth exercise feel very small, more like a game than a growth plan: we can't help sinning, but lucky for us our sins have been paid for, so we can repent and be forgiven. Repeat, repeat, repeat. There needs to be a larger point to it, doesn't there?

So I think the point of this life must not be the sheen of perfection, but the mess of growth. If I drill that down further, rather than becoming spotless, I'd say the point probably *is* our 'spots.' The things we perform with exactness and can't get better at don't grow us at all. It's the things we don't do so well. Clinging to the iron rod doesn't pull us forward; instead, movement occurs in our falling but getting up anyway and starting again. Every time we go down, every time we inflict or incur a wound, we learn a little more about ourselves. And if we engage in the repentance process, we learn a little more about grace, a little more about God.

Cynthia:

I am stuck on that idea—that repentance, or changing one's mind, can help me learn more about God's grace. And grace, the unconditional and infinite love of God, can in turn help me to grow and become a better version of myself. Grace envelops me, giving me the safety to be who I am in this very moment. Grace is my soft place to fall. Because of it, I know that nothing can change my worth. That's fixed. And that love, security, and safety—that God loves me just as I am right now—then allows me to change and move forward. It's like a looping circle that gives me a glimpse of what 'eternal progression' might look like.

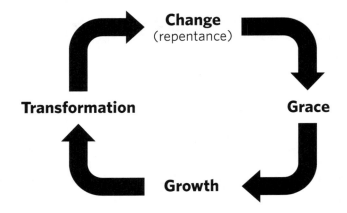

In religious terms, we call this 'grace', but in psychology, this is called the 'paradox of change.' This idea popularized by psychologist Carl Rogers explains why accepting myself as I am is the key to changing my behaviors and how I think about myself.[30] How many of us believed the opposite though? That we need to see ourselves as awful and wretched *and then* we will change? Grace tells us that *acceptance* is actually what fuels repentance and change.

I credit LDS philosopher Adam Miller for jump-starting my grace journey. In his fifth book on grace, *Original Grace,* he talks about how we often speak of grace and justice being opposites—you either receive grace or you receive justice. But Miller posits the idea that the answer to justice is simply *more grace*. In other words, grace is always the answer. I love the idea that even in our falling, movement is occurring and in that movement of falling—what we might call justice or consequences—we just keep rubbing up against God's grace. Grace all the way down, or as our pioneer ancestors sang, "Grace shall be, as your day."[31]

Susan:

Thank you for using that line from one of our pioneer hymns! I have a hunch that grace was more in favor with them than it is now, and I think it's because as a church we were entirely pieced together from converts who, probably in most cases, brought their previous flavor of Christianity with them, which of course included grace. And good luck stamping grace out of people once they've embraced it! We grew up in a church where generations of official teachings had been refined to replace grace with works in the common narrative. I can't be sure what the majority of members believe, but I do know what the majority of leaders talk about, and it's more likely to be works and worthiness than the kind of grace that is freely given and wholly undeserved.

But it's interesting to see what happens when I start to magnify grace in approaching repentance. It may be easier to accept the idea of grace for ourselves, or to allow it for others, depending on how we think. But if we're worthy of receiving grace, then they are. Or if they are, then we are. Once grace creeps into our view, there's really no containing it. That's one reason I think it's so unfortunate that grace receives almost no emphasis in our church. It really is the great equalizer, and changing the way we think about ourselves in relation to God has a big impact on how we think about everyone else. Those white clothes we wear in the temple? Aren't they meant to, at least in part, symbolize that we're all alike in God's eyes? I believe we can't 'live the gospel' of Jesus Christ without getting to a place where we realize our equal footing. Allowing grace a bigger role and retooling the way we think about repentance can help us begin to see others through a more godlike lens.

I think all of this speaks to two different mindsets: fixed and growth. People with a fixed mindset love being complimented on how accomplished—maybe *perfect?*—they are, while people with a growth mindset focus on effort. A fixed mindset is results-oriented, and a growth mindset embraces feedback with a willingness to try again. Which sounds more like what we're supposed to be doing on this earth? Isn't repentance the endless opportunity for us to fail, change something, then try again? Unfortunately, I feel our focus on being spotless is much more in line with a fixed mindset than a growth one. And I know a little something about that.

One day my daughter was getting ready to go on a first date and I asked what they were planning to do. She said they'd probably go bowling. Now I don't think I'd bowl in front of my own mother if I could help it because any game involving a ball is never going to show me to my best advantage. I asked my daughter if she was a good bowler. She laughed, "I'm a terrible bowler!" So I said, "Why would you agree to do that on a first date?" I'll never forget her answer: "Because it's fun!"

She may as well have been speaking a foreign language—that answer did not compute. Nothing is fun for me if I'm not good at it, one of my deepest, most unfortunate personal truths. So I'll never forget the day I learned about fixed versus growth mindsets because it exposed one of the most consistent stumbling blocks in my life. I like looking perfect or at the very least slightly better than I am. It's on the short list of traits I still want to grow out of, and I hope shifting the way I think about repentance is a baby step in the right direction.

I should pause here to say I've never been that good at repentance, so for me to be telling anyone what repentance should be is a bit rich! It isn't that I have a hard time believing God can forgive me—I can accept grace; I have a hard time forgiving myself. Repentance generally hasn't caused me to forget how awful I am. I think that's because I never really understood it, and I'm going to blame the misunderstanding on the messaging I received (or internalized) about sin and repentance having been mostly shame-based.

Repentance framed only in a perfectionistic context—the "spotless" ideal—makes us ripe for shame. It's where shame-based ideas like the chewed gum or the board with the nail-holes in it really get their foothold. These narratives not only warp the way we think about ourselves, they make it harder to extend grace to others. They are the ideas of people who think they need to be perfect to retain their value (even though you can't build anything with a board without putting holes in it—wood without nails just stays wood.) In my opinion, our approach to the whole topic is a demoralizing view of the human experience.

I was terrified to get baptized at age eight because I couldn't help obsessing about how long I would be able to stay perfect. I was worried about something bad I'd done in first grade and felt relieved that the icky feeling would finally be gone, *but* I knew full well it just couldn't last. Then the burden would be back. Through most of my adulthood, I still didn't have the understanding that would enable me to set burdens down and walk away from them.

Cynthia:

I remember that same feeling. I think I snapped at my older brother the day of my baptism and I thought, "Well there goes that!" Even though I don't think I was ever obsessed with perfection, I have always been concerned about being damaged goods. All the object lessons from my youth didn't help—chewed gum, a licked cupcake, the nail in the board, etc. Again, this goes back to how we define repentance—damaged and scarlet-stained versus an opportunity to change our mind. If eight-year-olds are worried about losing their perfection so soon after baptism, we have a problem with our repentance messaging.

I hope someday repentance can become firmly staked in the Growth Mindset Camp and we can once and for all abandon the Scarlet Sins Camp. But to do that, we're going to have to start believing our own stuff about repentance. And there is lots of good stuff! Alma the Younger in the Book of Mormon is described as the vilest of sinners, yet he became the prophet. Paul the apostle even condoned the stoning of the first Christian martyr, Stephen, but he too became a great leader in the early church. I don't see messy Alma-like leaders serving at the top in our church anymore.

I was specifically counseled never to teach with negative examples from our own life in a teacher development training at church. I understand that in a digital age, the church wants to protect their image, but we also need to ask ourselves: why do we prefer a squeaky-clean image to begin with? An institution whose central tenet is that the atonement of Jesus Christ changes lives should be the perfect place to have modern day Almas and Pauls at the helm. If the scriptures describe the vilest of sinners becoming a prophet, what are we afraid of? I can't help but think that the fear of less-than-perfect leaders with a known past would give the appearance of 'condoning sin.' Those are exactly the kinds of messy topics we should be having in all our church classes.

We teach that perfection isn't possible in this life, but also that ultimately it is indeed the goal—to be unspotted and pure. I can't help but see the goal post of perfection as a distraction to the real work of seeing the good, the bad, and the ugly as all a normal part of everyone's life experiences. Even in our most sacred ceremonies we are taught that *if* we yield to temptation, a Savior would be provided for us. Why isn't that 'when' instead of 'if?' 'If' implies that grace, repentance, and atonement is the spare tire when in fact we should all be driving through life, celebrating the good, the bad, and the ugly because that is where growth and change occur.

Susan:

I once heard Brian McLaren describe repentance as the "puncturing of confirmation bias." Confirmation bias is favoring whatever confirms our previously existing beliefs, so I think he meant it's hard to change our mind or our viewpoint—it's hard to *repent*—when we're all wrapped up in confirmation bias about ourselves. We must be willing to approach life with a growth mindset to maximize what repentance can help us achieve. It's got to be so much more than stain removal—Jesus already has that covered for us.

I don't see any evidence that we're lost because we sin. We're engaged in exactly the process we've come to earth to experience.

Barbara Brown Taylor sums it up like this:

It's a completely human response to want someone who can save you from falling, which may be why Christians have always been more attracted to the rising part of the gospel than we are to the falling part. . . .

When you wake from the dream of falling to find it's not a dream, you can actually choose to open your hands, along with your battered heart, which is how you discover the front edge of the good news: not the life after falling, but the life in falling—all the life you'd have missed if you had clung to the one you had. If you can trust that, also trust this: God will know what to do with you next. [32]

WORTHINESS

Cynthia:

When my husband and I were new parents in our west Provo ward, a member of the bishopric asked if he could meet with us. He lived on our street so the interview took place in our home. Not one minute after sitting down on our pale blue couches he asked my husband, "Well, are you worthy?!" No asking us about our new baby, our new home, or our health. No pleasantries or get-to-know-you small talk. I internally rolled my eyes while my husband answered "yes." The bishopric member then extended him a calling to teach Gospel Doctrine. I've thought a lot about that evening in my home. How interesting that the number one thing worth knowing about my husband wasn't whether he would even have the desire to teach, but whether he was worthy to do so.

I am trying to think of a gospel principle that gets more airtime than worthiness in the church, and I can't. In the church's *General Handbook* the word 'worthy' is mentioned sixty-nine times. We have worthiness interviews starting at age eight to determine if little children are eligible for baptism. They continue at age eleven. Twice a year throughout the teenage years, men in bishoprics meet with minor children to determine their worthiness. Once we get to adulthood, these types of closed-door interviews happen every two years when a person needs to renew her temple recommend, or sometimes when she is issued a new calling. So yes, lots and lots of our precious time is devoted to assessing the worthiness of our church members. But what does it really say about us and about a person's heart, desires, or ethics?

If I had a magic wand, the first thing I would wave away would be our use of the actual word—worthy. I think we need a completely different word. Words matter, and worthiness is tied to *worth*. It's a terrible thing to suggest we somehow earn our worth. It's damaging to have to earn worth for ourselves or to demand that others earn theirs. I'm not sure 'worthiness' can ever *not* be a flawed concept at church because I believe the word is fundamentally flawed. I'm not even sure worthiness is a real word as every time I type it, Google underlines it blue as if to suggest a more appropriate word. Google is confused and I am confused.

It seems impossible to develop healthy love of self when our spiritual worth is measured in external validation. The church doors may as well have marks up and down both sides of the doorframe where we step up to get measured by each other every Sunday. Elder Uchtdorf gave that now-famous talk where he said there's no sign saying your testimony must be "this tall" to enter the church doors.[34] But once inside we do measure how you'll be able to participate.

Instead of using the word 'worthy,' I have heard others use the phrase 'spiritually ready.' So instead of saying a person is 'worthy to enter the temple,' we could say a person is spiritually ready. I think that's better, but again, this brings us back to the subjectivity of it all. It doesn't seem possible for anyone to be able to determine another person's readiness.

Also, determining one's worthiness is subjective. Two different bishops can determine the same person worthy or unworthy. Who is right? In the case of my worthiness being determined, whether or not I deserve a temple recommend, why should the human frailties and worldview of one man determine the covenants I can make? In reading the *General Handbook*, it stipulated a couple of times that bishops and stake presidents need to be satisfied that someone is worthy.[35] What satisfies one man may not satisfy another.

It's telling of a flawed power structure that a woman's 'worthiness' is always dependent on certification by a man. It's never the other way around. It's also never a woman determining another woman's worthiness. Some men judge, all women accept.

As a young college student at BYU, it wasn't uncommon to hear from girlfriends who had 'chastity' issues with their boyfriends, only to have much harsher punishments given by their respective bishops to the woman than to the man. Like stated above, this could be the subjective view of worthiness by different bishops. It's also worth noting that there exists a culture where women are seen as the 'guardians of virtue,' thus harsher punishments often are given to women because it's on them to draw the line in a dating relationship.[36]

Personally speaking, it was this concept of worthiness that triggered a big change for me. Simply put, what the organization of the church taught me about worthiness stopped making sense. It wasn't until I began to experience in my own life, and also witness in the lives of loved ones, that sooner or later everyone's imperfect and messy life will affect the lives of those around them. Every one of us knows someone who either received an ordinance, performed an ordinance, or accepted a calling who wasn't 'worthy.' Receiving baptism, blessing the sacrament, receiving your endowment, performing a sealing, receiving a calling—seeing and experiencing scenarios like these caused worthiness to unravel for me.

For example, if a man isn't 'worthy' to baptize his child but does so anyway because he withheld information from the bishop in his worthiness interview, we still believe in the validity of that ordinance. But why? Why don't we require the child to be re-baptized? Is it because God is merciful and won't punish the innocent child? Is it because untold numbers of baptisms would need to be redone, creating a logistical nightmare? Is it because worthiness standards have changed throughout time, so what was allowed 150 years ago is now considered unworthy? (Ahem, drinking coffee or even whiskey.[37])

My first run-in with worthiness was when I was thirteen years old. I attended an English-speaking ward but our youth program was combined with the youth from the Spanish branch that also met in our building. Our youth group had a temple trip planned to the Los Angeles Temple in late January. I went to see my bishop for my temple recommend interview. He asked me the usual questions, including the one about tithing. I explained to him that over the holidays I lost track of all the babysitting I did and had spent all the money on gifts for my family. Trust me, I was the most obedient-rule-keeping child ever, but for that one month of December I didn't pay my tithing. The bishop asked me if I could back-pay my tithing and I explained that all the money was now gone, due to Christmas. He denied me a temple recommend. I was mortified at being deemed unworthy. When I explained this to a friend in the Spanish branch, she explained to me that she had never once paid tithing but that her branch president said she was fine to go do baptisms with our youth group. I stayed home from that year's temple trip. (Youth in my stake only went once a year in the 1980s.) Was I really unworthy? And was my friend worthy?

When it comes to invalidating ordinances, mercy is shown. The ordinance stands. So if mercy can be shown to the sinner who wasn't worthy to perform or receive baptism looking backward, then can we not also show mercy looking forward? If an ordinance always counts, regardless of whether the performer or receiver is worthy or not, then can we even say that worthiness is a real and true principle? Why not let all dads baptize their kids, or let a thirteen-year-old go to the temple with her friends, if that's *what they desire*? Either worthiness always matters or it never matters. Once I began to see the tangled mess that ranking myself and others caused in my life, the concept of worthiness never made sense again.

Now let's really zoom out and look at worthiness from a divine perspective, or as close as a human can possibly get to a divine perspective. I've heard my entire life that God's love for us is infinite, that nothing "will be able to separate us from the love of God." (Romans 8:39) Conversely, I've also been taught that "no unclean thing can dwell with God." (1 Nephi 10:21) Putting aside the fact that people aren't 'things,' I really question whether an all-loving God, a perfect parent devoid of ego and impatience, couldn't stand to be with me if I were 'unclean.' As a parent myself, that just doesn't make sense to me as I would always welcome my child's presence. Whether that is the case, or whether the atonement of Jesus Christ is what makes us clean so that our Heavenly Parents can tolerate being with Their imperfect children, aren't we covered?

Jesus never talked about worthiness, but He did talk about the characteristics of those on His right hand versus His left. Those on His right hand (who will inherit eternal life) are simply those who took care of the suffering. "Then the king will say to those on his right, 'Come, you who are blessed by my Father, take your inheritance, the kingdom prepared for you since the creation of the world. For I was hungry and you gave me something to eat, I was thirsty and you gave me something to drink,'" etc. (Matthew 25:34–35, NRSV)

Those are not the metrics I see modeled today. Jesus didn't say 'if you believe this' or 'if you avoided this beverage,' you're worthy to be with me. His list? Visiting the lonely. Clothing the poor. Alleviating the mental and physical suffering of others. Not one of those is a metric used today to enter the temple, the House of the Lord Jesus Himself. If there is a qualification to living again in heaven, to being deemed worthy of God's presence, this is a qualification quite different from today's worthiness metric. This scripture story is the closest Jesus seems to get in defining righteousness and worthiness. To be honest, I still think Jesus might eyeroll at even this discussion as being one of worthiness because, duh, His grace is sufficient. (2 Corinthians 12:9 KJV)

And that's what worries me in this climate of worthiness. That we've forgotten that we are saved by grace even after all we can do. That *"no one is good but God alone."* (Mark 10:18)

Section Notes

1. R. Scott Lloyd, "Elder Nelson Delivers Spiritual Thanksgiving Feast to MTCs," *Church News*, December 4, 2013, newsroom.churchofjesuschrist.org.

2. Eugene England, "Why the Church Is As True As the Gospel," *Sunstone*, June 1999, 61–69. The Eugene England Foundation, eugeneengland.org.

3. Pema Chodron, *When Things Fall Apart: Heart Advice for Difficult Times* (Element Books, 2005), 14.

4. Dale G. Renlund, "Abound with Blessings," April 2019 general conference.

5. Kate Bowler, *No Cure for Being Human: And Other Truths I Need to Hear* (Random House, 2021), 191.

6. Kate Bowler, *Everything Happens for a Reason and Other Lies I've Loved* (Random House, 2018), 21.

7. Jonathan Merritt, "Anne Lamott Offer Sneak Peek into Forthcoming Book," Jonathan Merrill, October 22, 2014, jonathanmerritt.com.

8. Thomas Jay Oord, *God Can't: How to Believe in God and Love after Tragedy, Abuse, and Other Evils* (SacraSage Press, 2019), 85.

9. "I, the Lord, am bound when ye do what I say; but when ye do not what I say, ye have no promise." Doctrine and Covenants 82:10.

10. Terry Tempest Williams, *The Open Space of Democracy* (Wipf and Stock, 2010), 32.

11. Sharon Salzberg, "When Fear Arises," *On Being*, June 23, 2015, sharonsalzberg.com.

12. Krista Tippet, host, *On Being* podcast, episode 611, "Choosing Curiosity Over Fear," May 24, 2018, 52 minutes. Guest Elizabeth Gilbert.

13. Gilbert, interview with Tippet, *On Being*.

14. Dieter F. Uchtdorf, "Perfect Love Casteth Out Fear," April 2017 general conference.

15. *At Last She Said It* podcast, episode 10, "We Don't Believe Our Own Stuff," May 12, 2020.

16. Uchtdorf, "Perfect Love Casteth Out Fear."

17. Rachel Held Evans, *Searching for Sunday: Loving, Leaving, and Finding the Church* (Thomas Nelson, 2015), 73.

18. Sharon Salzberg, *Faith: Trusting Your Own Deepest Experience* (Riverhead Books, 2003), 62.

19. Salzberg, *Faith: Trusting Your Own Deepest Experience*, 48.

20. Lowell Bennion, "Faith: Values and Limitations, 1959," in *The Best of Lowell L. Bennion Selected Writings 1928–1988*, ed. Eugene England (Deseret Book, 1988), 182.

21. Salzberg, *Faith: Trusting Your Own Deepest Experience*, 67.

22. Alan Watts, *The Wisdom of Insecurity: A Message for an Age of Anxiety* (Vintage Books, 2011), 24.

23. Cynthia Bourgeault, *The Wisdom Jesus: Transforming Heart and Mind—A New Perspective on Christ and His Message* (Shambhala, 2008), 44.

24. Peggy Fletcher Stack, "No apology? Really? Mormons Question Leader Dallin H. Oaks' Stance," *The Salt Lake Tribune*, January 30, 2015, sltrib.com.

25. "Repentance," *Gospel Principles*, chapter 19, The Church of Jesus Christ of Latter-day Saints, available at churchofjesuschrist.org.

26. Scott Neuman, "The Pope's Apology in Canada Was Historic, but for Some Indigenous People, Not Enough," *National Public Radio*, July 25, 2022, npr.org.

27. Gabriel Pietrorazio, "Biden Apologizes for Government's Role in Running Native American Boarding Schools," *National Public Radio*, October 26, 2024, npr.org.

28. Dew, "What Do LDS Women Get."

29. Kate Bowler, host, *Everything Happens* podcast, season 7, episode 8, "The Scandal of Grace," October 5, 2021, 35 minutes. Guest Philip Yancey.

30. Quoted in Jared Byas, *Love Matters More: How Fighting to Be Right Keeps Us from Loving Like Jesus* (Zondervan, 2020), 62.

31. W. W. Phelps, "Come, Come, Ye Saints," *Hymns*, The Church of Jesus Christ of Latter-day Saints.

32. Barbara Brown Taylor, *Always a Guest: Speaking of Faith Far From Home* (Westminster John Knox Press, 2020), 250.

33. Brené Brown, "Brené Brown: 'There Are No Prerequisites for Worthiness,'" appearance on Oprah Winfrey Show, YouTube, posted Oct. 6, 2013, youtube.com.

34. Dieter F. Uchtdorf, "Receiving a Testimony of Light and Truth, October 2014 general conference.

35. "The leader does not proceed with readmission *until he is satisfied* that the person has repented and is ready and worthy to enjoy the blessings of Church membership." Also in the same section: "When the bishop or stake president *is satisfied* that the person is worthy and sincere in wanting to be readmitted, the person may be baptized and confirmed." *General Handbook: Serving in The Church of Jesus Christ of Latter-day Saints*, section 32.16.2, The Church of Jesus Christ of Latter-day Saints, available at churchofjesuschrist.org, emphasis added.

36. Elaine S. Dalton, "Guardians of Virtue," April 2011 general conference.

37. FAIR, "The History and Implementation of the Word of Wisdom," The Foundation for Apologetic Information and Research, Inc., fairlatterdaysaints.org, accessed January 22, 2025.

IT'S COMPLICATED

THE ULTIMATE BIG DEAL

"Do you not know that you are God's temple and that God's Spirit dwells in you?"
—1 Corinthians 3:16 (NRSV)

Susan:

Are you ready to talk about the temple? I call it the Ultimate Big Deal because I can't think of *any* topic in our church that I've been more uncomfortable being open about, and I don't think I'm the only one! But I had an experience that got me started talking and apparently I'm not done yet.

My favorite church calling was my most recent stint teaching Relief Society, which I was lucky enough to do monthly for more years than people usually get to keep callings. Because I had time to really grow into the job, I developed specific goals as a teacher and one was to make room for a diversity of experiences in our discussions. I hoped in that room we might approach old ideas in new ways, creating space and expanding the conversation.

One Sunday I was assigned to teach from a general conference talk about temple work.

I've struggled with the temple for a variety of personal reasons since my first experience at age eighteen. I never felt I could say so out loud in a church setting, and rarely even among friends or family though I know I'm not alone. I want to summarize my own temple issues very simply, just for context: 1) I struggle with claustrophobia, and the temple is a perfect setup to push every anxiety button I have. 2) I've had a couple of bad experiences in the temple that have reinforced my anxiety. 3) My own beautiful children are excluded from the temple, and I was completely blindsided by how much pain this caused me.

But the temple is our church's centerpiece: the Ultimate Big Deal. When you struggle with something so reverenced, it feels like there's almost no one with whom you can be honest about that. I did not look forward to teaching that lesson, as you can imagine.

When teaching, I always pray to find a way into our conversation that might help women wrestling with the topic feel seen and welcome to contribute. In this case, that was me. So I took my inspiration with a deep breath, anxious but hopeful that at the very least, I might create a little space for myself.

I started by passing around a better-than-usual bag of chocolates. I talked about the importance of bringing our whole selves to these discussions. I admitted approaching the lesson with more than a little trepidation. I also shared that, for personal reasons, I hadn't used the recommend tucked in my purse that day one single time, and it would soon expire. I asserted that the temple is complicated and painful for people for a lot of reasons that are actually easy to understand, but we just don't talk about it. Women began to shift in their chairs. I was clearly making them uneasy.

Elder Renlund provided me with the perfect doorway:

> Family relationships can be some of the most rewarding yet challenging experiences we encounter. Many of us have faced a fracture of some sort within our families.[1]

With these words holding the door, I felt like I could invite everyone to step through by saying, "Let's get a clearer picture of who's in this room." Then I asked a list of questions, requesting that women raise their hands:

> Who has something that could be described as a 'fracture' somewhere within their family?
>
> How about someone who isn't eligible to attend the temple?
>
> Someone who hasn't experienced the sealing ordinance?
>
> Someone who is not a member of the church?
>
> Someone who has left the church?
>
> Someone with whom their relationship is difficult?
>
> Someone who identifies as LGBTQ+?
>
> Who has divorce in their family?
>
> How about someone with a sealing that creates a sticky situation we're asked to trust God will sort out later?

Who has polygamy in their family tree?

Who fully understands *all* the implications of the sealing ordinance, as it pertains to what our next life will look like?

Who has unanswered questions about *any* part of their temple experience?

Who has felt sadness because you or someone close to you was excluded from participation in an important family experience or event because it involved the temple?

Who has experienced *any* kind of pain in association with the temple?

Almost every hand was up for every question, and by the end of the list I could see there were already tears. I said, "Now that we've brought our whole selves to this conversation, let's talk about the temple." In the discussion that followed, our Relief Society room broke open in one of the loveliest ways I've ever experienced. I was reminded again of one of the foundational convictions driving my personal church engagement: if Latter-day Saints could get comfortable being real with each other, it could transform the church.

I've thought a lot about why that lesson felt like the most impactful one I ever taught. I guess it's because I pointed out something so easy to see and widely relatable, exposing pain that was in the room already, but had never been allowed to speak. How could challenges so common and so emotionally fraught go completely unacknowledged across my decades of church classes and discussions?

My list of quite benign questions brought into focus reasons why, for some members, the temple might bring more anxiety, uncertainty, or heartache than peace, answers, or spiritual experiences. Although it provides comforting promises for the next life, the temple acts as a dividing line here and now—sharply drawn, vigorously defended by members and the organization, the line divides families and separates people who love each other. The exact opposite of the way we commonly talk and are taught to think about it.

Cynthia:

The temple does indeed provide comforting promises for the next life, but I am more interested in a church for the living, not just the dead. So many of the temple ceremonies have caused pain to me now, in this mortal life. Kicking the can down the eternal road does nothing to help me get through today. The first time I went to the temple after my husband and I received an infertility diagnosis is the first time I realized how much of the temple caters to fertile couples. Every word and promise felt connected to fertility.

From the initiatory through the sealings I heard phrases such as multiply and replenish, joy in your posterity, and a promised blessing in the initiatory that your loins may be fruitful. Why did I have to hear that line, a harsh reminder of our infertility? Why did my sister, Patricia, who suffered five miscarriages have to hear that line? And why did my single sister, Carolyn, now in her forties, have to hear that line as part of her temple worship experience? And this is just one family of sisters! What pain were other families experiencing in our most sacred ceremonies? I wanted answers to these questions so one time I decided to go ask the temple matron in the Provo Temple. She wasn't available so they referred me to the temple recorder, who is a man. And for what seems like the millionth time, he reminded me that some blessings are eternal and not for this life. I pushed back and asked how they helped to alleviate all the pain of my sisters and myself *today*.

I began to wonder what other life experiences caused other women and men to feel pain in the temple. My blinders were removed and I began to seek out all experiences of women and men who found pain instead of peace in our most sacred places. And just as important as realizing there is pain for many, would there ever be a safe place to express that hurt? Or will we always default to the generic answer that God will work it all out when we're dead? I don't expect the church to have all the answers in this life, but I do expect my temple experience—at the very least—to not exacerbate the pain of those unanswered questions.

I'll never forget learning that there really was no safe place to voice my sadness and discomfort about the temple. I was at a family reunion in a large cabin at Yellowstone National Park. The adults were visiting after we put all the children to bed. The discussion turned toward the temple. I bravely—or tiredly—had the courage to finally admit out loud for the first time in my life that certain aspects of the temple experience were quite the opposite from the other glowing experiences in the room. Nobody was unkind, but my concerns were not met with empathy or validation. I learned then and there, in my thirties, not to speak out loud about my temple concerns. I know that you and I are not that unique, so if we are struggling with the temple, then other women are as well. Your temple lesson perfectly demonstrates that struggle.

Unfortunately, the panacea to many temple problems seems to be 'just go more often.' For years, I had a stake president proclaim from the pulpit that the temple would make more sense and hold more meaning to us if we made a commitment to go more. Once my children were all in school full time, I decided to commit to going more often in an effort to resolve these concerns. However, hearing the temple ceremonies even more frequently only exacerbated the problems. Specifically, over the years I talked with kind bishops about the pain I experienced in covenanting to 'hearken' to my husband. It felt so unequal! Does God really require women to covenant to listen and follow their husbands? If so, why aren't husbands required to do the same? My bishops couldn't answer my questions either.

Finally, I remember being in the temple one day and having the strongest impression that it was okay to stop doing things that hurt my soul. Whether it was from God or my own inner compass, I am not sure. Nor does it matter, because for the first time in my life I felt at peace about the temple. God didn't require my misery! Not six months later, 'hearken' was removed from the temple ceremony, among other sexist language. Words cannot describe the relief I felt with that change. Not so much because the hurtful covenant was gone, but because this gave me the courage to trust my inner compass from then on. Yes, it was nice to have my concerns validated with their removal, but I realized then that I didn't need anyone's permission to follow my intuition again.

Susan:

'Just go more' has been one of the most frustrating messages about the temple I've received. If something doesn't sit well with me, why would I want to do it more? I'm not in a parent-child relationship with the church organization or leaders. This isn't like I'm a child who's fussing about practicing piano, and my parents have the authority to make me do it anyway—I feel empowered to examine and make judgments about what kind of fruit a thing has yielded in my life, and the temple is a pretty mixed bag for me. To state it most simply: *I dread it for days before, and I'm extremely anxious while I am there.* So at this time in my life, I'm not attending regularly. That may change at some point, but I'm the one who will know when or if it is time to return. In the meantime, being told to go more feels like complete invalidation of my feelings and personal judgment about what is right for me. My decision to take a temple break for the time being felt like having a thousand-pound weight lifted off me. At last I could breathe.

We're not all having the same experience in the temple, full stop.

When I went through for the first time, I had no idea what to expect. I was eighteen years old, mostly just interested in getting married, and knew I had to jump through that hoop to do it. In hindsight, eighteen feels perilously young for making promises intended to govern every choice for the rest of a person's life. In preparation, I was given Boyd K. Packer's book, *You May Claim the Blessings of The Holy Temple.* I read it thinking I was going to gain valuable insight and understanding of the great secrets about to be revealed to me. Instead, it was full of general platitudes and promises like this:

> Be faithful to the covenants and ordinances of the gospel. Qualify for those sacred ordinances step by step as you move through life. Honor the covenants connected with them. Do this and you will be happy.... Your lives will then be in order—all things lined up in proper sequence, in proper ranks, in proper rows. Your family will be linked in an order that can never be broken.[2]

I believed it. I envisioned my life planted in neat rows like a garden that would never grow weeds because I was making the choice to marry in the temple. I know, I was seriously naive. And that promise of order and unbreakable family appealed to me because I was running headlong into adulthood in part to escape a childhood that had so often felt precarious and uncertain. I'd experimented with different kinds of choices in response to my young unhappiness, but soon settled on an early marriage as the most reliable path to the safety I craved. And by having gotten my wild-ish teenage self back on track, I believed I'd basically fixed everything forever. Having struggled with anxiety and depression even in childhood, the 'you will be happy' part meant everything to me. I was willing to jump through any and all hoops for that promise in adulthood.

Having the temple be yet another source of painful anxiety in my life was disappointing, to say the least. I assumed I was the one with the problem. I never heard anyone else talk about their temple experiences being miserable.

So I remember the exact moment the idea came into clear focus for me that actually, the temple might be causing *many* people pain, despite all the hushed, glowing adjectives we use to describe it with each other. It was the rededication of the Nauvoo Temple, twenty-two years after I'd taken out my own endowment. I'd spent those twenty-two years carrying my discomfort in silence, thinking I was the only one. There were no church meetings that day at our ward. Of course you needed a recommend to attend, and one of our three daughters did not have one so the rest of us went without her. She wasn't welcome there. I experienced the reality like a tear in the fabric of our family; the pain was something wholly new, a deep, personal wound. I cried all the way through the dedication ceremony, wondering why I couldn't seem to stop, wondering how she felt, alone at home, standing on the other side of the line—a gash, really—suddenly made visible within our family. As I looked around, noting the people I knew who were there (or more importantly weren't) from my folding chair in the stake center gym, I remember seeing for the first time that no matter how wonderful the temple might be, anything with an edge sharp enough to cut straight through families would also cause some people very real pain.

So much for the garden rows I'd tended so carefully, with every bit of love and faithful devotion I had. So much for order that could never be broken.

Cynthia:

Ironically, it was the Nauvoo Temple rededication that began to shift my views of the temple as well. My husband and I got a babysitter for our toddler and infant and went to the stake center to stand in a long line that wrapped around the parking lot, waiting for our turn to enter and watch the dedication. I saw a neighbor approaching and told her to just butt in line with us so she wouldn't have to wait alone. I asked her why her husband wasn't there, assuming they had a hard time finding a sitter as well for their two babies. She looked at me embarrassingly and said, 'It's just one of those … things.' I instantly felt about one inch tall. I had violated my friend's privacy, cornering her into explaining, even thinly veiled, that her husband didn't have a temple recommend.

It was in that moment, standing on the sidewalk with my friend, that I realized certain things that should be private, like having a temple recommend, never really can stay private for long. If you don't attend a family temple wedding, people will know. If you don't attend your sister's endowment before her mission, people will know *something* about you. They will know that you are either not 'worthy' in the eyes of the church, or that you have unresolved sins, or that you don't pay your tithing, etc. I think you're right in using the word 'gash' to describe what occurs in families when some can enter the temple and some cannot.

In addition to the lack of privacy and the gashes that can result in dividing families, the temple became even more difficult for me once I figured out that I learn better through discussion and sharing with my fellow saints. Once I had learned all I could in the temple on my own by being silent and just listening to the scripted and pre-recorded ceremonies, the boredom of attending the temple set in. We have a temple preparation class to prepare you for the first time you go, but there is no post-temple prep to help you after you've gone. Add in the extra layer of secrecy surrounding what happens in the temple, and what can be discussed?

My greatest communal experiences have happened at church when perspectives and experiences are shared and discussed from the pulpit, in lessons, or comments. All of that is absent from the temple so it's hard for me to pay attention, year after year, decade after decade, to the same scripts. I do learn in silence and meditation as well, but those lessons have always seemed to come through reading in solitude, or when I am in nature, surrounded by God's handiwork. I willingly make space for those who love the silence and lack of discussion in the temple. All I am asking is the same space in return.

Susan:

That's it in a nutshell, isn't it? All so many women are asking for is a little space around the temple to hold the complexity of our own feelings about it. To be allowed to fully feel our own anger, confusion, disappointment, grief, loneliness, discomfort, and whatever else may be tangled up with the love, joy, peace, faith, and hope we also feel and reliably project. We give voice to the latter while hiding the former, sometimes for a lifetime. I was well into my fifties before I felt I could broach my struggle out loud. That kind of secret makes for a lopsided emotional bundle, the kind that can take a lot of energy to package and repackage as we try to make it appear tidier and less unwieldy than it feels. Not being able to set a thing down for decades is exhausting.

Not being able to admit things even to ourselves is heartbreaking. Not being able to help others carry their own complicated bundle because we don't know they're struggling with it is tragic.

So why all the secrecy? Is it just to maintain an amped-up air of sacredness? Any time you have so much pressure on a thing as you do the temple, change is going to be really difficult, but could eliminating some of our reticence to speak plainly help dial back the ultimate big-dealness, making it a little easier for women who struggle to find peace? I feel confident that freedom to talk about all the reasons the temple has been hard for me across my lifetime would help defuse some of my personal anxiety. If there's nothing like not being able to talk about a thing to give it the wrong kind of power, I know of nowhere that is more true than with the temple.

THERE ARE WORSE THINGS THAN BEING WRONG

"Press forward with a steadfastness in Christ, having a perfect brightness of hope, and a love of God and of all [humans]."
—2 Nephi 31:20

Cynthia:

In 2019, on the eve of my daughter moving out to attend college, she told her dad and me that she is gay. In that instant I knew that I would love and support my baby girl in whatever she needed to be mentally healthy and spiritually whole. I was also pretty sure that she would want to establish her own family someday. A family that looked differently than ours. Although, maybe not? Our family consists of two parents and three adopted children. Her family could look similarly. But I digress, this isn't an essay about all the amazing shapes and sizes of families.

I had already been an LGBTQ+ ally for several years by then, but as I attended different support groups I heard LDS parents, also affirming of their gay kiddos, say out loud, "But what if I am wrong?" I could hear the wrestle in their voices. I heard them explore out loud the divinity and goodness of their child—that they too deserved a family of their own someday—yet feel the conflict from church leaders who called gay marriage 'counterfeit' and worse. In that instant, 'experimenting upon the word' became necessary for these parents.

That's when the thought came to me: *There are worse things than being wrong.* Way back in our second podcast episode, I said that is one of the things I know for sure. My daughter wasn't out publicly yet so I couldn't explain in front of my microphone exactly what was behind that surest thing that I knew, but I did say that being unkind is worse than being wrong. President Hinckley once said, "I constantly hope and pray that if we err, we will err on the side of mercy."[3] Time and time again this is what I see in my fellow LGBTQ+ parents—mercy toward their children who simply want what they've been taught their entire life to want: a family of their own.

As podcasters we get a lot of feedback through email and social media. We often save the messages and divide them into categories for future reference. One category we never created but maybe should have is, "But what if I am wrong?" I guess we shouldn't be surprised when we talk about old things in new ways that our listeners may want to make some changes in their own lives. And while those changes might be seemingly neutral, we Mormons have been conditioned to believe that every choice is either 'right' or 'wrong.' My entire life I have sung this line from our beloved hymns, "Do what is right, let the consequence follow!" So yeah, I get it. Doing what is right is a very big deal.

Now what you need to know about the women that write to us—who pose that hand-wringing question—is that these are women usually between the ages of thirty and eighty. Women who teach Sunday school. Women who have jobs. Women who keep small humans alive. In other words, they are already functioning members of society. I don't know a more practical bunch of law-abiding, morality-based citizens that make the world turn than Latter-day Saint women. I don't think my life, or the life of *most* regular Mormon women, would make great reality TV. Who would sponsor such an everyday kind of show except maybe fabric softener, or even more boring, multi-vitamins?

No, these aren't eighteen-year-old girls who can't decide their life's path. We're hearing from Grown-ass-Adult-Functioning-Members-of-Society kind of women who want to address God differently when they pray. Or who want to support their gay child if they enter a same-sex marriage. Women who want to think and pray about a calling before immediately telling a bishop yes. Women who are finding God's presence and guidance sitting under their favorite maple tree instead of in the temple. (Ahem, that last one is me.) These are not women who want to leave their families, light a match, burn it all down, and then backpack around the world living in monasteries while making goat cheese. Although now that I typed that last sentence, that doesn't sound half bad. Whether we're talking about women who make goat cheese or buy plastic-wrapped American cheese, what we hear in that question—*"but what if I am wrong,"*—is that women want to lead autonomous lives, trusting their inner voice and trusting that God will lead them. But the terror of being wrong halts their progress. Here's just one comment from our social media:

> "I so struggle with this idea … because what if I pick to live the principles that aren't truly from God, and then I am leaving out the stuff I actually should be doing? I am so afraid to get it wrong. #guiltmuch"
>
> My reply: "So sorry about the guilt. You've heard us ask our guests the question, 'What do you know?' And maybe you've heard me answer it—that what I do know is that there are worse things than being wrong."
>
> Her reply: "I have. And I agree—but what if I'm wrong for the eternities? (I know, such a Mormon concern.)"

When I read messages like that one, I think, "So what? What if she is wrong?" In Alma's famous sermon comparing the word to a seed we are encouraged to experiment upon the word (Alma 32:27). Experiment used as a verb in that scripture requires us by definition, "to try or test, especially in order to discover or prove something." We are to conduct little experiments and even what the commenter described as eternal ones. These are women who want to experiment with experiments, but they don't trust themselves to conduct the experiment! I get it. It's easier to trust someone else's experiment, especially when we've been taught our entire lives that our leaders know better, even that they see what we can't see.

Maybe that's true, but our church leaders still have their human lens and filters like I do. I can give weight to their words while still running my own experiment. I am the only person who will live with the consequences of my choices—not one single prophet ever has been affected by my choice to attend the temple, pray under my trees, or even if I choose to eat a healthy diet. Shouldn't the one who lives with my consequences have the majority say in how those choices are bodied out?

What if some choices are just … choices? I have stopped using 'right' and 'wrong' to describe my choices, or the even heavier weight of 'eternal' versus 'temporal' choices, and have started to use the descriptor of 'healthy' or 'unhealthy' choices. I am not saying that is always the correct barometer, but as a middle-aged woman my moral compass is pretty much set. Be kind. Commune with God. Eat oatmeal because it's good for my heart. Be a helper. Let people merge into my lane on the freeway. Forgive others.

Ninety-nine percent of my decisions now are whether something would be healthy for me, would benefit me, or would benefit the lives of those around me today. Not eternity. *Today*. I live in the Now and as such my choices need to be based in the details of the Now. It's the only kind of decision I know how to make anymore, as those consequences are usually measurable, visible, and understandable. Eternity? That's a different chapter.

Brian McClaren said, "We're not talking about individualism here, we're talking about basic adulthood."[4] I've thought about that a lot—the difference between rugged individualism and just basic adult-like decisions. After speaking to thousands of women at this point, I can safely say that women's choices are falling into that latter category of basic adult-like decisions.

What secured my mantra—there are worse things than being wrong—into my toolbelt of things I know for sure, came from one such experiment. We have a series on the podcast called "We Don't Believe Our Own Stuff." The idea behind these episodes is to explore the many beautiful teachings in The Church of Jesus Christ of Latter-day Saints that we can't seem to grasp and incorporate into our lives. Sometimes I wonder if we truly believe our own stuff about forgiveness. Good grief, Jesus couldn't stop telling stories about U-turns, forgiveness, and second chances. If we really believed our own stuff—the stuff of Jesus—maybe we wouldn't be so afraid to experiment upon the word? If I believe in a God of endless U-turns, and I do, why does the idea of a U-turn scare us so badly? If an experiment eventually leads us to asking forgiveness of our loved ones and of God, is that the end of the world? And wouldn't God prompt me about my errors anyway? Won't that still small voice I have heard about since Primary be my guide? And absent those promptings, won't the natural consequences of running such experiments tell me whether this was a healthy or unhealthy choice?

On the church's website, there's a video called *Wrong Roads*, narrated by Elder Holland, describing an incident when he was out enjoying the wilderness of southern Utah with his young son. At the end of their adventure, they headed back home but encountered a fork in the road. He and his son both felt through prayer that they should take the right fork. But after five hundred feet, they realized it was the wrong road. They had reached a dead end. Elder Holland summarizes that it was only through their experiment that they now knew that the left fork was the correct road to have taken, even though their previous answer to their prayer had intimated otherwise.

That seems to be a pretty realistic metaphor for life, that we often make wrong choices, even with careful thought and prayer. If we believe our own stuff, if we believe in forgiveness and second (and third, and fourth, and one hundredth) chances, won't it all be okay?

Are our experiments foolproof? Will we always make the right or healthiest choice? Even when we involve God? Of course not, but is anything foolproof in an imperfect world? Every choice I have ever made, on my own or with God's help, has been filtered through my own imperfect lens—my past experiences, my personality, my cerebral wiring. When I think about the enormity of some decisions, it can sometimes make me feel like finding the nearest bed, pulling the covers over my head and playing depressing songs from The Smiths while I cry into my pillow. But when I can apply what I know for sure—that there are worse things than being wrong—I know that through the grace, mercy, and atonement of Jesus Christ, somehow making those small and big decisions seems less daunting. Maybe, just maybe, I can press forward having a "perfect brightness of hope." (2 Nephi 31:20) Not because I am perfect, or my choices will be, but because God's perfection allows me to have my imperfections.

WHEN WOMEN ARE THE PROBLEM

"There is a special place in hell for women who don't help other women."
—Former Secretary of State Madeleine Albright[5]

Cynthia:

I once had a visiting teacher who came into my home and with what seemed like genuine sincerity, asked me what my issues were with equality in the church. I gave her a brief synopsis of all the things I noticed and experienced in the church. Two days later, I opened my mailbox to see that she had left me a general conference talk by an apostle about how much the church loves women—printed, stapled, highlighted in yellow and carefully annotated by her as to why she believes the men love the women of this church. (Never mind that loving someone and treating them as your equal are two different things.) She was a young woman in her twenties, so I smiled and thought, "Let's talk in a few decades," and tossed the printed pages into the recycle bin.

Even though this happened over a decade ago, again the lesson reinforced to me that day at my mailbox is that most often women are the problem. A 2010 survey of church members found that 90 percent of Latter-day Saint women opposed female ordination, whereas only about half of Latter-day Saint men opposed female ordination.[6] Why the huge discrepancy? We could spend a lot of time analyzing the gendered differences in that one statistic, but a quick summary could be this: we women are complicit in our own marginalization.

I'll never forget a podcast conversation we had with James Jones, a Black man, a Latter-day Saint theologian, and host of the *Beyond the Block* podcast. He said:

> I think every marginalized community deals with it to some extent where we have to talk about the members of our community that are often complicit ... When you have a significant number of the population (most women?) say they're fine, how do you overcome that?[7]

Like we said in our previous discussion of ordination, we are never advocating for women (or men!) to take on responsibilities that they don't want or that go contrary to their values. What we are asking women to think about are the ways that we may possibly hold each other back, like James suggested.

Susan:

I remember exactly where I was when the thought first occurred to me that women are complicit in our own marginalization within the church; it was one of those moments that gets burned into your brain. The realization was sickening—at first it was hard to even say out loud.

We hadn't been at the ALSSI project long when I started to notice how many women seemed to have happily become 'hall monitors,' policing each other to stay inside acceptable cultural and organizational lines in all kinds of subtle and less-subtle ways. Like the proverbial crabs in a bucket, as often as a woman expresses ideas beyond the party line, other women are quick to pull her back. In talks, lessons, and private conversations, Latter-day Saint women defend the status quo by bearing their testimonies of it, a move that may be intended to teach or persuade, but is probably just as often intended to shut down discussion.

Let me be clear that I respect women's testimonies of the things they believe and that are deeply meaningful and significant in their lives. But I also believe there has to be space left around a testimony for the beliefs and experiences of others.

So I want to talk about complicity: what we mean by it and what its origins and implications might be. But also definitely what we might do to change it. How can women better support other women in our church? Because the church of the shutdown—a church where the members refuse to see or listen to one another—is not a church I want any part of. Could we even call that church?

A church where members accuse other members of being influenced by 'the adversary' because their experiences have been different, and therefore their needs and their ideas are different too, is also of no interest to me. I can't imagine it's a place my beloved god-of-diversity would hang out.

Rabbi Sharon Brous writes, "Err on the side of presence."[8] She's talking about the requirement, as people who think of ourselves as God's people, of 'showing up' for each other in all our life experiences.

Life brings a full diversity of experiences, good and bad, and that's everyone's life no matter how much we pretend otherwise. No matter how worthy you think you are—or you're told you aren't—life is coming at all of us hard, and the Christianity I believe in and want to practice requires that I try to be a soft landing place for others. But I think the crabs pulling other crabs back down into the bucket are less concerned about the feelings, ideas, and experiences of others than about defending their own. The message they're transmitting is *not*, "I'm here with you."

It costs us nothing to sit with someone whose experience is different from our own, but we each gain a measure of soft space in a hard world when we're willing to do it. The magic of presence is the magic of Jesus—He stopped, He asked, He healed! We have the same power, but in my experience it's often not the chosen approach.

I'm always disheartened to see women make no room at all for the possibility that other women are having a different experience, or can legitimately—righteously!—need and want something more from the church organization. It's a human organization on a human earth required to grow and change, adapt and update in order to stay alive. If there's anyone who loves where we are collectively at this moment enough to want to stay here the rest of eternity, I'd listen to them make their case. But personally, I want more for all of us.

Cynthia:

The crabs-in-the-bucket analogy makes me wince not because it isn't true, but because I don't want it to be true. Over and over, I witness women pulling down other women who dare to do, think, or say things differently. In my own ward's Relief Society, there was a young teacher who told us about her personal revelation to return to her career as an elementary school teacher even though she had a young son at home. Her vulnerability was not rewarded by the sisters. Over and over, comments were made that prophets have told women to not work outside the home. Never mind church leaders hadn't said anything of the sort in over a decade on the topic of women working. No space was given that day to this young mom to differentiate. By the end of the lesson she was in tears, and not happy tears.

Why do we pull others back into the crab bucket? Who deputized the women of the church? We might as well have been handed a sheriff's star and told to enforce the law that we had no input in drafting. In her book *Down Girl,* Kate Manne explains, "Misogyny should be understood as the 'law enforcement' branch of a patriarchal order, which has the overall function of policing and enforcing its governing ideology."[9]

I realize the use of the word 'misogyny' seems very harsh in this context. Misogyny is usually defined as a form of sexism that is manifested as hatred, contempt, or prejudice against women or girls. I don't think LDS women hate or have contempt for other women in the proverbial Relief Society room. But I do think many women are prejudiced against women who are not 'well-behaved' Mormon women. Manne makes a distinction between misogyny and sexism though. She theorizes in her book that misogyny enforces patriarchal norms, whereas sexism rationalizes them.

That aligns with my experience as a Latter-day Saint woman. Misogyny, in the LDS context, divides women into good women and bad women. Those who follow the counsel from the brethren—the patriarchal norms—are the good ones. Those who follow their own intuition and revelation and speak out about the harms of patriarchy are the bad ones. These deputized women (and men) use sexist ideology masked as pseudoscience, or worse, as God-ordained differences to draw very strict and narrow boundaries around the duties, talents, desires, and responsibilities of women.

When women step outside those narrow boundaries, it's a threat to the entire ecosystem. After all, if one woman can be successful outside those boundaries—for example, working moms—then maybe the very real sacrifices of the 'good women' who sacrificed careers didn't matter after all? Thus, we double down on our choices and go after women who differentiate because it's too painful to reassess our own life's choices.

Susan:

When I started to think about LDS women and complicity, I realized our church experience may not be that different from what many women experience in the world. For instance, some of feminist writer and philosopher Simone de Beauvoir's ideas on this sound all too familiar to me. She asserts that not only do women have fewer resources and fewer opportunities than men, but at a more universal level we are "unfree" because we are "conceived of as the Other." To be Other in this existential sense means to be the passive object to man's active subject:

She determines and differentiates herself in relation to man, and he does not in relation to her; she is the inessential in front of the essential. He is the subject, he is the absolute. She is the Other.[10]

This idea of being 'the inessential' while men are the 'essential' is really stark and painful when I place it in the context of some of our temple narratives, particularly historically. Beauvoir asserts that men cast women into this position, but find in us "a deep complicity." In other words, we don't reject our passive and dependent position, rather we accept and even embrace it.

Research has shown that when women's voices are disregarded, it affects how we think about ourselves, which in turn affects how we use our voices. It's a cycle. I posit that our acceptance of women's roles as defined by men shapes how we view ourselves and our own capabilities, opportunities, and potential. A distorted view of ourselves might lead us to become complicit in ways of life we would not otherwise choose. Though a limited role may not be what she would select for herself from the broad range of life's possibilities, a Latter-day Saint woman knows to choose something different might involve rejecting the agreed upon narratives and understanding of what it means to be a woman, and that's a very difficult thing to do. Beauvoir describes this as women "clinging to their chains," or "actively playing the role of passivity," out of certainty that things can't be different from how they are. I believe a lot of women in our church would tell you just that: some things simply will not—indeed cannot—change.

This is not the place to argue whether the doctrinal specifics behind that viewpoint are true or not, but I do want to point out it is a view that is weaponized to squash hope. Hope of even simple organizational changes that many members (women *and* men) feel are long overdue at church! It also flies in the face of changes that have already occurred around women's roles in the world, the world in which our daughters and granddaughters are living and by which their choices will necessarily be shaped. The difference between their experiences and my own point to an evolution I feel we cannot deny and we must not ignore. One of my favorite quotes on hope comes from Krista Tippet, who describes it like this:

It's not wishful thinking. It's not assuming that things will turn out all right. It's an insistence, looking at the world straight on as it is and rejecting the idea that it has to be that way, and then throwing your light and your pragmatism as much as your spirit at [that]. What does it look like if you don't accept it? That's how I think of it.[11]

I'm not sure many of my sisters at church are willing—perhaps even able—to do what she's describing, to actually *invest* in the possibility that things could indeed be different. But it's precisely that kind of hope that fuels the ALSSI project.

Cynthia:

I have hope as well. Hope that more women can and will reject the idea that things have always been this way so they need to stay this way. We never started our podcast project with any hope of changing the organizational church, but rather that we could help women have hope that things could be different for them personally and spiritually in their individual lives. Whether that possible groundswell of personal empowerment and change eventually changes the church organization is not our focus. The latter could take years. But individual women can change today.

We received a voicemail from a mom whose daughter said she couldn't wait to pass the sacrament. Her immediate thought was, "Have I not taught you your proper place in this world?"[12] And then she was instantly horrified at her own thoughts because she realized the world wasn't holding her daughter back—the church was. But I also think her voicemail has stuck with me because we've all (mostly) had similar thoughts—wanted or not—that men and women need to know their place in the church organization. We just have different responsibilities! Never mind that those differences in responsibilities leave men and women unequally yoked, as men are in charge and women follow. It's not a difference of responsibilities where women hold equal power and representation with men. But I digress.

If Sharon Brous is right—that we should err on the side of presence—why can't LDS women just be present with their sisters who yearn for change? Why do we police other women in the form of conference talks left in mailboxes?

Susan:

Unfortunately, other women may be the biggest obstacle we face. I remember the training of our Labrador Retriever puppy, which my husband did so diligently because he wanted a well-trained hunting dog. He studied the best ways to achieve the behavior he wanted, then became passionate about developing the relationship.

One tool he used was an e-collar, also known as a 'shock collar.' It's a good tool for a dog with impulse control challenges and is most useful after the dog has already been trained—they need to understand basic commands like sit, stay, and come, then the e-collar acts as reinforcement. There's a tone setting, a vibrate setting, and different degrees of shock. The idea is you only need to use the tone to warn the dog when they're violating behavioral boundaries and that's enough to bring them in line.

I mention this because, as women who are well trained to our own behavioral boundaries in the church, we've developed a culture in which we may as well all be wearing e-collars. All the time, women sound the tone to other women who are perceived to be pushing some limit. Occasionally, the reprimand goes to vibrate. Our interactions with men may occasionally progress to shock because they have the ultimate power to discipline in the church setting. But plenty of women seem happy to keep their fingers on the control button, zapping others with the tone in lessons and conversations.

Cost is another obstacle to change. A woman must ask, "What would it cost to give up what I have now?" As it stands, we are in an alliance with the 'caste' in charge—we're rewarded for our complicity, right? If you can't get on board and support, there's not really any meaningful place for you among the Latter-day Saints, and I think that's particularly true for women. Upsetting that equilibrium comes with consequences. I want to note that men are also complicit in this structure, but women's complicity has greater negative effects for us. For instance, being an active member of the church does dictate things for a man's life; however, accepting your role as the patriarch and 'presider' in your home is different from accepting your role as the one who does *not* preside.

Cynthia:

The consequences to speaking up are so real and can be so life altering. For many years now, you and I have had a front row seat to how this plays out in the very real lives of women around the globe. A woman confides in her bishop about her faith struggles and she's released from her calling. She can also lose her temple recommend. Speaking up at church can sometimes cause us to lose our influence in our ward.

Losing relationships can also be a very real threat. One woman we know in her sixties wrote to us and said that her husband doesn't know a single thing about her complicated churchy feelings. She said: "You're the only person I can say this to. My husband is all the way in and it would crush him if he knew. I am living such an inauthentic life, but I'll do it to keep the peace. My husband and I both have stake callings and we've served a senior mission together. I deserve an Oscar award for my performance sometimes."

The price can be high. So I understand why so many women choose to keep silent, although that silence also has its own repercussions. The internal cost is to realize you could have had a different life. I hate the idea of sunk costs in describing a religious life, but I do think for so many women that is a real factor in doubling down on a system that hasn't served us well. One way the idea of sunk costs manifests, for example, is requiring young women to kneel down at dances to see if their skirt touches the ground. Is it embarrassing? Yes. But the idea is that if I had to endure this, the next generation of girls should have to endure it as well. It's just what women have to do.

To renegotiate rules around 'modest' clothing might seem daunting. Maybe you wonder if there is a better way? The fear of the unknown can seem, well, fear inducing. So in the end you stick with what you know. I endured, my mom endured, and thus my daughter will endure.

Susan:

Ouch. That last sentence rings so true to me! I see that kind of double down in all kinds of places outside church, which means it must be human nature. But what has my attention now as it relates to church is this: there are many young mothers who are not willing to ask their daughters to put up with all the things they and their own mothers and grandmothers have accepted! We hear this all the time: young mothers write to tell us there are some things they simply refuse to pass along. Many are not sure how that refusal plays out exactly within the current structure of the church. They struggle with how (and whether) they can raise their daughters within it. Maybe this has happened before; maybe all women's progress throughout history has been a result of one generation rising up to say about something, "This stops with us."

But men have been telling women who we are supposed to be from the beginning, and I continue to see that pattern play out. We have yet to arrive at the generation that has never heard, internalized, and in some ways been subject to at least some of the tired patriarchal narratives that have shaped the world.

I think overcoming this obstacle within our LDS culture will require a twofold approach: changing the way women think about ourselves, and changing the official narrative that drives our expectations for women. In a church of continuing revelation, I don't think it's too much to expect that when the first happens, the second will follow. To me there's great hope in finding our daughters simply don't think of themselves in the same ways older generations have! For any organization to remain relevant in their lives, it's going to have to be willing—also able—to adapt accordingly.

The quote at the beginning of this essay is a strong indictment of women who hold back other women. I've thought a lot about the kind of complicity that keeps some women invested in policing others and how it manifests in our culture. There's a huge diversity of experience even within our highly correlated church. Two women who grew up as Latter-day Saints and spent their whole lives progressing through the same programs may have entirely different experiences. And there's something about a 'true' church—as ours claims to be—that I think leads members to expect uniformity of experience, so it's hard to sit with different perceptions and outcomes.

We encounter someone whose experiences are very different from our own and automatically assume they did something wrong; if they had done everything right, they'd have achieved the ideal—the happy results the church promises. This inability to tolerate difference presents a challenge when it comes to having meaningful discussions that could move us forward. If we're always assigning fault or aberration to the non-ideal/nonconforming experience, how can we ever identify problems or agree on ways to address them? We must be willing to begin with the assumption that there is no 'right' experience. There are only women's experiences, and each is real and valid. If we can't allow for different experiences and outcomes and show up for each other in that difference, how can we feel, not to mention express, the kind of unity that might lead to change?

In a patriarchal church structure, members are socialized into be-lieving—and consequently acting—as if women are less valuable based on power, privilege, and priesthood. Some men, and more important to this discussion women, push back on that statement, insisting women are valued equally. But it's a statement of fact that men are privileged within the existing organizational structure, which is what I'm talking about here. As women, being in this position might make it feel hard or risky for some to truly support others. However, that support would only require women to be willing to sit with each other in our experiences, and allow the full expression of diverse ideas. Can we imagine together? Can we enlarge our collective vision? How about just our vocabulary?

Cynthia:

Let's get really specific and talk about some of the ways women could just sit with different feelings in the proverbial Relief Society room. What does women's lack of support for other women look like? Here are a few scenarios I have personally experienced with other Latter-day Saint women:

Scenario 1: *"I would never want that kind of responsibility!"*

Me: I think that women belong in every place that decisions are made—bishopric meetings, disciplinary councils, stake presidency meet-ings, etc.

Female Friend: Well, personally, I'm glad I don't have that responsibil-ity! I would never want to be in a bishopric!

Me: I would always prefer to have more free time as well! But that doesn't mean that I don't want to be represented in every church meeting. Can you see that diversity is a good thing? That *some* men and *some* women would make great leaders? And also so many, maybe you as well, would prefer to be helpers? Hooray for diversity of talents!

Scenario 2: *"Women would make lousy bishops!"*

Me: Can you even imagine a bishopric made up of men and women? Wouldn't that be amazing!

Female friend: I would never want to see women in a bishopric. Women are too emotional! Heavenly Father just made men and women differently, I am okay with that.

Me: Is it possible you have trouble seeing women as clergy because for your entire life you've been socialized to only see men as clergy? There are biological differences between the sexes, but I think for too long we've used those differences to exclude women from decision-making jobs and church callings. Can you stay open and curious and leave some room for maybe changing your mind on this issue?

Scenario 3: *"I have never felt less-than as a woman in this church!"*

Me: It's hard for me to see women released from callings when their priesthood leaders disagree with their opinions on women's equality, LGBTQ+ issues, etc. It feels like unrighteous dominion. Like being a woman with different opinions makes her 'unworthy' to serve.

Female Friend: I have never experienced that. I have always felt loved and listened to. You're being too sensitive. The men of this church love the women!

Me: Can you accept that I have had different experiences? That I don't need to be put on a pedestal and told I am loved? That due to my negative experiences within our patriarchal church I see equality as the antidote, not hollow praise and love? Every woman's experience should be recognized as valid.

Having personally experienced each of these scenarios with friends, I can tell you the common denominator in all three. It feels demoralizing. Women who can't show empathy for their fellow sisters and insist there is not an equality problem in the church leave me feeling that since this is the way things have always been, things will always be this way. In a church that believes in ongoing revelation, that's not good enough for me. Change should be an inherent part of the system.

Women desirous for change often second-guess their very real lived experiences when they're met with doubt, disbelief, and disapproval by women who are content with the status quo. It's easy to understand the second guessing of feelings. First of all, there is usually a long history with a specific policy. Since this is the way things have always been done it stands to reason that it's because God wants it this way. Otherwise God would tell the prophet to change. On the rare occasion when women do admit change would be good, they very often add, "but I will be patient until God and the prophet authorize a change." This can make women like me feel less-than because I am the one labeled as impatient and lacking faith in God's timing. It is a no-win situation.

Another argument I hear from many women is that men and women simply have different and divine roles in the church—roles put in place by God. But we should look skeptically at a system where men are always in charge of women. There is not one decision a woman can make in this church that cannot be overruled by a man. Not one. Let's just assume, though, that men and women really do need to have separate roles in the organization of the church. Much could be done to work towards equality of power anyway. For example, the late LDS historian Melissa Inouye suggested the following:

> We could do so much good if [the women's organization] Relief Society, for example, were in charge of distributing our humanitarian aid and could coordinate those local projects in their areas. Or if, for example, to preserve some sort of complementarian difference but to make sure that women had significant power, if men were in charge of like the sacerdotal priesthood—you know, call the men for the ordinances type things—and women were in charge of the finances, then we would have a true kind of codependent relationship.[13]

Unfortunately, we do not have anything even resembling the type of interdependent relationship that Dr. Inouye suggested. Instead we have a system where men are the gatekeepers for all the spiritual and organizational involvement of women. Women are completely dependent on a man's approval of her worthiness to participate in our highest ordinances, her ability to interact with the organization through callings and assignments, and the list goes on.

Kate Manne, in her book *Down Girl*, says, "Sexism wears a lab coat." Meaning, women and men cling to outdated ideas about gender roles because they believe it's just science that women and men are different. Do we women really believe that those differences somehow make men more capable of leading and women more inclined to follow? But in our church we have that lab coat *and* the prophetic stamp of approval. Those are two huge hurdles to overcome! No wonder LDS women with concerns about equality often feel alone. Belonging to a church with members who believe in 'separate but equal' can feel like an insurmountable brick wall that stands in the way of a woman being understood by her fellow saints.

Susan:

How could we change it? How can we make a shift toward women supporting each other, regardless of where we sit on the question of women's representation or roles in the church organization? I think getting in the habit of pushing beyond the 'warning tone' when we're speaking up could bring change. In other words, some of us (looking in the mirror here) need to become a little more resistant to being shut down. I watched our chocolate Lab pup glance back over his shoulder before making the decision to do what he wanted anyway enough times to know that warning tone wasn't much of a deterrent if he truly wanted to chase the rabbit.

I believe our stories hold the key to changing our culture and eventually our church. As often as we share our personal experiences, we can open space for ourselves and others. Eventually there will come a tipping point—enough voices cannot be silenced. I've sat through so many church lessons without commenting, even though my feelings or experience didn't line up with the message I was hearing. I know I'm not alone in that. Like the woman who couldn't help herself from 'testifying' in my Relief Society lessons—but eventually gave up—women will stop pushing that tone button when enough other women refuse to wear the collar.

My hope for the church's women includes all the women in the church. It's not a vision of one group of women silencing another. It's a Relief Society room in which we collectively hold the diversity of experiences and ideas of all the women in the chairs. I'm willing to make room for the fact that plenty of women are happy with things exactly as they are. I'm not necessarily here to change their minds, I'm here to make space for myself and others by asking those who are happy with the way things are to sit with women who are not, and acknowledge the very real pain many have experienced. I think willingness to sit with one another in difference was what Lucy Mack Smith meant when she said, "We must cherish one another, watch over one another, comfort one another, and gain instruction that we may all sit down in heaven together."[14] She was describing unity, a Zion mindset. Most simply, she was describing love.

Cynthia:

I love the very practical and doable ways we could change this. By now you know me well enough to know that I have a propensity to want women to drink from a firehose about this topic. Okay, on lots of topics! Dang my Enneagram 1 personality! I want to spray down anyone who will listen to the research that shows women do better throughout life when they have female leadership mentors, including female clergy as children. I want to give them a quick history and rundown of patriarchy and the ills of it. But as I have thought about this, I think we need to start with a drinking fountain approach. Offer women to come and sip, no harsh firehose needed. The drinking fountain approach could be as simple as asking a few questions of the woman who defends the status quo.

First, can she just sit with and allow other women to feel differently without judgment? Can we agree that all experiences and feelings are real to all women, and as such those feelings and experiences deserve to be heard out loud? Second, can she stay curious? She may not understand, and she may even have great feelings and evidence to prove the opposite—that LDS women are equals in every way—but can she make an effort to stay curious because at least one LDS woman in her life is hurting. It might be her eighteen-year-old daughter, her older sister, or a dear friend. Would she read a book, a blog, or listen to a podcast about this topic to hear another perspective? Third and last, can she at least celebrate diversity? The Body of Christ is strongest when we all contribute our diverse talents, thoughts, and beliefs—a Zion mindset, where all hearts are knit together in unity and love.

WORKS FOR ME

"Someone can believe in an organized religion and still have qualms about certain aspects of it. There's a nuance to everything."
—Kelly Corrigan[15]

Cynthia:

At the Encircle House in Provo, a new friend admitted to me that she had judged me for being an active Mormon.[16] After thinking more about it, she wanted to apologize to me for that judgment. Umm, okay! I didn't even know I had been judged! She said to me, "I get it Cynthia, the church works for you." I bristled. My friend, a gay woman about my age, had been deeply harmed by the church. I can see how she would think that for a straight woman who is active, it's because it all works for me.

As I drove home that afternoon, I kept thinking about her words—works for me, works for me … but does it work for me? I thought about it all week. When I went to Encircle again the next week and saw my friend, I said, "About last week. I am not sure 'it works for me' is the right descriptor." I blabbered about why that was an itchy phrase and she said, "Well, when you do figure it out let me know, I really am curious!" Yeah, me too.

As I have thought more and more about that phrase—works for me—I have thought, my car works for me. My beloved Kitchen Aid mixer works for me. My car and my mixer make my life easier, kneading my bread so my arms don't have to, or getting me to stores and appointments so I don't have to walk or wait for a bus. But I'm not sure my affiliation with the church makes my life easier. Perhaps assessing the value of something as making my life easier isn't the metric for choosing, or sticking with, a religion. There are certain aspects of my lifelong association with The Church of Jesus Christ of Latter-day Saints that have 'worked for me'—not in the sense that they've made my life easier, but that they've added meaning and richness. Here are some ways the church has worked for me and continues to do so.

Mormonism is my spiritual language. It's where I knew as a child that God loves me. That I was divine. That I had individual worth. As a woman who went through the Young Women program and then served in it for many years, I always said to the girls I taught, "If there is one thing you should take away from the Personal Progress program, please let it sink into your bones that you have worth. That you are divine." I naively thought that any woman who came through Young Women ... gracious ... anyone who even came through Primary, knew that divinity was their spiritual heritage, that their worth was great in the sight of God.

Of course, life circumstances are complex, and for many their association with Mormonism taught them the opposite. Some of my own siblings feel this way—same DNA, same parents, same bishops, many of the same leaders, but not the same results. We're all now gray-haired adults and we've spent hours talking to each other about our varied experiences growing up in the church. I honor and respect that their experiences are indeed different from mine. And maybe I would've always thought I was worth a million bucks no matter where my faith home had been. I can't answer that, but I am grateful for the church that taught me (and I absorbed it!) that I matter. That I am known. That I am loved. Knowing that God loves me 'works for me.'

I'm not even that great at anything to have such a great self-esteem. I describe myself as a Jackie-of-all-trades and a master of none. I'm pretty proud of my mediocrity, actually. I only got one A in my four years at Brigham Young University. One! It was in Economics.

I play the piano, but very poorly. I took piano lessons from a sister in our Chino, California ward. Like school, I wasn't that great at the piano either. But playing the piano gives Mormons lots of service opportunities. For one of my Personal Progress Laurel projects, I played the piano for the Relief Society in our local Spanish branch for six months. I also played for Young Women musical numbers in sacrament meeting. One time, my sheet music almost blew off the piano during a musical number. (Dang our constant air conditioning!) Afterward, someone said to me, "I love the way you added feeling with that dramatic pause!" No, I'm just lousy at improvising when I need to.

At age forty, I decided I wanted to get better at playing the piano, without any dramatic pauses to mask my 'meh' skills. One of the pieces my teacher said every pianist needs to learn is *Claire de Lune* by Claude Debussy. She said, "Everyone can get good at this piece, once you do, offer to play it in sacrament meeting!" After three months of careful tutoring by my instructor, she said, "We've played this enough, you can just keep practicing at home." Playing the piano in public never made my life easier but knowing I can do hard things in public in church has definitely 'worked for me.'

Mormonism is my heritage. My mother joined the church in 1960 in Los Mochis, Sinaloa, Mexico. According to my mom, the church saved her life. We can, and we should, talk about colonialism and being White Saviors but I have to respect my mother's experience, and her experience is that The Church of Jesus Christ of Latter-day Saints brought light into her life where there was none and lifted her from utter poverty. Through her associations with her new-found faith, she and many of her siblings later emigrated to the US through different missionaries they had associated with. I grew up hearing my mom praise those missionaries by name and praising the church, almost like a repeated bedtime story. Mormonism definitely *worked for my mom*, and hearing her testimony deeply affected me.

Speaking of my Mexican heritage, it wasn't uncommon for kids of my generation in the 1970s to grow up *not* speaking the native language of their parents as assimilation into American life was *the* goal. I'm so glad that's changing. I have a grandson being raised speaking more Spanish than English. Even though both my parents were fluent—Mexican mom, gringo dad—they only spoke Spanish in code with each other to hide conversations from us kids. During the pandemic many people learned to make sourdough bread but I already knew how to do that, again with mediocrity, so I decided to learn Spanish, to be a real Mexican girl.

I have a Venezuelan online tutor. When we start each lesson, we exchange pleasantries like the weather. I speak the weather language of Fahrenheit, she speaks Celsius. She might tell me it's twenty degrees Celsius, but I have to do a quick math calculation in my head to get the feeling of her day. Twenty-nine degrees Celsius. No feeling. But eighty-five Fahrenheit? Now we're talking, now I'm feeling it! To me, eighty-five Fahrenheit means long sleeves are not needed! (Unless you're indoors with A/C). Eighty-five Fahrenheit gives me the feeling of popsicles, pools, and sandals. Happy Cynthia! Likewise, being LDS is my language, a context for how I feel my way through life. When I attend other churches I enjoy the experience, but the feeling isn't one of familiarity. The feeling and language of Mormonism continues to 'work for me.'

I feel like I've tried, on microphone, to answer the question of why I stay—a lot. It might be the number one question we're sent through social media when somebody finds our podcast. I get it—two women who say all the hard things out loud but still get asked to speak in sacrament meeting and teach Relief Society lessons? What an odd mix.

I can't remember when it dawned on me that it's not so much why I *stay*, but rather, why do I need to *leave*? I already believe what I want in my brain, do what I want in my life, don't do what I don't want, shrug my shoulders at what I want, wear what I want, drink what I want (chai tea is so good!), so why leave?

I have completely embraced the custom-fit clothing approach. As a tall woman, I could rarely buy skirts and dresses off the rack at the mall. Thankfully, a favorite seminary teacher taught me to sew. Learning to sew for my specific body type was essential. I know how to custom fit my faith now as well. I can't get by with off-the-rack Mormonism anymore, so I've been using my spiritual sewing skills to hack, splice, spread, and lengthen.

I still prefer to practice those metaphorical sewing skills in my local LDS ward. I totally resonate with Melissa Inouye's idea that she had a rock-solid testimony of the local Mormon ward. It would be so easy to craft my life in such a way that I only deal with like-minded people. But my life doesn't need to be an echo chamber—I already think my way is best (duh, if it were not I'd change my ways!)—so to be part of a community that stretches me to 'love one another,' the ultimate boots-on-the-ground commandment from Jesus, still 'works for me.'

I was in a Relief Society lesson where we discussed a general conference talk about apostasy, and that studying the Book of Mormon can help us avoid collective and personal apostasy. I raised my hand and said, "Most of you know I have a complicated relationship with the church organization. I am good with God, but many here, if they knew about some of my choices, (ahem . . .chai tea!) would think, She's definitely on the road to apostasy!" I went on to say that it's hurtful for me to think of my daughters, who would *not* describe themselves as followers of Jesus, as apostates. Apostasy and apostate are really harsh and judgy words. I said, "Please when I am done, don't comment with any silver linings about kids who step away from the church and eventually return, because me and God are good and I am at peace with my girls' decisions." I ended my comment by saying: "I guess I'm just trying to say that I am able to hold those two paradoxes—that I love the gospel *and* I respect that for many, the organization is not right for them. I see my young adult daughters as fellow travelers now; they chose their way, I chose mine. We're equals."

The teacher thanked me immediately, saying, "Wow, I never would've thought that word—apostasy—would be hard for so many. I can see that now, thank you."

A few affirming comments followed, and the woman who gave the closing prayer said, "We're so grateful that we can all show up as ourselves."

I don't need to have everyone in the room agree with me. We don't need to have many beliefs in common as long as we have love in common. Eugene England said, "The Church is true because it is concrete, not theoretical; in all its contradictions and problems, it is at least as productive of good, as is the gospel."[17]

That day in my Relief Society, the church felt concrete.

I realize I have lots of privilege in that area. I've lived in the same west Provo neighborhood for twenty-seven years. For most of those years I was very orthodox so I built up a huge capital reserve—having girl's camp fundraisers in my front yard, cooking bacon at 6 a.m. for those same girls in the mountains—and now I am strategically spending that capital, wearing pants and a rainbow pin while still doing dishes at funerals with sisters I love.

I like to joke with my husband that after being in a million wards due to boundary changes, I could run for mayor by now! I love my ward, and my ward loves me. And love will always 'work for me.'

As a very practical person, some things right off the LDS rack have fit me beautifully, as is. When I say practical, don't think practical as in 'boring,' but as in efficient. (Remember that one A that I got in Economics? Love me some measurable graphs!)

There's an episode of *Modern Family* where Manny, who is turning eleven or twelve, is celebrating his birthday and his stepdad Jay says to him, "You were born a sixteen-year-old," meaning Manny was never a kid. In many ways, I'm like Manny. I have never been a kid. I was born practical and a rule keeper, and could always see the consequences of bad decisions ten steps ahead of me. The church fostered that practicality with a strong 'choice and accountability' framework. (Gosh, I loved those Young Women values!) Mormonism was really a fantastic model for raising kids like *me*. And now that I have raised kids *not* like me, I can also see the damage.

Speaking of kids not like me, one of my kiddos has always been the complete opposite of me. When she was thirteen years old, she told me that she didn't even think there was a god, or if there was, what would a god even be like. I never asked those kinds of questions until I was forty. I was told what God was like and I accepted that idea, straight off the rack. But in that moment, I already had enough experience with this child to know that the Primary Answer of who God is would not work for her. So I tried to cast a really wide net to let her creative juices about the Divine ... just flow. I said, "Sweetheart, you are allowed to think anything you want about God. You can think God is a talking rock. If that gives you comfort, go for it."

I've heard it said by comedian Pete Holmes, who heard it from Barry Taylor, the road manager for AC/DC of all people, that "God is the name of the blanket we throw over the mystery to give it shape."[18]

I was trying to give my daughter permission to name the mystery because after a lifetime of wearing LDS theology straight off the rack, I needed a custom-fit God too. So together, my daughter and I sat in that mystery, trying to give it shape.

By now you might be thinking, this sounds very much *not* LDS at all, but at the same time, how could I have been raised on ideas like Kolob; how could I have highlighted lines in my patriarchal blessing that said, "The mysteries of god will be made plain to your soul," and *not* feel free to speculate about a cosmically large and expansive God?

At the same time that my LDS roots have allowed me to think more deeply about God, I have also felt free to think more about Jesus, the Galilean preacher, and less about The Christ. I taught youth Sunday School from 2020 through 2024, and teaching the New Testament was my favorite year. To teach those young people the fleshy stories of Jesus will remain one of the highlights of my LDS Church callings. Author and Episcopalian priest, Barbara Brown Taylor, said, "I don't speak of the Christ, but I'm happy to talk about Jesus."[19]

That deeply resonated. I have no idea if I need someone to redeem me or pay for my sins so that justice can be met and God can stand to be in my presence again, but I do resonate deeply with the way Jesus moved through His life, bumping up against messy humans, particularly the marginalized. And don't get me started on His parables about grace. The number one trophy-winning-parable of all time, in my opinion, is the parable of the prodigal son. A child insults his parent, takes all his inheritance that he probably shouldn't get until his dad dies, blows said inheritance, lives on pig food, then decides, hey, maybe my dad could love me again? We all know the story—he goes running to his dad with some ridiculous speech in hand about how he's willing to just be a servant. And when his dad sees him afar off, runs to him, thwarts the giving of that dumb speech, and says, "For this my son was dead, and is alive again; he was lost, and is found (Luke 15:11–32 NRSV) As Rob Bell says, he was always at the party.[20] You are always at the party. I have always been at the party. "Grace shall be as your day." God, Jesus, and His grace, 'work for me.'

As I consider how I can help those on the margins, I find a perfect blueprint in how Jesus moved through His life. Hanging out with adulterers, tax collectors who worked for The Man, liars, know-it-all church dudes, as well as woman after woman after woman. All those people seemed to be his jam. Terryl and Fiona Givens wrote: "The gospel Christ taught was spectacularly designed to unsettle and disturb, *not* lull into pleasant serenity."[21]

I don't want to pick on the Cynthia 1.0 version, but I definitely like myself, my 2.0 version better, or what Richard Rohr calls the second-half-of-life version. To be honest, the organization had lulled me in pleasant serenity with all my friggin' amazing box checking. But now? I don't want to say my serenity is gone, because duh, *grace,* but I am definitely being stretched more now. It's one reason I wear a cross around my neck. I really think this one question—Am I moving through this world the way Jesus did?—is enough to power my daily walk as a Christian. As author Flannery O'Connor said, "What people don't realize is how much religion costs. They think faith is a big electric blanket, when of course it is the cross."[22]

I am not the only religious person who holds tensions. I don't have to leave because I don't like the way the proverbial off-the-rack, mass-market skirt fits my body. I despise patriarchy. I despise homophobia. I despise that as a church with the name of Jesus on every building, we hoard billions of dollars.

I love the foundation the church has always been for me. I love the lifestyle and I love being a follower of Jesus. I don't need to leave because I personally don't feel trapped by what doesn't work for me. Author Kelly Corrigan said, "Someone can believe in an organized religion and still have qualms about certain aspects of it. There's a nuance to everything."[23]

Lastly, I couldn't have stayed were it not for so many 'fringy pioneers' who modeled that nuance for me. Barbara Brown Taylor said, "Like campers who have bonded over cook fires far from home, we remain grateful for the provisions that we have brought with us from those cupboards, but we also find them more delicious when we share them with one another under the stars."[24]

To my fellow fringy Latter-day Saints who are under those same stars with me, thank you for sharing your warm fire.

THE COLOR OF NUANCE

*"Did he believe that God wrote stories with only one kind of meaning?
It seemed to me that a story that had only one kind of meaning
was not very interesting or worth remembering for too long."*
—Chaim Potok[25]

Cynthia:

I have a pretty good talent for picking paint colors. What I have learned after twenty-five years of painting furniture and walls is that having a paint fan deck is essential. For best results, you can't just grab those one-inch paint swatches at the hardware store and expect to have success. I take my fan decks (yes, plural!) to friends' homes too when they need help picking out paint colors and ask them what color they're thinking of—because often when someone is thinking 'dark blue,' they're thinking of a gradation of blue. Do they want a cool blue, like a gray-blue? A green-blue, maybe leaning towards turquoise? It helps to choose the color swatch you *think* you want, then follow that color all the way down the fan deck to the darkest color and compare it to the ones on either side. It's the only way, for me anyway, to see that what I am choosing is actually what I want for a specific project. To better understand my choice I have to see what shades are on my left and also which are on my right. That's nuance: understanding that there are hundreds of varieties of blue paint. In fact, that is actually part of the definition of nuance in the dictionary: *a very slight difference or variation in color or tone.*

Susan:

I love the fan deck image as it applies to being in a church—the idea that there are members all over the spectrum when it comes to almost any tenet of our faith helps me feel more at ease with my own version of my religion. In any class or discussion, I can find belonging in the understanding that there are people to the right of where I land on a question, and people to the left. All the shades of blue are there, and belong there! The fan deck gives me a concrete way to get my head around the idea of unity: when you describe nuance as understanding that there are hundreds of varieties of blue, I can see unity as understanding that there are hundreds of varieties of faith. Mine doesn't need to look exactly like yours for us to both be blue.

However, in our church, many members still insist blue is blue. Rather than appreciate the diversity of the fan deck in our pews, they classify other members who approach belief or practice differently with labels like "cafeteria Mormon." As if we're not all picking from the faith cafeteria line, institutionally as well as individually!

As a church, we focus on some things while ignoring others. Look at the Word of Wisdom, for instance: it's full of good counsel of which we emphasize certain aspects while generally ignoring others. When studying the scriptures together, we focus on the same stories and verses year after year, while there are some weird and uncomfortable things in there we never really unpack or talk about at all. Even our own history is full of things previous prophets have said or done that we'd prefer people to forget about now.

As individuals, we're really good at some things and not so good at others. Life makes it impossible to focus on everything, so we pick a few things and try to do our best with them, right? But what's important to you or to me is never going to be exactly the same—we have different experiences and needs, not to mention unique personalities.

There's always going to be a whopping dose of personal humanness in our individual approaches to religion. Even operating under one basic goal—Love God and Love One Another—there will be many shades of nuance in the expression of that love in people's lives. Even within such a succinct statement, there's room for us to not be in agreement about what is most important.

Nuance isn't easy and for some it will not come naturally, requiring a very intentional stretch. Stretching can be painful, especially if we're old and stiff or we've held one position for too long. But I believe leaning into the discomfort of difference is how we grow toward each other. Nuance is the pathway to unity.

Cynthia:
If nuance is the pathway to unity, why do we resist the idea that every

shade of blue is already in the pews at church with us? Deep down, if we're honest with ourselves, we already know this—even in Mormonism we have an abundance of rich shades of blue. The real question is, am I going to celebrate this by scooting over on my pew so there is room for more? Or am I going to spread out with my One True Idea of what the correct shade of blue should be? Maybe there are a few unicorns out there who naturally welcome the already-present diversity, but in my experience, most of us have to set intentional stretching goals.

Will you forgive me for pointing out that you are one decade older than I am? You once gave me an invitation to stretch: "Go ahead Cynthia, bend over and touch your toes, then repeat that in ten years and call me." Not only is that great physical advice to stay limber, but it's good spiritual advice to avoid what the Book of Mormon calls 'stiffnecked.' A refusal to see what's on my left and on my right, literally and metaphorically, is to be unyielding to an invitation to take in the full periphery of all the blues of this world.

In my experience, sometimes we prefer a stiff neck over a limber one because humans just want to avoid discomfort. Adding to this, we have our own Latter-day Saint teachings and culture that tells us discomfort comes from Satan. The scriptures teach that contention is of the devil (3 Nephi 11:29) but conflict is not. Hugh B. Brown described conflicting perspectives as exercising our 'freedom of the mind':

> More thinking is required, and we should all exercise our God-given right to think and be unafraid to express our opinions, with proper respect for those to whom we talk and proper acknowledgment of our own shortcomings. We must preserve freedom of the mind in the church and resist all efforts to suppress it. The church is not so much concerned with whether the thoughts of its members are orthodox or heterodox as it is that they shall have thoughts.[26]

Being unafraid to not conform (heterodox) is to simply acknowledge that I prefer a greenish-blue and my friend prefers a grayish-blue.

One of my healthiest life lessons in dealing with discomfort has been in my quest to become a better listener. I learned about the skill of active listening from David Ostler.[27] It felt like a very helpful exercise to help me develop my nuance skills. Developing genuine listening skills has been essential in seeing, accepting, and loving all the shades of blues in my friends and family. It isn't something that has come naturally to me, but I have worked at it long enough now that listening to people talk about uncomfortable things—from religion to politics—has gotten easier. (Not easy, but *easier!*) It's becoming my default goal when I interact with others.

Learning to really listen—not in an effort to form my reply but in a real effort to understand the person across from me—has been some of the hardest work I have ever done. In the beginning I would actually have to say to myself: "You're uncomfortable, shut up and listen anyway." Especially when I was parenting teens, I sometimes had to say to myself as they were speaking, "active listening, active listening." My default reaction was otherwise to enter Mom Mode and jump in with advice and commentary. Now that my children are young adults, this skill has become even more essential. Learning to listen, acknowledge, and accept my own children's shades of blues has been the deep work of discipleship. It's the stretchiest way I have stretched. I give it a one-star review for fun but a five-star review for results. May my flexibility only increase. I'll call you in ten years and report back.

Susan:

When you do, I'm going to make you stretch while I'm on the phone so I can hear the noise you make. That will tell me everything I need to know. I used to wonder why my grandparents moved through the world with painful sound effects—now everyone knows when I have to bend. But as my physical joints get less stretchy, thank goodness my mind feels able to move more freely than it used to. I hope my heart is becoming more pliable too. So far, that kind of stretching is about the only thing I've found to like about aging.

I love the mantra, "active listening." I wish I'd had that concept when I was raising kids, but would I have been able to implement it? It feels aspirational for me even now. It's so hard to not fall into old patterns, especially in old-shoe relationships. You know, the kind you've worn for so long, you don't actively notice them anymore? I've learned that close relationships with the people I love can so often benefit from me being willing to keep my mouth shut but my mind and heart open while listening.

Besides relearning how to listen to others, I've also been trying to learn to listen to myself, because let me admit right here: I'm a person who, as soon as discomfort starts to speak, turns my inner voice all the way down. So what I'm trying to practice now is just letting the discomfort tell me what it came to say, and getting curious about why that feeling was the first one to show up. I haven't been good at allowing discomfort in my life, probably because somewhere along the line I was sold the idea that discomfort is negative. I've spent a lifetime in church settings where the correlation is drawn between discomfort and 'the Adversary.' But you know what? I've learned discomfort is actually not of Satan. In fact, quite the opposite—my discomfort shows up to ask me to go deeper, to help me identify ways I might stretch, learn, or grow. Shutting down those feelings was just a way of remaining safe and small.

And if discomfort is not of Satan, I believe there are a few other things I've misunderstood, things that have been mischaracterized to me, and I accepted the negative spin without question because my own discomfort (yes, the same discomfort I chose to mute rather than listen to) convinced me it was true. But my experience has taught me that questioning isn't of Satan, disagreeing isn't, keeping an open mind isn't, active seeking isn't, exploration and experimentation aren't, changing my mind isn't, shifting my opinion to make room for new information isn't, trying new things isn't—it turns out many things that feel scary or uncomfortable, and therefore sometimes get demonized at church, aren't actually bad or dangerous at all. In fact, they're tools for growth. It may sound cynical, but I can't help but think if someone was going to try to scare me away from possible growth by drawing repeated rhetorical connections with 'the Adversary,' I don't think it would be God. Do you?

Cynthia:

No! All the invites I have had to increase my curiosity have felt like they actually came from God. That is saying a lot for someone like me who can count how many times I have felt actual capital A-Answers from God. If thirty-something-year-old Cynthia could peek at fifty-something-year-old Cynthia, she would be shocked. And not just at her sun-damaged skin, but because fifty-something Cynthia flies a pride flag, wears pants to church, and reads more books by Episcopal priests and Lutheran pastors than listens to LDS general conference. So be careful in choosing what ruler you use to measure others because someday you may fail your own measuring tests. It pains me to admit I naively thought that once I was married and had kids—once my testimony had solidified—it was about simply enduring to the end. I never would have planned on changing this much, nor could I have imagined the richness of seeing all the shades of blue that have come into my life. My previous faith seemed perfect for an unchanging robot, but lousy for a woman committed to the kind of discipleship Jesus requires of us. It's not that I didn't think I would change, but I thought my testimony would never change—and for good reason! In high school I memorized Helaman 5:12 in seminary. The words of Helaman so resonated with me that I ripped a piece of graph paper out of my geometry notebook and scribbled out his words. It became my mantra:

> It is upon the rock of our Redeemer, who is Christ, the Son of God, that ye must build your foundation; that when the devil shall send forth his mighty winds, yea, his shafts in the whirlwind, yea, when all his hail and his mighty storm shall beat upon you, it shall have no power over you to drag you down to the gulf of misery and endless wo, because of the rock upon which ye are built, which is a sure foundation, a foundation whereon if men build they cannot fall.

In my defense, is it any wonder I felt that I could be immovable? That the winds and storms of life could never move me? I coupled that scripture with teachings from President Hinckley that the church "is either right or wrong, true or false, fraudulent or true."[28] Where is the room for flexibility and nuance in Helaman's or Hinckley's words?

Sometimes I wonder if in my youth, flexible thinking and nuance had been taught and modeled for me in my faith community, could I have avoided a crash later in life? Or are crashes just inevitable as they signal an end to old ways as new ways come into focus? I don't know the answer to that, but I do see society headed toward a less black-and-white approach with children. For instance, we can ask children more questions to encourage nuanced thinking, rather than giving them prescribed answers. Questions such as:

> "Would you feel the same way if you were someone else, in a different place, time or situation?"

> "Is there another way to answer this question?"

> "Do we have all the information we need?"

> "Is there anything that might make you change your mind?"[29]

That last one really gets me because it asks for just a bit of curiosity from a more black-and-white thinker. It's a safe enough thought experiment, to give space for the idea that just maybe, like the choose-your-own adventure books I loved as a child, there will always be alternate endings depending on my current situation today. I once heard biblical scholar Peter Enns ask, "What if God delights in curiosity?" When I hear it phrased that way, I want to facepalm my former self because of course God wants us to be curious! Looking back, I am not so sure my natural wiring is to be a black-and-white thinker, but I do know that my faith community encouraged it, rewarded it, and I ran with it. And that worked perfectly well for me—until it didn't.

Susan:

I learned to rollerblade when I was forty years old. I was a really good roller skater as a kid, but rollerblades became popular during years when my days were completely consumed with small children. When my fortieth birthday rolled around, I had a daughter going through a very hard time who needed a distraction in her life. I needed a distraction from my age, so as her gift to me she offered to teach me to rollerblade. Thank goodness she was patient and not too easily embarrassed. I thought it would be a breeze since I had been so good at skating as a kid, but I really struggled teaching my old legs that new trick. I tried so hard to control them, and by extension control every bump in the road. I was rigid and tensed and laser-focused on anticipating any possible thing that might trip me up. The key to success was actually the opposite approach—like a building can survive an earthquake with the right kind of flexible foundation, my legs needed to relax a little to absorb the bumps in the road and keep me upright.

I had a similar experience learning to drive. I took the wheel in a white-knuckle death grip and focused on the road *directly* in front of me. Steering was continuous and keeping the car exactly where I wanted it was much harder than I thought it would be. I didn't think I could ever master it. One day my grandpa took me out driving. We hadn't gone very far at all when he said in exasperation, "What are you ... doing?" I said, "I'm driving the car." He said, "You can't drive like that! You don't look at the road right in front of you, you look *down the road to where you want to go.* Forget about the road here and keep your eye on the road up there!" That piece of advice changed driving instantly for me. I was able to get comfortable, and to my surprise, enlarging my focus made steering easy, almost like the car just knew where to go.

I wish I'd understood he was also teaching me a life lesson. Giving up my controlly grip gives me the flexibility to be responsive to change without being destabilized by it.

Cynthia:

I love your two examples, because they demonstrate that learning any kind of new skill, be it driving, rollerblading, or nuanced thinking, requires that we be humble, curious, and open minded.

A friend told me about her niece who came out as queer to her grandparents. The grandparents, in all their humility, told their grand-daughter, "We are old and there are a lot of things that we don't understand, but we love you and you are always welcome in our home. And please, bring whomever you love." How often do we respond with that kind of intellectual humility and unconditional love, instead of doubling down on what we currently understand? These grandparents, like your granddad, saw the road far ahead of their current view. By widening our vision, we widen our capacity to love.

I was a youth Sunday School teacher for years for the twelve and thirteen-year-olds in my ward. One of my main goals was to encourage open mindedness. To encourage a diversity of answers I used comments like, "Ooooh, I like how you think, tell me more!" or "There are no wrong answers here, just tell me where your brain is going."

Pastor David Hayward said, "I now understood that questions unlocked the barriers of the mind and that these questions could pull us down into a deeper understanding and appreciation of this mystery. But the mind wants answers. Many religious and spiritual people want to be told how and what to believe."[30]

This is what I wanted for my young Sunday School class—to unlock their minds with questions that encouraged critical thinking before that predisposition Mr. Hayward speaks of—to be told how and what to believe—could take root in their young minds.

Our mutual friend Jeralee Renshaw is fond of saying that she sees a full spectrum of colors now. I like that much better than just saying there's a 'gray area.' Life isn't drab and gray! It's colorful! And learning to see that spectrum of colors—all the shades of blue—has brought richness to my life.[31]

Susan:

I think that's a great way to look at it. The creep of gray in my worldview—including my faith life—has corresponded well to the creep of gray in my hair. In my experience, the gray whole is much bigger than the sum of its black-and-white parts, and I'm more comforted than troubled by that. But add color to the black and white and I suddenly feel like the possibilities become endless. Other languages have whole flurries of words for snow—I think the Eskimos have fifty and the Scots have over four hundred. Well, who doesn't want hundreds of shades of blue, not to mention every other color, instead of just one? The ways we see, think about, and discuss ideas can be as rich as we are willing to allow them to be. There is no limit to how many times we can reconsider a thing, looking at it from another angle or in light of new information, or even our continuing experience. We can change our minds! And wake up tomorrow and change them again. In a life over which I often feel I have little control, this feels empowering to me.

I talk a lot about getting comfortable with change because I really have to work at it, and being able to tolerate change in our circumstances can start by being able to allow it in ourselves. No one can do that for us. But counterintuitive as it may seem, peace doesn't actually come from controlling everything and making it go exactly the way you think it should. That's where angst comes from, because you can't do it, but you will make yourself crazy trying.

Peace comes from not needing to control everything. This has often felt like two steps forward and one back—you'd be surprised how many times I think I'm getting better at it, only to look down and find the same white knuckles.

Rigid thinking is a control game you play with your head. When I'm set against any nuance that might come along and change all the things I'm sure of, I'm trying to control not just the events in my life but the ways I'll respond to them. How can I know that in advance?

Sometimes stuff just happens and feelings rise up to meet the stuff, and we find ourselves knocked off our feet because what we 'knew' suddenly isn't able to accommodate the experience we're having. Even though this is actually an invitation to growth, it's terrifying, so I fight it.

Speaking of stretching, Amy Watkins Jensen talked with us about 'stretchy faith,' remember?[32] She described a kind of faith that makes room. I haven't stopped thinking about that—about how a whole church of 'stretchy saints' might feel compared to what church has often felt like to me. She explained that stretching makes us stronger and more agile, helping us with mobility and balance and stability. I loved her metaphor because I feel like stretching is something I can practice and improve at. We've already established that if I'd been better at it across my lifetime, I'd still be touching my toes with ease and I'm first to admit that's not the case. But spiritual flexibility is something I have worked hard at developing and maintaining because it makes me less vulnerable to having my faith pulled out from under me by whatever happens outside my control. If I'm stretchy, I'm more likely to take bumps in stride. Maybe if I'd apply my own advice more broadly in my life, I wouldn't have to make that noise every time I get out of my Miata.

Section Notes

1. Dale G. Renlund, "Family History and Temple Work: Sealing and Healing," April 2018 general conference.

2. Boyd K. Packer, *You May Claim the Blessings of the Holy Temple,* (Bookcraft, 1981).

3. Sheri L. Dew, *Go Forward With Faith: The Biography of Gordon B. Hinckley* (Deseret Book, 1996), 390.

4. Pete Enns and Jared Byas, hosts, *The Bible for Normal People* podcast, episode 174, "The Four Stages of Faith," July 26, 2021, 33 minutes. Guest Brian McLaren.

5. Madeleine Albright, "Celebrating Inspiration," keynote at Women's National Basketball Association (WNBA) All-Decade Team luncheon, New York City, July 12, 2006.

6. Josh Coates, Stephen Cranney, "New Survey Shows Strong Cross-Generational Faith Among Latter-Day Saints," *Deseret News,* February 9, 2024, deseret.com.

7. *Beyond the Block* podcast, Bonus: *At Last She Said It,* July 11, 2022.

8. Sharon Brous, *The Amen Effect: Ancient Wisdom to Mend Our Broken Hearts and World* (Avery Publishing, 2024), 15.

9. Kate Manne, *Down Girl: The Logic of Misogyny* (Oxford University Press, 2017), 62.

10. Charlotte Knowles, "Beauvoir on Women's Complicity in The Own Unfreedom," *Hypatia: A Journal of Feminist Philosophy* 34, no. 2, (April 1, 2019): 242–65.

11. Clay Skipper, "'Hope is a Muscle': Why Krista Tippett Wants You to Keep the Faith," *GQ,* July 21, 2022, gq.com.

12. *At Last She Said It* podcast, episode 198, "What About Women Leaving the Church? / Revisiting Messages to Our Daughters," October 1, 2024.

13. Tamarra Kemsley, "Five Days Before She Died, LDS Scholar Shared Her Wildest Dreams for the Church," *The Salt Lake Tribune,* April 24, 2024, sltrib.com.

14. *Daughters in My Kingdom: The History and Work of Relief Society* (The Church of Jesus Christ of Latter-day Saints, 2011), 25, available at churchofjesuschrist.org.

15. Kelly Corrigan, host, *Kelly Corrigan Wonders* podcast, "On the Meaning of Life," November 9, 2021.

16. Encircle is a non-profit youth and family resource center dedicated to helping LGBTQ persons and their families, encircletogether.org.

17. England, "Why the Church Is as True as the Gospel."

18. Holmes, *Comedy Sex God*, 149.

19. Gary Alan Taylor, host, *Holy Heretics* podcast, episode 58, "Becoming Fully Human," December 13, 2022, 49 minutes. Guest Barbara Brown Taylor.

20. Rob Bell, host, *The Robcast* podcast, episode 216, "Jesus H. Christ | Part 7—You Are Already At the Party," October 28, 2018, 51 minutes.

21. Terryl and Fiona Givens, *The Crucible of Doubt: Reflections on the Quest for Faith* (Deseret Book, 2014), 27.

22. Flannery O'Connor, *The Habit of Being: Letters of Flannery O'Connor* (Farrar, Straus, and Giroux, 1988), 354.

23. *Kelly Corrigan Wonders* podcast, "On the Meaning of Life."

24. Barbara Brown Taylor, *Leaving Church: A Memoir of Faith* (HarperOne, 2012), 224.

25. Chaim Potok, *Davita's Harp* (Random House, 1996), 331.

26. Hugh B. Brown, "An Eternal Quest: Freedom of the Mind," Brigham Young University devotional address, May 13, 1969.

27. Richard Ostler, host, *Listen, Learn & Love* podcast, episode 514, "Principles for Families to Remain Strong When One Leaves the Church," April 8, 2022, 1 hour 17 minutes. Guest David Ostler.

28. Helen Whitney, *The Mormons: American Experience*, Public Broadcasting documentary, April 30, 2007, pbs.org.

29. "Why We Need to Teach Nuance to Little Thinkers," Red T Kids Media, March 21, 2019, redtkidsmedia.com, accessed January 22, 2025.

30. David Hayward, *Questions Are The Answer: nakedpastor and the Search for Understanding* (Darton, Longman, and Todd, 2015), 86–87.

31. *At Last She Said It* podcast, episode 11, "Women on the Edge of Inside," May 19, 2020.

32. *At Last She Said It* podcast, episode 187, "Embracing Your Journey," June 25, 2024. Guest Amy Watkins Jensen.

EMBRACING YOUR JOURNEY

SPEAKING UP

"I thought that being faithful was about becoming someone other than who I was, in other words, and it was not until this project failed that I began to wonder if my human wholeness might be more useful to God than my exhausting goodness."
—Barbara Brown Taylor[1]

Susan:

When I was a kid, Primary was on Tuesday afternoons. I climbed the long hill to our ward, swinging my school bag in a gaggle of chatty friends, hoping there was a treat and wondering what it might be. After a long day at school, I mostly wished we were on our way home instead.

Opening exercises were in the chapel. The church building of my childhood was much bigger than any I've attended since, a cavernous midcentury space presided over by a bone-rattling pipe organ. I loved feeling that the big echo-y chapel was just for us on those afternoons, our small songs, our childish voices. We got birthday pencils and brought our pennies for Primary Children's Hospital. We heard stories from *The Children's Friend*. We sang Popcorn Popping and Sing Your Way Home and Jesus Came to John the Baptist. We loved the songs with actions the best. We sang, "The chapel doors seem to say to me," taking special delight in adding too loudly the "Shhh, be still." Our chorister had a cool visual aid that looked nothing like our church building with Gothic-arched doors you could open. If you sang sincerely enough, you might be called up to fold back the cardboard doors and expose the picture of reverent children inside, arms folded and heads bowed.

In those days, the song continued, "For this is a reverent place to be, Shhh, be still. There are many things we can do outside, we laugh and play and we romp and slide, But when we come through the chapel doors, Shhh, be still."

I'm afraid I may have taken that last line a bit too much to heart.

Members of The Church of Jesus Christ of Latter-day Saints live under a curious code of silence. How did it begin? How is it enforced? How have we bought into it so unquestioningly? As the world has become more open to talking about things that were once taboo, how has it continued to maintain its grip? Not just at church, but sometimes even at our own family tables?

Perhaps I was in some ways a victim of my time. I announced excitedly at the dinner table one Tuesday night that my Primary teacher had told us she was pregnant. My mother shushed me with her eyes as well as her mouth. "We don't say *pregnant*," she said. "We say, *expecting*." Were other people in my 1970-something Salt Lake neighborhood saying 'pregnant' at their dinner tables? I have no idea. But I remember being seen more often than heard in that childhood world, and being corrected with perhaps a bit more disapproval than I deserved.

"For this is a reverent place to be." Okay, perhaps there will always be limits inside the church building itself. I suppose there should be. But what about the rest of our lives? How was I taught to bury my burning questions, silence nagging doubts and discomfort, squash my desperate needs, and shush my yearning for something bigger? In a church that failed to meet my most basic spiritual longings, why have I chosen, even in my adult life, to leave them mostly unuttered, unexpressed?

I've struggled to have a relationship with prayer because the words I was taught were appropriate for prayer didn't summon my heart to meaningful participation. Another Primary song says, "I begin by saying Dear Heavenly Father, I thank him for blessings He sends, then humbly I ask Him for things that I need, in the name of Jesus Christ, Amen." That reflects exactly the format I was taught. Why didn't I ever feel at liberty to try bringing language of my own—my words, my song—to that most personal, foundational practice, and thereby to my relationship with God? Whose disapproval could I fear, while metaphorically—even literally—kneeling in my own closet?

And why, even today, when I raise my hand to make a comment surrounded by the members of my ward, almost all of whom I know and love, does my heart still pound? Why, despite vigilant pre-screening of my own comment for acceptability, does my voice still waver?

There's nothing like feeling you can't talk about it to give a thing the wrong kind of power. That principle explains a lot about my relationship with the LDS Church. Living my whole lifetime of faith within the confines of its chapels, it was difficult to untangle that negative power from my own spirituality when I realized I had to do it.

People talk about experiencing a faith crisis. I don't describe myself that way—my wrestling has been ongoing and amazingly consistent. But about ten years ago, I did experience what I call a Silence Crisis. I realized that for my spiritual self to survive, I was required to break my silence. I'm not sure what triggered it, I only know that the urge to talk and write—to finally speak up—about my church experience in a more honest way than I had before became overwhelming. I couldn't continue to wrestle in silence with the tension between my personal faith and its uneasy Mormon context.

Not that I hadn't expressed problems—sometimes loudly—as I went along. If you've listened to the podcast, chances are good you've heard about me yelling at my Sunday School teacher as a ten-year-old that I refused to be a baby factory for eternity, or being branded 'Drano-Mouth' by another teacher a few years later. It was a loving reference to what he described as my caustic personality. My young years were peppered with outbursts designed for their shock value that were really a reflection of mighty conflict raging in my young heart.

I eventually grew out of that kind of speaking and acting out, never having resolved any issues that fueled it. As an adult I've always known where the acceptable lines are, observing them with a wide margin when addressing my concerns or airing my complaints. For one thing, important relationships have been on the line as an adult. I had responsibilities to our children who were being raised in the church. I'd made marriage promises to my husband. I knew what my parents and siblings expected from me, and I needed those relationships to be comfortable and loving. I also wanted to maintain some influence within my ward family. I'd noticed through the years when people I respected and admired had spoken outside the lines and become suddenly voiceless in the ward.

A Danish writer said something to the effect that, "All sorrows can be borne if you put them into a story, or tell a story about them."[2] I know this is how I've made my way through life. By the time I was in second grade, I had already realized that if I could build the right receptacle with words to hold my difficult childhood, squashing it into what I constructed could improve its shape into something I liked

better. Or at least something less unwieldy. Something more acceptable. Something I might manage to hold and carry. Like Fred Rogers
said, "If we can mention it, we can manage it."[3]

It's no surprise that when it came time to break my silence, I approached it in writing. I started a blog, a small yawp in the online
universe. That beginning continues to inform my journey today. Since
I first hit 'publish' with a shaky finger, I've been able to use my words
in a variety of ways to find new space in my ward, in my family, and
perhaps most importantly in myself. Starting that insignificant blog
felt like the scariest thing I'd ever done. One day across the lunch table,
I told my sister I was thinking about doing it, and the look that flashed
across her face was unmistakable.

Was she afraid for me and my faith? Afraid for her own? Worried
that I might set in motion something over which I might not be able
to maintain control? I don't know, but as much as I want to say her
fears were unjustified, I can't say that and be entirely truthful. Daring
to live my faith life out loud has had consequences for myself and for
my family. The fruits for me have been good, but nothing exists in a
vacuum and the words that have healed me and helped others may
have weakened the faith of someone else within earshot. One of my
daughters confided to me that her relationship with the church became more strained as a result of my speaking up. That was never my
intent. But we can't control where or how our words land or how they
sit once they do. When I read those old blog posts now, I laugh. There's
nothing in them that anyone could really object to. I think the reason
they seemed so dangerous to me is I knew all the emotions and ideas
stacked up behind those carefully chosen words.

The blog was short-lived, about eighteen months. During that time,
I had many people approach me to say that my words had thrown a
lifeline of some kind, given them just an inch more breathing room,
and that filled me with enormous hope. I realized there were a lot of
people struggling in the same ways I was, and doing it in the same
self-imposed silence.

My first post, titled *Bring More Chairs*, was about how my beloved
father-in-law had supported me through many difficult times with a
powerful testimony of his personal motto, "There's room for everyone in the Church." People reached out that I hadn't heard from in
decades. I was encouraged. My second post was a light but heartfelt

personal essay about … Jell-O. That's right—I needed to recover a little from having put myself out there with the dangerous idea that we might need to open our doors and our hearts a little wider. My husband's response was most telling. He said, "Your Jell-O post was great! I think it's important to do a positive post in between the negative ones." So "bring more chairs" was not a positive message? Note taken. Of course I understood that he was right—after all, he voiced the very fear that had cooked up my Jell-O post to begin with.

I loved writing every scary, freeing post of that blog but the project ended abruptly. When the November 2015 LGBTQ+ exclusion policy was announced, I wrote a piece clearly stating I was utterly at a loss to find Christ anywhere in it.[4] I was getting more comfortable speaking out by this time. I'd joined some online groups and was in the daily habit of sharing my struggle with all-things-church. But only with strangers.

What I said, in part, about the policy is this:

> Many members would tell me to pray about it and I can receive a confirmation of the Spirit that these changes are indeed Christ's intended direction for His church. That's becoming the climate, as near as I can tell—I find myself increasingly in situations where Mormons tell other Mormons that sustaining the Brethren means trusting that they always speak on God's behalf, accepting what they say without question, or praying ourselves into agreement. But I don't believe that's what God intends for us. In fact to me, that idea has more in common with a different plan.
>
> So I've decided to change my personal approach. Rather than sitting in the discomfort of implied agreement, fearing to express the ways I struggle or disagree with some of the things I hear, I can question those things, including the ones from Church leaders, and even openly disagree while continuing to sustain them. After all, I sustain them by showing up on Sunday, and by trying to follow Jesus. By trying to ensure that my neighbors' lives are better as a result of their association with me, and by contributing to my congregation and looking after those over whom I have direct stewardship in my family and my callings. Those things are my responsibility as a member of the Church. I do not have a responsibility to agree.

Nothing terribly damning, right?

But the next day, I got a phone call from my father. My parents have always known me to be an uneasy Latter-day Saint—they were the ones raising the kid nicknamed Drano-Mouth by her Sunday school teacher, so how could they not know? But there was something about this post that crossed an invisible line. The phone call can best be described as a phone *spanking*, delivered kindly but unmistakably.

It was enough to silence me or at least send my voice underground in closed online groups, safely out of earshot of anyone who knew me in real life. For a while, that freedom to speak was enough. But in my online interactions with others facing similar challenges, it quickly became clear that the hard things in my life I hadn't been allowed to talk about had perhaps become my greatest gift. In order to survive, I needed to work them out, to make them okay somehow for myself. In doing that, I seemed to have become equipped to help others make them okay for themselves too. It was a gift I felt called to use.

I'd thought of offering God many things over the course of my life. Some out of a desire to repent, to please or appease, some out of a hope of becoming better, some because I felt I owed something out of gratitude, and some because I thought they might ease my fit in my family or religious community.

This was the first time I'd considered offering my whole self.

What I mean is that it had never occurred to me that my whole self might be an acceptable offering. That I could offer it for no reason other than it's the thing I have, the thing God and I have crafted together, and the thing that's hardest for me to give. Not because I love it more than anything, but because I don't tend to love it enough. Who wants to give a gift they're not sure they want themselves?

Did I hold back because I wanted to be better before I offered myself? Because I planned on giving the Perfected Me, once I got it finished? I can see I'm not really any closer to perfect than I've ever been, and it doesn't look good for happening any time soon. So besides showing up to perform my callings, when would I begin to really give to the people with whom I worship?

It is entirely possible that in all my waiting, in all my withholding, in all my self-protecting silence, I was missing the point. All the parts of myself I've held back are the parts that might create space or ease the way for someone else. It's the same thing that makes great literature great: in telling the human story, suddenly everyone is in the club. I'd been squeezing into such a tiny space on Sundays, I didn't even leave room for myself, let alone scoot over to offer someone a seat next to me. I was miserable squished; I never complained out loud. I accepted being squished in silence.

I'm a big believer in putting the things I need into the world, but somehow church has always been exempt from the rules that define my approach to life generally. It has taken me decades to fully understand and accept that languishing in silent want for all of my Mormon life has been at least, in some part, my fault. That's actually good news. It means I have, in some part, the power to create change.

Let's remake the church with our words.

Let's stop talking about the things we've talked about and start talking about the things locked in our hearts, say out loud for ourselves the things we need to hear.

The change must begin with what happens before we show up and start talking. First we need to want real relationships. We need to come to church as whole people, expecting to see others who also arrive in full. We need to be willing to sit together as we are. To always be scooting over to squeeze in one more. And when we open our mouths, let our storytelling inventory the pieces we lack as well as the ones we remembered to bring. The parts we can't fit as well as the ones that drop effortlessly into place without oil or explanation.

Raising our hands, our voices, and most importantly our stories— we cannot remake the church without reclaiming our stories. First our collective story, our history: that reclamation has been essential and is ongoing, both through official channels and as a consequence of the internet. But next our individual stories, the lives we've given to a silence that did not respect or invite (let alone reverence) our personal experiences. Even our unique encounters with the Divine are governed by guidelines. For me, my church family has never felt like a safe repository for the truest or trickiest details of my story.

"There are many things we can do outside ... But when we come through the chapel doors ..." I built large barriers between my Latter-day Saint self, and my ... well ... *Self*-self. It was almost like being two people and only one had permission to speak.

Yet the unruly human experience is the essence of living in a body. According to our own theology, our inherent messiness sits at the heart of the so-called Plan of Happiness. But don't we clean it all up and even pretend it isn't happening for the purposes of our participation at church? We put on our Sunday best like a warped version of the armor of God, stuffing our scriptures and lessons into a church bag, but leaving the messier parts of ourselves at home.

I want to talk about my real things. Can't heavenly parents handle the retelling of my story, a story they already know by heart? What would it do to our fellow saints to share a few of those details except to say, "You are not alone, I'm also hurting and I need you to sit with me and by the way, did I mention that despite all the messy things I've just told you, I'm still here, as you are, seeking? Perhaps if we looked together, we might see further?"

It's not that I want to turn church into therapy. It's that we cannot lift the thing we don't see or ease the burden we will not touch. In understanding the person we're sitting next to, in holding their story, sitting-with becomes ministry. But in a culture steeped in the practice of never sharing our real selves, true ministry becomes impossible, doesn't it?

These are the feelings that powered my most recent stint as a Relief Society teacher. I had the luxury of having the floor for a while and was able to really build something, carefully, deliberately, and over time. I'm not sure why I was given that opportunity, and especially not sure why the call magically coincided with my Silence Crisis. I wasn't sure what I believed, if anything, at the time I received it. I had just emerged from a wholly unexpected dance with cancer during which I realized (with no small amount of shock) that I wasn't at all sure there is an afterlife. You might call the realization I describe a faith crisis, but it struck me that I'd never been sure and I actually knew that—I just hadn't felt at liberty to admit it to myself. (See, my silence extended even to things I could not say to Me.) Anyway, although my hope had been enough to keep me walking, that's a pretty foundational doctrine to suddenly turn up missing. Still, I felt a spiritual nudging that I could, and should, teach.

So it was with a lot of trepidation that I accepted the call. It was time for an act of unselfishness and courage—or maybe utter selfishness, but still courage—time to reclaim the dignity of my own story, to hold it up right in the face of the enormous cultural silencing that had kept it invisible in my church life. To show the ways that messiness is actually integral to the plan, not the enemy of it. I felt I owed it to myself to explore some deep questions too—I obviously had some stuff to figure out and decided to do it out loud in hopes there might be someone else in the room who was having trouble asking their questions or admitting difficult things to themselves. Perhaps we might take a look at things together and describe what we each see.

I was assigned to teach conference talks, which had drawbacks but also advantages. I pray before preparing lessons—I want to be inspired to know what's most important, what will benefit the specific women in our group, and if I might have a unique slant to explore that could open us to a broader perspective or understanding. I've found that no matter how difficult the topic, if I come at it from a position of vulnerability, I can find a way in for both myself and others. I might begin by saying, "Here's what's hard for me about this," "Here's what I struggle with," or "This talk was difficult for me because_____." No one ever seems to want to pick a fight with my personal feelings or experience, even if I'm beginning the lesson by throwing the talk under the bus. Reading the general authority's own words of testimony at the end saved me many times from having to testify to things I don't know, ending the lesson on a note with which no one in the room would argue. I know, that's a little sneaky. Because other than that, I take lessons wholly in the direction I'm inspired to go. It's my own brand of teaching, in which everyone leaves feeling better than they did when they came in, if I do it well. This approach, coupled with a big bag of candy bars, was amazingly successful. It's not a stretch to say I had a real impact on the overall culture of my ward's Relief Society.

Through teaching, I've learned an important truth about human interaction in general: in pursuit of carving out a safe place for ourselves, we get further by making ourselves a safe place for others. Any time I succeed in bringing my own whole self to the lesson and invite someone else to do the same, it's like opening twice the space at once.

I want to make more room for my own ideas, but not create that space by edging someone else's out. To do so would erase any gain, and the goal is to enlarge the whole. So often it has felt as if people were waiting to step through the door, if I'd just open it. And why not? I've been standing outside waiting to be invited to the conversation for decades; why have I automatically assumed I was standing outside alone? Probably because we were all waiting in silence.

With so little variety in the script at church, it's hard to read between the lines. The silence in the room translates as agreement, when in reality there are as many different thoughts in every meeting as there are people. By assigning the same meaning to each individual silence, we've made a grossly erroneous assumption. While assuming we agree, we're actually having a misunderstanding. But as it's a silent misunderstanding, no one knows.

If our silence were to give way to expression of those thoughts, would the resulting conversation and inevitable lack of agreement be dismissed as contention? Perhaps, at first. It takes time to grow used to saying things, to hearing our own voice, to become accustomed to following unfamiliar ideas to new understanding. It would require love to allow ourselves to engage in that process with willing hearts and open minds. But real unity is not in finding agreement, it's in figuring out how to love anyway. We've been mistaking our silence for agreement, our mistaken agreement for unity, and our mistaken unity for love, when in reality this way of being together should probably wear much less flattering labels. Poet William Carlos Williams said:

> Their story, yours and mine—it's what we all carry with us on this trip we take, and we owe it to each other to respect ... and learn from them.[5]

I tried to help the women in my ward glimpse this truth in one memorable Relief Society lesson. We were talking about adversity being the 'homework' of earth school—the lessons unique, unfairly distributed, and ongoing. I wanted to communicate the idea that through our own adversity, we learn to love and understand others.

I wanted to move beyond the abstract and really get a snapshot of the specific adversity in that room. So I asked the women to think of the hardest things they'd experienced, the biggest burdens they carried, then I asked them to call them out. I went first—again, the critical ingredient in the success of my lessons has always been the invitation to other women to bring their whole selves to the discussion by leading with my own vulnerability. I was hoping it would work well in this case, and it did. I started by offering my own struggle with mental illness. Almost like I'd turned on a faucet, the burdens began to pour. Death of a child, divorce, loss of spouse, sexual abuse, alcoholism, drug abuse, child in jail, faith crisis, suicide, ongoing unemployment, cancer, chronic illness—these things and more tumbled out. I don't think there was anyone in the room who wasn't caught up in the emotion of it. How can you not be moved when the woman sitting next to you shares that she was repeatedly molested as a child? Something happens to collapse the space between you in that moment. So many previously unseen, real-world things were suddenly there in plain sight, wearing the faces of people we knew and loved. We moved to discussing how surviving these things had changed us and everyone agreed that the number one lesson they had learned from their adversity was to not judge others.

I didn't know what to say. I couldn't make sense of that. I told them I've spent my entire lifetime at church feeling judged, and many said they felt the same. But why? How? Who taught us this way of being? If we taught ourselves, don't we also have the power to learn a new way?

That exercise exposed a jarring disconnect between our culture—or maybe perceived culture?—and the individual, very real people in the pews. I told them if I'd only learned that lesson when I was eighteen, my entire church life might have been different.

I will never stop saying this: If we can get members to be real with each other—to actually meet where we are and walk a bit together—it would change everything. How could it not?

My teaching experiences were transformational for me and continue to power a deepening acquaintance with my own spiritual voice, spilling over into other areas. I've been able to speak some things of my heart in my marriage and family for the first time in my life. It's a huge shift, an enormous weight lifted. It didn't happen all at once. It happened a little at a time, here and there a daring new word or idea expressed.

It has helped that the church has offered a few more avenues into some difficult conversations. If we can meet on the neutral ground of an essay on an official church website to begin, we can usually find our way along a conversational path that's beneficial to both of us. Even if it's only a step or two at a time. Curiously, the more I've been willing to say, the less fear and suspicion the people around me seem to have. Yes, the blog that raised everyone's eyebrows was scary at first. But we've come a long way since then and I feel there's almost nothing I can't say out loud. When I first summoned my courage to speak, I dared not even imagine the things I talk about now.

A few years ago, I decided to reclaim prayer for myself by coming at it from a new direction. I spent a month writing a prayer every day. I wanted to use words completely different from anything I'd been taught to say. I wanted to put my prayers into the void under their own power, unfettered even by the constraints of a prescribed destination. Recipient unknown. They consisted of my everyday observations— small things I found worthy of note as I went, things I wanted to write and hold and even share, but not with anyone I could identify. When I'd feel a nod from the universe, I wanted from these prayers a tangible way to acknowledge it with a nod in return. Here's a prayer sitting at the heart of the project itself:

TO WHOM IT MAY CONCERN:

You have given me a voice from the beginning. Did you not expect that I would want to use it? Filled me with the press of questions, with wonders deserving the honor of my attention but also my words. Trusted me with children who could not grow strong under my silence, in addition to yours. We must both tell them what we know.

You've demanded—commanded—my honesty, but not the kind that speaks in my language, not the secret begging for daylight. How could you have placed me here within this world's tangled knot, asked me to let the thread ends lie helpless on the table?

Am I meant to walk in silence? Am I meant to notice only the things pointed out by someone else? When will it be my turn to point and name, to ask but also answer, to speak my way to the front of the question?

Let me draw close to you with my mouth, press my shell heart against your ear. You'll know when I have said what I needed to say. When my foot finally rests from its eternity of nervous beating. When my silence becomes listening, rather than marking time.

My project to remake prayer did make a difference for me. It wasn't easy. I didn't have trouble thinking of them as prayers, but I did have to give myself permission to write them. New permission, every single day, as if the prohibition of such a radical act was deeply imprinted somewhere too complicated to reach.

Since that project I've added other practices to my prayer life, additions to the Mormon-style prayers that continue to punctuate my days and from which I draw real comfort. I've started having conversations with God right out loud and whenever I like. We call ourselves by our first names in these conversations. We use whatever kind of language suits us at the moment. We can each say what we need to say. It's the closest I've come yet to something that feels like two-way communication. Somehow, my heretical experiment with written prayers got me out of my own way just enough to finally let myself speak directly to something or someone larger.

I've spent many years thinking, "I wish the church would/were ____." You can fill in that blank a million ways. Things I'd like to hear more of, things I'd like to hear less of, ideas I wish we'd explore, ideas I wish we'd erase, policies I wish we'd change, people I wish were nicer, and on and on. Probably about forty years' worth of daily ideas. What I'm still just figuring out is that if I want more *anything* in my church experience, I do have some power to put it there.

For instance, if I'd like to hear comments in Sunday School that are more like the thoughts I'm having, I should express my own. Suddenly that thought becomes living. It's in the room. Someone could even say they "heard it at church." And maybe someone will surprise me and agree. Maybe not, but it's out there nonetheless.

What am I protecting myself from by keeping my unique feelings and ideas under wraps? From people deciding I don't fit in? I knew that decades ago.

Here's a thought: put more of myself into my ward and automatically there would be more people at church who are *like me*. There would be one, anyway, creating a better, more inclusive environment— for myself—one Sunday at a time. And who knows? By speaking up, maybe I'll create an opening for someone else who's been quietly waiting, dying to end their silence but listening for just the right break in the conversation.

Let's remake our church experience. "It's kind of fun to do the impossible," said Walt Disney.[6]

Let's be whatever way we "wish the church were ..." Do things we "wish the church would ..." Say things we "wish we heard people say" at church. The church belongs to all of us, and our Sunday meetings belong to everyone who shows up.

The way forward is through difficulty and discomfort though. Our own, but also that of the people shifting uncomfortably in their chairs every time we open our mouths. We'll each get used to it if we do it enough. Church will feel different if we change the conversation. Unfortunately, Latter-day Saints are people who seem to prefer church to always be the same. Still, big changes are afoot—in vogue even—and we should capitalize on any hint of fresh air in the room. One breath at a time, with the good of the whole always foremost in our minds. Culture grows and develops over time, and it will only be changed over time. We don't have to say everything we need or want to say at once. In fact, we can't.

There is other work to be done. We must also create a space capable of receiving and worthy of holding the stories of ourselves and others. The only way I can see to do this is by beginning to put the stories into the space we hope to create. As Muriel Rukeyser wrote, "The universe is made of stories, not of atoms."[7]

It's easy to bat a doctrinal idea you believe is mistaken back to the person who says it, armed with whatever evidence supports your view. It's not personal, you didn't invent the doctrine. It's a lot harder to throw someone's story back onto them, however, once it has been offered to you. Even if you didn't want it, once it's in the room, there it sits. Throw enough of them on the heap and we're bound to hit critical mass at some point. In my experience, once the stories begin to pile up people become eager to add their own. Sharing is gradually less hard the more you do it. As I said before, this holding of another's story is really just a different name for ministering. In our willingness to hold it, they are no longer alone. In our collective carrying, their burden is lightened. I believe that if we got in the habit of going home from church on Sunday feeling our burden had in some way been made less, we'd come to value our church time more. Rather than a *must do*, it could become a *want to*.

Perhaps you're not like me. Perhaps you haven't felt silenced in all the church meetings of your life. If not, thank you for the things you've shared that have kept me alive for all the years I've been unable to share myself. If you were one of the people who was willing to go first, know that you invited me in and after years of hearing your invitation, I've finally stepped into the space you held open. I only hope I can ease the way for someone who is still sitting in silence, hoping for a turn to speak. If you're not yet ready to speak, that's okay. Keep listening. Without listeners, our speaking is useless. We'll wait for your story until you're ready to share and welcome it when you do.

I believe our words have real power. In fact, I believe that in our stories we hold the key to healing this church. We show up trailing only hints and wisps of who we are. The very real pain, experiences, questions, and relationships we shoulder on our daily walk are largely left outside the chapel doors every time we enter the building. Learning to fully inhabit my Mormonism is the lesson of my adult life. So far, I've not been a quick learner. I'd almost suffocated from decades of self-imposed silence when I finally had no choice but to speak. What I understand now is the silence that had always seemed the safe path was actually leading me nowhere. Without my story, I'm not equipped to share myself with others. I can't partake fully of the fellowship offered. I can't contribute the largest part of my heart. I can't heal or be healed. I'm there in body but I've kept my spirit to myself. My silence does nothing but add weight to the suffocation of the brothers and sisters who also came to church looking for that thing they need most.

I heard a photographer once talk about *qarrtsiluni*, an Inuit word that means 'sitting together in the dark waiting for something to happen.'[8] I think that makes it another word for church. I'm afraid we most often think of church as sitting in light, waiting smugly for the things we know to materialize just as we've said they would, and pitying those not in the light with us. That's what it feels like to me. But I prefer to think of church as sitting patiently in the dark, comforting others, waiting in hope, appreciating the small gradations of darkness, the cracks of light that illuminate briefly, the faint glow of promise when the door opens so someone else can come in. I can only make this shift for myself, and to do it has meant I've had to bring my whole self—my feet and my faith—to my dark place. And then I've had to look around and talk about what I've found there. It's a different stillness than the kind in the Primary song. A kind that enlarges rather than shushes. A kind that opens me rather than shutting me down. I'm remaking my church experience one word at a time and in the process, it feels like I'm also remaking my relationship with God. I don't have it all figured out, but I think we're allowed to share glimpses ahead of where we are, to envision the places we want to go next.

I want to rewrite the words to that old Primary song. I'm going to need a new tune because I want to deliver the message the way I need to hear it. To speak the unruly phrases of my heart. I haven't yet imagined the notes, but the lyrics would say something like this:

The chapel doors
Seem to say to me, come in
Bring yourself and sit where we
Can both talk and listen, sing
Even the uncertain hymn, here
Let me take your coat—
Once you have spoken your fill
Eaten at my table, only then
Be still, let us reverence

Each other, let us be easy
Together, let us witness
The truth of your story,
The slip of its hand into mine.

There is still so much to be said, so much to be written, to be learned, and shared, and understood. This will require our words as well as our presence. The full participation of minds, ears, mouths, and hearts. When—at last—our stories are allowed to speak alongside our scriptures, we may finally experience wholeness and unity. As individuals, and as a church.

WHY I WEAR PANTS TO CHURCH

"Will my personal direction from God be the same as yours? I don't think so. We're individuals. God deals with us as individuals. This is the same God who made not just apples but pears and apricots and persimmons and grapes. He likes diversity. He invented it."
—Chieko Okazaki[9]

Cynthia:

When I was a little girl, a widow lived next door to us—Marion Shaver. She was a retired teacher who had a prosthetic leg which caused her to walk with a limp. One Sunday my siblings and I were challenged in Primary to invite someone to church, so we decided to invite Mrs. Shaver. She was always kind to us, letting us eat all the walnuts that fell from her large black walnut tree in her yard and ours. She was so kind and patient with me and my four siblings. We surmised that she'd be a perfect addition to the Chino 2nd Ward. However, upon asking her to come to church with us, she told us she couldn't come because she didn't wear dresses. We had never ever in our short little lives seen a woman wear pants to church, so we assumed it simply wasn't allowed. We dejectedly walked away, our first missionary experience not one that would be featured in *The Children's Friend* magazine.

In 2013, I was in my ward's Primary presidency. I started hearing a buzz in the LDS bloggernacle that feminist members asked all women to wear pants to church on a specific Sunday. I didn't know much about the movement, nor did I do any follow-up research. Wanting to support women who were trying to broaden even the tiniest cultural norms for women, I talked to the Primary president I was serving with about wearing pants. She emphatically told me she would support me no matter what I wore. As a counselor, I often conducted the Primary meetings, played the piano, gave a small lesson during sharing time, or did all the usual running around that Primary leaders do on behalf of children. Feminist or not, I thought how much more sense it would make for Primary workers to wear pants because, more than any other adults at church, they are constantly wrangling little ones into their chairs, feeding them snacks, bending over to pick up spilled crayons, and often sitting on the floor with them. I knew if I received any criticism about wearing pants that the president, also my friend, would fiercely support me. In the end, I never did wear pants while in that presidency. I was too self-conscious, too worried about being misunderstood, and still too much of a rule keeper, even if they were unwritten cultural rules.

Fast forward to 2018, I was in a full-blown organizational crisis. I was questioning everything about the patriarchal organization of our church, and I could not only see how it harmed women but I had firsthand experience of how it had hurt me. Consequently, I began questioning our strict gender roles that Mormonism proudly proclaimed were God-ordained. I was also questioning our policies towards LGBTQ people, and suddenly, pants felt like the least of my worries. My always-safe-church life had crumbled around me and suddenly my formerly nervous thoughts about wearing pants to church made me guffaw, like I was playing a game of jacks on the floor while my Mormon world burned down around me. I went from "people might think I am wicked" to "I dare them to think I am wicked." A lot can happen in five years.

At that same time, I was serving in the library, a calling that as an extrovert I affectionately like to call "which friends can come out and play with me today?" Everybody knows folks in the 'Hall Class' wander aimlessly from the foyer to the library to the drinking fountains. And even though I only passed out scriptures and crayons, and made copies, I loved my quick (or long!) visits with my fellow saints who stopped by. Those days seemed like the best time to strategically begin wearing pants to church. I say 'strategic' because I always made sure I was dressed to the nines—brightly colored slacks, heels, sparkly jewelry, and my signature red lipstick. I was doing my best to redefine Sunday best.

As a recovering Rule Keeper, I was frustrated that my heart still beat like crazy those first few Sundays. Maybe nervousness is simply a hazard of bravery. It must be, because whenever we talk about wearing pants to church on our social media accounts, the comments abound! Here's a favorite that normalized the nerves for me:

I was so scared the first time I wore pants to church. I had to hype myself up and I needed the example of another sister in the ward. But when I did it, it wasn't that scary. Church culture always makes it seem like any deviation will be the end of the world, somehow. But really it's pretty easy and most people won't say or do anything to you for being a little different. Wearing pants to church actually helped me make more friends. The ward feminists saw me and decided I was an ally.

Thankfully, the nerves didn't last long, and before I knew it, women were stopping by the library and making comments such as, "Well, now I want to wear pants too!" and, "Hey I didn't know we could wear pants?" To each of these comments I replied, "your body, your rules." A couple of women eventually followed suit.

Seven years later, and I have never received a negative comment yet. Plenty of glances but only from visitors as my own ward members are used to my counter-culture ways. I am sure anyone reading this who lives in Boston or Berkeley is rolling her eyes. She should. Because the debate between wearing fabric wrapped around each individual leg versus fabric that wraps around both legs at once is laughable to be discussing in the 21st century. But I live in Provo, Utah, which I affectionately call Mormon Mecca, where traditions run deep. If you live in an area close enough to walk to church, my guess is your local ward is fairly traditional as well. The higher the concentration of homogeneity, the harder it is to break the norm in favor of diversity.

If that diversity is never modeled, how can we create welcoming spaces for all? Even though I am a girly-girl who loves all things feminine, I rarely wear a dress anymore and not just because I am thermally challenged, though it does feel great to finally be warm at church in the winter. (Sidenote—I am actually colder in my church building in the summer where men who wear layered suits control the thermostat, literally keeping it under lock and key. Just one more reason to wear pants year-round!)

Perhaps the best outcome of pants wearing is the solidarity I feel with the women in wheelchairs, the women with colostomy bags, the gay women, the women who want to send a message of equality to the patriarchy, the legging-loving girls in Young Women, or simply the thermally challenged.

I can easily blend into my conservative and homogeneous Provo surroundings, but I have chosen to model the diversity I want to see through the clothes I choose to wear, the comments I make, and the rainbow pin that adorns my bag. I'd like to think that my pioneering-pants efforts have made room for other differences, seen and unseen. We don't get many investigators in my Provo ward, but I'd like to think that if Mrs. Shaver came to my ward today, she'd fit right in. All are welcome to sit by me.

WHY I WEAR A CROSS

"Anyone who gets to the end of their life with the exact same beliefs
and opinions as they had at the beginning is doing it wrong."
—Sarah Bessey[10]

Susan:

It's a Sunday morning in deep springtime, and I'm sitting in a church with a group of fifty or so other women. Before us is a wall of windows as tall as trees, new leaves the only color in the room, except for two slim red lines: a cross that reaches almost from floor to ceiling. I can't take my eyes off it. This is rebirth spelled out plainly: an unbroken line of green, gracefully punctuated in red. I can't imagine a more perfect setting for worship than this.

My eyes follow the red line that extends up, up, uninterrupted until near the top where it meets its other line. I'm thinking about roots, and about reach, about the point in the center, where I sit, wishing my arms could extend forever. I want to embrace it all. The morning, the women, the birdsong, our hymns. For a moment, I feel completely taken in by that cross, two simple lines clearly marking my place in the great whole. It nudges me inward and onward, gently pointing every way at once.

It's hard to believe I'm not only comfortable but deeply nourished there. Looking back at my young self, I see a kid who could have reeled off a list of things Mormons Don't Do without even thinking, and Sunday morning spent in a church with a cross would have topped the list. In fact, in my neighborhood the Don'ts functioned as a playground retort, a semi-automatic way to elevate yourself above whoever you wanted to put in their place. "Mormons don't drink Coke," we'd sneer at the kid in our ward we saw holding one. Or "Mormons don't play cards," or "Mormons don't swear." We poked each other with pointed one-liners of our righteousness all the time.

The list of cultural prohibitions changed and grew as I did. Even after I stopped hurling childish weapons, jabs and judgments continued in my head. I'm ashamed to admit that to observe other church members was to classify and sometimes scold them—it happened almost automatically. "Good Mormons don't wear spaghetti straps," I'd think when I saw a girl dressed in a way I didn't feel allowed to dress myself.

New rules would emerge now and then after a general conference talk, or whenever a prophet singled out a specific idea like double ear piercings or R-rated movies. These weren't doctrinal prohibitions, more like instant taboos—markers of 'valiance' and 'righteousness' and 'exact obedience' that took on a life of their own. Something no one thought much about (like two earrings/one ear) could become elevated to a deeply held tenet of our faith in one fell prophetic swoop. For many LDS kids who were taught to avoid even the appearance of evil, believing meant adopting these cultural markers ourselves without question.

From a young age, one thing I knew for sure was that Mormons Don't Wear Crosses.

No one I knew wore them, anyway, and I'm embarrassed to say I would have felt distrustful of someone who did, even though I wouldn't have understood what was behind those feelings. I had no idea that historically crosses had been used in LDS architecture, and that wasn't all. Early Utah Mormons wore crosses as jewelry, decorated with them during celebrations, sewed them into quilts. They assembled flowers into cross-shaped funeral arrangements, etched them onto gravestones, erected them as monuments to the pioneers, and printed them on marriage certificates.[11]

I didn't know the history of crosses within my religion, nor much about it as a symbol in wider Christianity. I'm not sure anyone ever specifically told me I couldn't wear a cross, but it was something I absorbed as surely as if I'd heard it from a prophet himself. I associated Catholics with crosses and crucifixes, but never felt I needed to look beyond that one fact. It didn't even occur to me to ask why they wore them or why we didn't, or even the difference between those two symbols. I just accepted the prohibition I had absorbed as somehow True.

As a young teen in Salt Lake City, I went to visit a friend in Holy Cross hospital. As I stood by his bed, I couldn't keep my eyes off the crucifix on the wall above it. It made me so uncomfortable, I wondered whether I would ever be able to sleep there. I felt sorry for him—not because he had endured an appendectomy, but as an extension of my own discomfort. It never occurred to me that the same symbol making me anxious might bring great comfort to the one in the bed.

Even the word 'crucifix' felt wrong or dangerous somehow, like a word whispered in a slumber party conversation I wouldn't want my parents to hear, the "x" pricking my young conscience like a pin. Even peace signs, ubiquitous on clothing and bumper stickers and jewelry of the time, were guilty by association—a "broken cross" my parents managed to make clear wasn't welcome in our home without ever elaborating. Not that I dared to ask. Crosses were simply verboten.

If you told seventh grade me that sixty-something me would wear a cross almost every day, I'd have laughed, and not just because I didn't believe I'd ever be so old. I couldn't imagine finding any positive connection with that symbol at all. I wouldn't have even known how to start.

Fast forward half a century and I find myself made weepy by its grace, planted at the head of a small chapel in the woods. The cross has become deeply meaningful. Although some Latter-day Saints see it as a symbol of Jesus's death, I experience it as a symbol of my own living faith.

As recently as 2022 we were reminded in general conference that our church does not use cross iconography.[12] But when my life dropped me on bare ground scraped clean of my inherited faith and I realized I didn't know what I believed, or even wanted to, I had an opportunity to rebuild from scratch. One of the first things I picked up to reexamine was Jesus. Not long after that, I also chose to pick up His cross as a symbol of my desire to walk after Him.

I bought my first on a vacation because I thought it was really beautiful, and I also wondered what it would feel like to not feel prohibited to wear it. It was scary for me—I was a little afraid for even my husband to see it as I uneasily unpacked my bag from the trip. The first time I wore the necklace to lunch with my sister she looked like she might fall off her chair. Her eyes got big as she shouted to be heard across the table in the noisy restaurant, "What? You're wearing a CROSS?!"

She reacted just like I expected she would. However, what I found with that first cross was that I loved how I felt every time I caught sight of myself in the mirror wearing it. It reminded me that I am a woman of faith and I've chosen to follow Jesus. I liked that it told others the same.

We may as well get this out of the way now, because I think my sister would probably tell you this about me: I'm rebellious by nature. She probably sees my cross in that context, knowing me as long as she has, and she has a point. At first, the idea that wearing a cross as a way of being Mormon-rebellious filled me with more than a little glee. But putting a cross on a chain around my neck has come to mean so much more than that for me. This is spiritual progress, not rebellion: a symbol of my own growth, upward and outward.

After a lifetime of feeling like a misfit at church, like maybe my faith was defective, I had come to the realization shortly before I purchased that first necklace that I am actually a woman of great faith. Still in the pews, still reaching for God. That was a new way of seeing myself, and I wanted to be reminded of it every chance I could. It's not an overstatement to say that realizing the depth of my own faith—and that I could actually call it faith—was life changing for me.

Having come through a time of not being sure whether there was a god, once I got to the other side of that experience I wanted to cultivate a relationship in every way I could think of. Wearing a cross became a reminder to myself to always be inviting relationship. It felt like an outward reflection of my inward desire, a signpost I could carry with me to mark my path even while walking it. I'd experienced a conversion to God's love and grace. I don't know another way to describe it, but somehow the cross described it for me. The symbol was new language for me, and I wanted new language to describe my new understanding.

Wearing the cross has expanded the ways I think and talk about God. It's a symbol I wear of the exploded box, as if I unfolded the packaging of my faith on the table and was surprised that what I'd always experienced as a box was, when you laid it flat, a cross. A visual representation of the larger god I'd spent my life yearning for.

Shortly before I started wearing the cross, I read Richard Rohr's *The Universal Christ*, and some of his ideas had a profound impact. He described Christians who "feel called to not hide from the dark side of things or the rejected group, but in fact draw close to the pain of the world and allow it to radically change their perspective. They agree to embrace the imperfection and even the injustices of our world, allowing these situations to change themselves from the inside out, which is the only way things are changed anyway."[13]

For all the ways I was still the same Latter-day Saint, my faith was completely new. So the cross became a symbol of my desire to be able to hold tension: in relationships, in religion, in life; tension which I found to be deeply resonant on a personal level. I had always experienced life as an intersection of profound darkness and breathtaking light. The cross gave me a place to stand in the middle of it all.

> The cross isn't just a singular event. It's a statement from God that reality has a cruciform pattern. Jesus was killed in a collision of cross-purposes, conflicting interests, and half-truths, caught between the demands of an empire and the religious establishment of his day. The cross was the price Jesus paid for living in a 'mixed' world, which is both human and divine, simultaneously broken and utterly whole. He hung between a good thief and a bad thief, between heaven and earth, inside of both humanity and divinity, a male body with a feminine soul, utterly whole and yet utterly disfigured—all the primary opposites.
>
> In so doing, Jesus demonstrated that Reality is not meaningless and absurd, even if it isn't always perfectly logical or consistent. Reality, we know, is always filled with contradictions, what St. Bonaventure and others called the 'coincidence of opposites.'
>
> … We are indeed saved by the cross—more than we realize. The people who hold the contradictions and resolve them in themselves are the saviors of the world. They are the only real agents of transformation, reconciliation, and newness.[14]—Richard Rohr

And then there's the symbolism of the vertical (a reach upward) and the horizontal (a reach outward) that I find to be such a simple reminder of what I want to be about. I imagine myself extending both directions while my roots go down, down, deep into my ground of self, held fast in depths I have only begun to plumb.

I don't have to understand all the reasons this symbol speaks to me in order to hear it. It is summed up in one last line from Richard Rohr. In a passage entitled, "Jesus speaks to you from the Cross," he says, "Embrace it all in me. I am yourself. I am all of creation. I am everybody and everything."[15]

That's it exactly: Jesus speaks to me from the cross. He says, "Follow me," then sets off without leaving detailed directions, which has me believing I can follow no matter where I go. His symbol reminds me that part of being human is suffering—that we're all in it together, and it's just as hard for everyone else as it is for me. This idea softens my heart, loosens my too-tight grip, and blurs the hard edge between me and the other. I take the cross up willingly. Its presence opens a crack in my preoccupation with my own problems to allow something bigger to enter, to urge me up and out. So this necklace I wear has become, for me, something that isn't at all about the thing I think most Latter-day Saints object to. It isn't a symbol of Jesus's death but is instead a symbol of my own living. It's a gift I wish I could give to everyone, but especially to the little girl I was who misunderstood so much in her naivete and misjudged her own faith so profoundly. I would clasp it around her neck with a whispered blessing that she can always find stillness in the center and growth in every direction it points.

GRIEVING AND GROWING

"There's something weird that happens to the broken hearted. There's a kind of inside-outness that happens that can make us the exact right kind of people that can help us live in unfinished times."
—Kate Bowler[16]

Cynthia:

When my son was a toddler, I told him that I was heading to the nursery to buy a tree for our yard. Up to that point, we had installed only a sprinkler system and some struggling hydroseed for our lawn. Buying a new home in 1998 was great; we happily picked out our cream-colored carpet and blue countertops, but it also meant landscaping in the desert. When I came home from the nursery a few hours later, my son took one look at that sapling of a tree, no thicker than his little arm, and with disappointment exclaimed, "Mom, I wanted the kind of tree you can climb!" Fair enough. I wanted shade and he wanted to climb. Sadly, neither of us would get what we wanted, at least not yet. It was going to be a while. A decade or more, actually.

We moved by the time my son was eight so he never got to climb a tree in that yard nor did I enjoy any shade whatsoever at that house, but I was determined to make both happen in our new home. Once again, we bought a home that required the arduous task of landscaping a yard. Before I had even unpacked our boxes I went off to the nursery to buy trees. We planted ash trees, flowering pears, aspens, redbuds, evergreens, maples, and honey locusts. Almost two decades later I do have my shade. And maybe my son, now an adult and married with his own little boy, is too big to even want to climb trees anymore but his son will get to climb our twenty-three trees someday. They'll be large enough by then.

Thankfully I do have shade now. I need its refuge. This sun worshipper is getting too old to sit bare-faced in the hot backyard anymore without a bit of respite from the glaring sun. As I sit under my trees, listening to the messages in the rustling leaves, watching the birds eat seeds from the feeders, I think about my little son and his desire to climb a tree that couldn't bear the weight of his tiny body and how everything worth having in life takes as much time as growing a climb-able tree. Trees take years but so do people.

A lot has happened between the years of hauling those trees home from Home Depot in the back of my sister's SUV, to now. My trees have added lots of growth rings and I would like to think I have as well. Here are some of my growth rings.

First, I've added the ring of faith. Well, I subtracted it, then added it back so maybe on this one I am neutral. I won't say much about faith challenges, because in many ways, that's what every other essay in this book is about: loving the gospel of Jesus Christ *and* being able to set boundaries between myself and the harmful and complicated things I experience at church. Peter Enns said:

> I wonder, too, whether our sense of losing faith is really more of an invitation to move toward a faith of a different sort, where 'holding on' to what you 'know' is decentered and exposed as an idol rather than a sign of 'strong faith.'[17]

Deconstructing is painful but reconstructing has felt like coming into my own self. My 100-percent-certain testimony about the church was an idol. One I would take out and polish and display loudly at church.

Second, I've added a growth ring to my relationships. Working hard at fixing and maintaining relationships, reading almost every Brené Brown book, and attending therapy with three different therapists has probably been the thickest ring I have added. Hopefully I keep adding rings here because the messy work of human relationships is never done. As Susan has said on the podcast, families are messy, even the best ones.

Third, I've also added the ring of curiosity as I felt a Godlike nudge to educate myself on LGBTQ Latter-say Saint experiences, or as we Mormons like to say, "I heeded the promptings of the Spirit." Indeed I felt prompted to throw out all my past (what I call) 'benevolent homophobia' and start fresh. That meant listening firsthand to the actual lived experiences of queer family and friends. Just when God had sufficiently softened my heart, humbled me, and I had fallen in love with the LGBTQ community, my own daughter came out as gay. I was ready for another new challenge. My trunk was growing thicker with each passing year.

Fourth, by far the most growth has come from healing from grief. Hands down, my grief has been the fertilizer to increase the size of all my growth rings. As I have looked around my surroundings more and noticed all the suffering that used to be in my blind spots, I realize there's a price to pay for wisdom. I once said to my therapist, "I paid a terrible price to learn these lessons." He looked at me and said, "Nobody says you haven't." Ecclesiastes 1:18 says, "For in much wisdom is much grief; and she that increaseth knowledge increaseth sorrow."

I wish it wasn't so. But working through my own grief opened up the grief of others to me as well. Grieving changed me. It meant I carried an extra weight, an extra burden—extra sorrow, as Ecclesiastes says. Jesus carried the weight of the world so if we are to be like Him, how can we not be expected to carry just a smidgeon of that sorrow and grief? In a weird kind of paradox, when we learn to really love and suffer with others we definitely get something in return. The *Les Misérables* musical states, "To love another person is to see the face of God." In Mormon-speak, we might call that sanctification.

I would like to think that all I have accomplished in the last few years would have happened anyway. Trust me, I am a shallow enough person that I really do wish I could learn to mourn and grieve without having to experience my own Gethsemane. Nobody leaves their comfort zone willingly.

Richard Rohr said, "All healthy religion shows you what to do with your pain, with the absurd, the tragic, the nonsensical, the unjust and the undeserved—all of which eventually come into every lifetime. If only we could see these 'wounds' as the way through, as Jesus did, then they would become sacred wounds rather than scars to deny, disguise, or project onto others . . . I am sorry to admit that I first see my wounds as an obstacle more than a gift. Healing is a long journey."[18] Dang Father Rohr, you nailed it again. Healing is a long journey.

Don't get me wrong. I would never go looking for grief. I'm not a masochist. Nor am I a Pollyanna-like person who wishes to put a positive spin on every crappy thing I go through. But when grief became my constant companion I learned to eventually welcome her. To lean into all the big feelings of sorrow. To stop shoving grief away and pretending everything would eventually get better with just more time. It's okay to not be okay. Grief wouldn't be my constant companion but she was a longtime companion. She was the teacher I never wanted and never knew I needed.

A few years ago I wandered a very old cemetery in San Juan, Puerto Rico. My teenagers were enamored with an old open grave, ooo-ing at what could be the story behind it. "I think I see bones! I think I see a ghost!" I laughed at their conversations. Once they had seen everything they wanted to see, they wandered away and explored something else. But I found myself lingering by a statue of a woman hunched in grief, clutching a wreath, mourning a loss almost impossible to bear. In that moment I realized I knew how she felt.

I raised my camera and took several shots. It was hot and humid from a rainstorm moments earlier. The heavy camera lens kept fogging up and I knew we had to catch a plane home soon, but for that moment everything was quiet. Just me and my camera. The cemetery was empty but my thoughts were full. I found another statue. A woman, head bowed in prayer, clutching her rosary in clasped hands. Age weighed heavily in the statue's face, weathered stains adding to her mournful look.

Grief has exposed me to another dimension I didn't really know existed. Or rather, it removed the blinders so I could finally turn my head and see it on my left and on my right.

Grief over lost dreams.

Grief over lost trust.

Grief over lost certainty.

Grief over loss of faith.

Grief over what was hidden in plain sight.

Grief over new realities.

Grief over the past.

Grief over the present.

Grief at what might be in the future.

I feel odd at remembering my life before—how invisible grief was to me.

Latter-day Saints don't 'do' grief very well. In fact, I believe we are lousy at it. We even tell fellow Mormons not to wear black to funerals because we celebrate life and we don't mourn death. Why do we do this? If someone needs to display their grief through their clothing choices, is it really up to us to tell them they can't, or even worse, they shouldn't even want to outwardly express grief?

I was trying to explain to my son, when he returned from his missionary service in the Dominican Republic, some of the sadnesses I've experienced as I sought counsel from priesthood leaders. I told him that it was traumatizing to be told to go home and write a talk on forgiveness instead of simply being allowed to grieve—for as long as necessary—for the pain inflicted upon me.

He said he can understand why these male leaders would do that because Jesus talked a lot about forgiving and not much about grieving. He said he was sorry I was treated that way, but in all honesty, that's how he dealt with people on his mission as well: a focus on forgiveness instead of giving people the time and space to grieve their losses, abuse, and injustices. I told him that since he is male he could be someone's bishop someday and I begged him to never mention forgiveness, to let the person bring it up when they're ready.

I shared with him my favorite scriptures on grieving: Alma at the Waters of Mormon admonishing us to mourn with those who mourn, Jesus weeping with Mary and Martha even though he would raise Lazarus like five minutes later, and my favorite, Alma taking care of Amulek after he was rejected by his friends: "therefore he took Amulek and came over to the land of Zarahemla, and took him to his own house and did administer unto him in his tribulations, and strengthen him in the Lord." (Alma 15:18)

Can we do better in grieving with our loved ones? We should meet people in their tribulations, like Alma. I can picture Alma bringing Amulek into his own home, making him homemade chicken noodle soup and hot bread, giving him a soft bed and telling him, "You've just lost everything, your friends and family, take all the time you need. I'll keep providing hot soup and a listening ear." That's what disciples of Jesus do. Mosiah 18:9 doesn't say to make happy those who mourn. It says to mourn with those who mourn. Right along with them.

In my grief and anguish, I found that the normal Mormony prayers did nothing for me anymore. But sitting under my still-growing trees became prayer. The messages in the fluttering leaves of my trees have taught me how God speaks to me—subtle but sure.

After all these years, some tree roots are now large enough that they are poking through my lawn. Last fall I planted tulip bulbs. As I dug holes all around my yard I kept running into the deeper but smaller—more spidery—tree roots. I did my best not to disturb them, to let them do their own thing, and to carefully plant the bulbs around the roots in our rocky Utah soil. Those thin little roots will get thicker and more stable year after year. They'll keep progressing and spreading, sending out more roots, like I am, even when, or especially when, growth seems to be negligible and even non-existent.

Have you ever hiked Kolob Canyon in Zion National Park? My family and I hiked there one year for fall break. There's a thin and narrow passage that in the fall is filled with brightly colored aspen trees. As we hiked, a gust of wind came through quickly and I heard that familiar movement of leaves that now signals to me stillness and reverence. My husband stopped and said, "I love that sound, the rush of wind through a narrow canyon." He heard wind but I heard God, once again whispering to me through rustling leaves, that everything is going to be okay.

My Heavenly Parents are aware of me. I matter. Be patient. Let my roots grow deeper. Let my rings expand. Grief and growing. Rings and roots. Humans and trees. We're really not that different. God has given me shade for now, and soon it will be time to climb.

METAMORPHOSIS

Everything that waits is also preparing itself to move.
—Margaret Renkl[19]

Susan:

I got married at 18. I don't think I need to explain a single thing about that sentence to you. There's plenty I could say: all the reasons my young marriage was, as Dickens might describe it, my best idea, and my worst. All the reasons it was a total shock for everyone who knew me, but unremarkable in the larger context of approved life choices for Latter-day Saint girls in 1981. I tell you that fact here so we can all start in the same place—at our beginning. I talk about my experiences in hopes of pointing to something bigger than my story; I want to help you locate yourself within your own. You may feel deep recognition in the things I share, or not connect with them at all, but either reaction can be a doorway to yourself.

I wore a pink cummerbund with my wedding dress. It represented the girl I had been. When I look at it now, I see all my teenage hopes and dreams. It was my last gasp rebellion against the white long-sleeved concession. In fact, my mom and I were asked to leave the bride's dressing room because we were still arguing about whether or not pink was appropriate on the temple grounds (and whose decision that should be) as I wrapped it around my waist for the photos. I really wanted to wear a white pantsuit to my wedding—I'd seen it in a bridal designer's window and knew immediately it was for me. When I floated the idea, my then-fiancé seemed equally hurt and bewildered. He said, "But my grandparents will be there …" I could have asked what that had to do with it; I didn't need to. But as the wistfulness in his voice closed the door on my pantsuit, the pink cummerbund took its place and became nonnegotiable.

About ten minutes after leaving the grounds of the Salt Lake Temple, I found myself (still in my wedding dress) at the doors of the Alta Club, having walked the few blocks up the street for our wedding breakfast. I had visions of gracefully ascending those front steps, the cake-topper of the whole world for one moment, but instead was informed that women were only allowed to enter through the back door. I was incredulous, indignant, but also exhausted, overwhelmed, surrounded by every authority figure of my young life, and not wishing to cause any embarrassment to my new in-laws who were hosting the event. I swallowed everything I was dying to say, opting instead for the death of *not* saying things. *How could I not have known? Did I really agree to this?* A girl who was keenly aware of effective ways to act out, I also knew when to get in line. In the moment, there was nothing to do but comply. I tucked my tantrum away in a pocket I didn't remember having before. Maybe it materialized in the temple.

Looking back, I can say it was at about the 10-minute mark in my now almost 43-year marriage that I began to form my chrysalis.

Often when I approach a topic, I begin by googling stupid questions about it. You might say there's no such thing as a stupid question—asking any question has its own value. But my search history would bear this out—you'd be astonished how dumb I can be, especially when I'm trying to get down at the root level of a thing so when I look up into its branches I can understand what I see. In this case, when I considered the word 'metamorphosis,' my first question was:

Q: Do caterpillars know they will turn into a butterfly?

The answer was exactly what my question deserved. I wondered if the internet ever tires of being everyone's second-grade teacher.

A: Like other insects, caterpillars don't reflect on what they're doing or ask questions about it. They don't know anything about their future, and they don't wonder about it.

I began to wonder what a better question might be. What question would I ask if I were a young caterpillar hearing crazy rumors on the playground and wishing someone would just be straight with me about the facts of life ... or even a grown-up human, wandering the halls of my adulthood wondering what the hell was happening but also trying to hide the fact that I had no idea?

In either case, I decided the question I could use an answer to would be:

Q: How does a butterfly become a butterfly?

In other words, how do I get from point A to point B? What exactly happens between here and there, between where I am right now and that magical far-off day when I wriggle my way out of this tired old shell to find I'm finally who I want to be? How can I guarantee my own transformation?

How do I become Me?

Unfortunately, neither my second-grade teacher nor the internet had that information for me. Nothing but my own life could equip me for the journey toward wholeness, and I was to pick up my equipment along the way, handed to me with no diagram showing how to use it. If I have felt unprepared—or grasping, or floundering, or terrified, or in the dark—it's because I have been. All those things. Sometimes even before I get out of bed in the morning, and often when I can't sleep at night. There are no instructions for becoming that I know about anyway. Like metamorphosis for an insect, becoming just happens.

Or as writer Ann Patchett put it, "Sometimes not having any idea where we're going works out better than we could possibly have imagined."[20]

I've seen the truth of that, even when 'working out better' has just meant being able to survive experiences I didn't think I could at the time I was going through them. Being able to wring a few drops of meaning or growth out of my worst things has been icing on the metamorphic cake—life was going to bring me this stuff regardless and I was never going to emerge unscathed. The meaning or growth hasn't usually meant I'd sign up to go through those experiences again. But I wouldn't give most of them back either. In fact, the older I get the more I like to leave my hardest things standing there, right where they happened, so whenever I need to, I can look in the rearview and see how far I've come.

If I can still see those things easily, does it mean I haven't made enough progress? Actually, for me a willingness to keep looking in the rearview is evidence of progress. Moving closer to becoming whole has required gathering in all my wounds with a willingness to include them in the inventory. The ones I caused myself, and the ones inflicted by a world full of people over which I had no control, but not for lack of trying. The wounds I thought I had gotten over, the ones I worked to overcome, the ones I buried under decades-thick layers of denial or shame, the ones I had been running from all my life and probably still am. As I unearth them, I place them where they belong in the story, knowing I'm going to keep seeing them, and even worse, others might find out about them too.

Living in that kind of plain sight has not been the way I've approached life for most of it. I'm a person who has loved to pretend I'm much more evolved than I am, a caterpillar who started trying on fake butterfly clothes years before I had any right to be shopping in that department. As a kid, I always wanted to be with the adults. I wanted to impress everyone. I wanted to be so unbelievably advanced people would wonder how so much maturity could exist in one small package. Regrets? Didn't have any. Resentments? None of those either, because everything was fine. I was always fine. Of course I was, because my fineness was proof of *doing-it-all-right*-ness.

The main problem with this is that looking fine and being fine are not at all the same things. One does not guarantee the other, and in fact, insisting on the first sometimes makes the second impossible. I'm embarrassed to tell you how recently it has come to my attention that central to our health, well-being, and ability to find happiness where we are is making peace with where we're coming from. In my case, and I'm guessing in yours—I don't want to presume, but I'm going to since I'm pretty sure I'm right—where we're coming from is complicated.

Fred Rogers said, "The child is in me still and sometimes not so still."[21]

When I was a kid, my bedroom had two doors. Both of them stayed open all the time; one of them was located next to a corner. It was a big old house with big old solid doors to match, and the corner door had a full-length plate glass mirror on it too. Punctuated by a heavy crystal knob, it probably weighed a ton. When that door was open, it blocked off the corner, creating a really convenient space for shoving all the things I was supposed to be putting away. This constituted cleaning my room. You could stack and pile, pile and stack as many things as you could get to stay on top of each other long enough to shove the door back against them. That big, beautiful door held the whole pile in place, keeping it nicely hidden. My mom would poke her head in to make sure I was doing what I was supposed to be doing, and she was fooled every time. Until she wasn't. Because sometimes even I would forget what was there. That door would get closed and then I'd be in trouble. But on all the days my mess didn't tumble out and betray me, I admired myself in the mirror completely unbothered by the stuff behind it. In fact, I was proud of it. In my mind, keeping a mess hidden was as good as cleaning it up; even better, because it avoided hard work *and* meant I was smart enough to put one over on people.

Speaking of hidden messes, I've done a few big stints of professionally supervised personal clean-up in my life. The first was in my twenties, when a skillful psychiatrist pulled back the door that hid the piles of my childhood and tried to help me find a place to put away all the things I'd shoved behind it, as well as things other people had left there that I didn't have the wherewithal to put away properly if I'd tried. Reconciling myself to those hard truths required years of painful sorting and repackaging. Some things I learned how to carry better, redistributing their weight and finding a handle where I couldn't quite figure out how to hold them before. Other things I tried to stop carrying at all, examining their contours carefully to understand as much as I could, then setting them down. My stated goal was to walk away lighter; I'm afraid I secretly hoped I might manage to walk away from myself. Though some of the girl had rocketed into adulthood, much of her was stuck in her old room, trying to keep the mess of her childhood from falling out on the floor.

I wouldn't say that doctor managed to help me see any of it as a gift, even though I began to see it that way later, which I think had a lot to do with his painful excavation. My mental health was in shambles well into my thirties, and most days it was hard to see much of anything beyond my own struggle and my growing family. Just being me felt hard, every minute of every day. Crippling anxiety and depression, panic attacks, agoraphobia, disordered eating, obsessive, intrusive thoughts—all came crashing into my life not long after my first child was born. I've always talked openly about mental illness, offering my story as a lifeline to anyone it might help and I think I've done some good. But there's a new wrinkle, and this is the important part here: I'm in my sixties now and that narrative—my most personal, my most precious, until now my most true—is changing. After decades of telling myself and the world the same story, a few big question marks have popped up right in the middle of it. *Are you kidding?* A subtle change of light, a shift in some bedrock, an unexpected noise from another room ... and suddenly the story that has served me so well is no longer sure of itself? It's bewildering and hard to accept or allow—how can truth change? How can I be so sure of one thing about myself for fifty years, and not only that, have it throw off all kinds of light and energy and goodness in my life because of how I've used it to help others and also leveraged it for my own growth, only to find out the picture I've been working from all this time wasn't the *whole* picture?

My mental health story is on the move, because other parts of me are changing too. Remember that chrysalis I was building ten minutes after I got married? Well, now I'm going to tell you something important about it, too: I misunderstood the assignment. That's right—I built the wrong thing! I will explain by giving you the shortest possible version of my best-decision/worst-decision, which is the exact opposite of what Dickens would do.

My marriage at eighteen was the best thing I ever did because it saved me in all the ways I hoped it would when I engineered it as an escape hatch from my childhood. I needed a scaffolding to build for myself the kind of nurturing life I didn't have as a kid, and I got that, and built it. The only part of the story I understood or knew how to tell for decades is that marrying at eighteen was a lifeline thrown straight from God.

I grabbed the lifeline, attaching every part of myself I could, then formed a strong chrysalis, one to keep me safe and secure (but also small), and prevent anything from ever changing. My unruly eighteen-year-old self who desperately believed women must be allowed to go through every door and should wear whatever they want to their own wedding couldn't fit comfortably, but by tamping things down *very* hard and trimming myself a bit here and there, I managed to just squeeze in. It was living in a corset, but I'm hardly the first woman to do that. However, like every other laced-up woman, I left myself very little room to breathe. Knowing me as I did, I thought that was probably safest, so I just wrapped and wrapped and wrapped. When parts of me poked out, I lopped them off and they landed in pockets I could never reach, being so squished.

And that right there is why it was also my worst decision. It's only now that I'm able to look at the arc of my life so far and see how all the lopping and squashing had profound effects on my mental health, my happiness, my faith, and most of all, my ability to grow. I had blamed my struggle for wellness on faulty wiring—six generations of mental illness in my family tree—but even if those genes provided the spark, some of my own life choices were gasoline I brought to the fire. (This is the first time I've told this part of the story, outside my therapist's office anyway. It's still pretty hard to say out loud.)

My choices have had consequences, and many of them were so, so good. It's almost unbelievable how well the ill-advised decision of an eighteen-year-old can turn out if she works hard but is also very lucky. I'm thankful every day and I have a lot of grace for that girl who took everything she'd been taught about the world, every hard thing she'd been handed, everything she knew about herself, and made a choice.

But this is my ultimate, most personal lesson in the truth and tension that so many spiritual thinkers describe using the words both/and: for all the ways it's turned out better than I could ever have imagined, I now see that some of the consequences weren't good—for the deepest, most essential parts of me—at all.

Here's what I've come to think of as The Chrysalis Problem: yes, they're built for protection but that word is too easy to misunderstand. The protection is not to keep you safe from change, but to defend enough space to change so completely that you can't even get your head around the magnificent thing you will become. Until you have them, you won't conceive of your own wings. Still, you must protect their becoming.

I think this problem is further complicated by the fact that generally, no one wants to change. Transformation? Absolutely. Change? That sounds kinda painful—I think I'll pass.

One of my mother's best bits of wisdom has always been this: "The one class everyone should be required to take is Change 101." I love her insight—if we can't get comfortable with change, we're never going to get very comfortable with anything about life. If I were designing the syllabus for the course, the first unit might look like this:

Change 101: The Chrysalis Problem
1. Nobody wants to change
2. It's not a tame process
3. You're not the boss of it
4. Sh!+ happens
5. You'll be changed by it

1) Nobody wants to change. This is pretty straightforward. Change is scary and uncomfortable. It requires things of us. Change is always pushing us forward, insisting we embrace the thing we haven't met. Grow-y times are not comfortable times! Remember when you were a kid and you'd get that growth-ache in your leg bones? Or if you've been pregnant, maybe your feet and hips hurt because your ligaments were softening in preparation for the big stretch? *Ouch.*

Also, we just like things how we like them. We may even choose the thing that isn't so great, if we're used to it, over the thing everyone assures us is better. But transformation is always going to require disruption of the old. I think the reason detective Adrian Monk is one of my all-time favorite TV characters is because he articulated The One Rule: "Never change anything ever. (It's not my rule. It's a very old rule.)" But when Monk was unable to control the loss of his beloved wife—the only safe and comfortable thing he'd ever known—he tried to control everything else.

2) Metamorphosis is not a tame process. It's a shape-shifter, in the most literal sense. Actually, when I first started to think about it, I wasn't sure whether metamorphosis would be best described as a cycle or a process. (You can also find that question in my search history.) I mean sure, I know it's part of the 'life cycle of the butterfly.' But it doesn't start and end in the same place.

A process moves from point A to point B. It's a description of what happens in between two things. I'm a process-oriented artist. I was raised as an artist, so to speak, by my mother-in-law who makes quilts 100 percent by hand. She would have no interest in doing it any other way—to her, the stitching *is* the thing. It's slow work, meditative and imperfect, a balm against the world's relentless insistence on speed and precision. Having come to art through that doorway, I valued the same thing I found in hand-quilting in all my work that came after. For me, the process became the thing. My small fiber pieces would often require a month of hand stitching. I loved holding the whole thing in my hand day after day, laying in thousands of tiny stitches through which a picture revealed itself.

As a child, the book I read more than any other was Madeleine L'Engle's *A Wrinkle in Time.* I was transfixed by the concept of the tesseract, a fifth-dimension kind of travel illustrated simply in the book by two hands holding a piece of fabric at points A and B for an ant to walk across. When the hands are brought together, the distance is erased. The ant can suddenly move from A to B in one step.

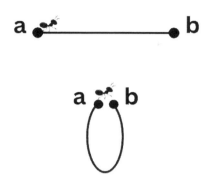

"Swiftly Mrs. Who brought her hands, still holding the skirt, together. 'Now you see,' Mrs. Whatsit said, 'he would be here without that long trip. That is how we travel.'"—Madeleine L'Engle, *A Wrinkle in Time*

I've thought a lot about why that idea was so appealing to small Me. Looking back, I can see all the ways I tried to get myself from the A to B of my young life faster. I skipped a year of high school. I got a job in a bank before I was old enough to get a driver's license. I lied about my age when I wanted to sing in a bar or date men instead of boys. I went through college impossibly fast, hardly slowing down enough to absorb what I was learning. I thought by achieving and impressing— with a little well-placed deception—I could travel at light-speed to adulthood. The middle parts of my youth were painful enough that by the time I hit seventeen, I wanted to leapfrog the rest of it altogether.

When you think of me on the steps of the Alta Club in my wedding dress, I am the ant, blinking in shock and surprise (and definitely fear) over having just successfully tessered. It's no wonder that my impulse was to double down, to hug the ground where I'd landed and demand, "Stop! Nobody move!"

It makes sense to think of metamorphosis as a process. The caterpillar goes in—things happen—the butterfly comes out. But what happens if you cut out that middle part? What happens if you ignore life doing its natural work and reject the attempts of all the uncomfortable parts, the stuff completely outside your understanding or control, to *change you*? It's nice from a comfort standpoint, but I don't think it makes a butterfly.

It's a miracle butterflies exist at all, but I think the most miraculous thing about them is not that they *are*, but how they come to be. For me, the metamorphosis-type of creation is evidence of a *process* God, not a *product* one. Such a god makes the Grand Canyon, a jaw-dropping spectacle, with drops of water so we can see that the end result, no matter how remarkable, pales a bit when you hold it up against the miracle of how it happened.

Sue Monk Kidd wrote, "Waiting is the missing link in the transformation process."[22] It would seem there's something about the patient passage of time that is an important ingredient in growth. And there's nothing we can do to speed it up.

Which has never stopped me from trying. I'm the first to admit, I've got some real control issues. One of the prayers I say most is only three words: *Open my hands.* I beg God to help me relax my grip at least once a day. Maybe on a subconscious level, this is why I find more healing in process than in product. It's not just in art—I'm happiest walking the same circular route over and over. It's clearly taking the steps that matters, not where the steps are taking me. Stitching on the same four inches of fabric for a month at a time over many years centered me in my own life and body—my specific place and time—teaching me more than the art I created with those stitches ever could. Process work is stepping into the present moment: the dish you're washing, the light across the sill. We need to be here now because, as I once heard someone say, the present is the only thing that goes on forever. Allowing ourselves to trust process is allowing ourselves to trust God. While I haven't always known how to surrender to the process of my own life, I think my soul has tried to help me practice, to teach me this in other ways.

But I think metamorphosis also has much in common with a cycle. A cycle is a circle. You begin at A, you loop around—and a lot can happen in that loop!—and then you come full circle. So much of life is the same thing over and over. "The tree looks a lot like the tree yesterday, and so does the baby," writes Rebecca Solnit.[23] I think that's profound, because trees and babies are change and growth at their most obvious, aren't they? So this tells me even when every day looks pretty much the same, time will still be doing its metamorphic thing with us.

We moved and moved and moved again while raising our family, and every time we landed in a new city, I unpacked all the same things and rebuilt the same home. The kitchen was different; the art on the kitchen walls and the table and chairs we ate at were the same. In a way, it was resetting to A again and again. This reinvention was a cycle, but it was also metamorphosis. Because each time we came back to A different, changed by all the places we lived and the people we met, by everything that happened in between A and A and A again. Resilience and faith were at work every time the boxes were filled and sealed, opened and unpacked. We started over, but larger somehow.

Richard Rohr talks about a principle he describes as "transcend and include." We grow from the things that become part of us. We cannot give them back, but we can come back bigger each time we return and reset, having onboarded new experiences that will continue to do their work on the next loop, and the next. Perhaps what looks like a circle is actually more like a spiral—it will eventually move us from A to B, but only because, as Mary Wollstonecraft Shelley is said to have written, "The beginning is always today."

Our progress may look and feel as much like the movie *Groundhog Day* as anything else. We begin again and again, but hopefully we can make the next loop with a little more grace as a result of what we learned from the last ... and eventually get to a new place.

3) You're not the boss of metamorphosis. It's a process over which you have very little control. Sure, you can change your habits, but transformation is going to be a result of forces working upon you, inside and out. You are a metamorphic rock. You may have started out as igneous or sedimentary, but some combination of stuff like heat and pressure will come along and it won't leave you how it found you. In this metaphor, heat and pressure is code for life, for all our rubbing up against the actions of other people and the unpredictable things they do. Unfortunately, as Anne Lamott rightly points out, "Nobody in isolation becomes who they were designed to be."[24]

The fact that we're not in charge also means walking blindfolded and that's uncomfortable. But it's what I like to call *holy discomfort*, which is better than the regular kind: it's worthwhile discomfort, discomfort that earns its keep. Not always in the moment, but eventually. The practice of tolerating uncertainty while continuing to move forward expands our spiritual capacity.

Holy discomfort is sitting with things we don't understand or don't know how to accept. It's sitting with opposition, with questions, with fear, with the unknown. It's feeling emotions that are so difficult you don't even know what to do with them, but letting them stick around anyway. Holy discomfort is the doorway to growth, an invitation to enlargement, to create new space within ourselves. It pulls us into the present moment by making us aware in our bodies of what we're feeling or experiencing in our hearts and minds. My therapist once asked me what happened to me that so completely disconnected my head from my body. "As near as I can tell, *all* of your living takes place here," she said, pointing to her head. "Where is the rest of you in your life?" I was completely taken aback by this question. She was right, of course, but how could something be so obvious to her and never register at all with me? I'm still working on an answer, but in the moment I knew it had something to do with desperation to turn off my own discomfort. Part of learning to reconnect to my body would involve being willing to tolerate everything I'd been refusing to include.

One of my favorite quotes comes from Stephen Harrod Buhner: "You cannot use the tools of a system to refine the system whose tools you are using."[25] I'm always looking for new tools to help myself. Discomfort is often the first clue that I'm stuck, that I need to find—or sometimes invent—a new tool; an approach, insight, or resource that can give me a push toward 'include' so I can eventually get to the 'transcend' part of working through a difficulty. But for discomfort to tell us what it's trying to get us to hear, we have to be willing to listen closely. Sometimes that's as simple as paying attention to your own body to see what it knows about you.

It can work in the opposite way too—sometimes new tools introduce themselves with gentle, loving voices that soothe a place I didn't even realize was raw. I went to New Mexico for the first time for my fortieth birthday, and I had what I can only describe as a spiritual experience. I thought I knew the desert, having grown up in Utah, and I didn't much like or care about it. But when my feet hit New Mexico, something started to speak and I realized the desert and I had some kind of connection; it satisfied a craving I'd carried my whole life without understanding it. I don't know what else to tell you except that I couldn't stop going back. For a few years, I was in Santa Fe so often I felt like a local. People asked me, "What do you do when you go there?"

My answer was, "Just *be*." It was the only place I'd ever been where I felt like I could. It was meeting myself. The desert soothed wounds I never knew I had with potions I didn't know existed. It was a new tool, completely different and wholly unexpected, and those pilgrimages—I call them that using the word in its most spiritual sense—fortified me for a lot of what has happened in my life since.

4) Stuff happens. Do I need to say much about this one? If you haven't figured this out yet, I pray your induction to the club might be a gentle one. We should actually say, "happens and happens and happens," because from where I'm sitting, life seems a little like an infinity mirror—you know, those mirrors you stand in front of in the temple sealing room? Like that, but with crappy stuff. Don't get me wrong, there's plenty of good stuff too, but the good stuff doesn't stick to your shoe and smell up whole years. If someone had told me everything I was going to go through in my life—and I'm just talking so far—I would 1) never have believed them, and 2) have been willing to do just about anything to avoid it.

I made a piece once that spoke to this. It's on the short list of art I would like to have kept for myself, but being a working artist requires certain concessions to the realities of the world, the first being that you sell even the pieces you end up in a relationship with. It's a blonde girl in a setting vaguely reminiscent of a stage. She's wearing a pearl necklace, hair done up in a pink headband (did someone say cummerbund?), because she wants to look like she's in charge, even if her face tells us she may not be sure she wants to star in this particular show. The caption says, "Things will happen you can't begin to imagine now." I made this shortly after the first thing happened in my life that I *really* couldn't have imagined (and would have run screaming from if I did) and I can't tell you all the ways it has come true since. For starters, the adage 'bigger kids, bigger problems' has been determined to prove itself repeatedly to me. More variables (read: other people) equals less control, math that's simple to understand but hard to live with. I was forty before it started to dawn on me that maybe I hadn't actually controlled anything since that one very light pink strip of rebellious satin at my wedding, and I had to fight to stay in charge of that. I've had a death grip on everything since, but even my best plans for myself and others are often ignored. Every inch of this earth is prime real estate for catastrophe, *but also goodness*, and we don't work the switch. Which brings me to my mother's other truest saying, "We always worry about the wrong things." Worry is practicing resistance. Bracing for everything that doesn't happen robs us of presence for what does.

5) You'll be changed by it. Yes, stuff happens, but so does metamorphosis. And I'm betting there are sometimes during that process where the insect looks like sh!+—like it's spent a really bad night alternating between the toilet and the bathroom floor, or maybe been in a weeklong bar fight. I don't think anyone bumps into the half-changed caterpillar and says, "You're looking well!" Do they?

The first round of changes from my hard things are what I'm forced to in order to survive, and I'd usually like to cry uncle when we get through that first phase because I'm so ready for the unpleasantness of whatever's happening to stop. But no, it is only the beginning—it may be the caterpillar's skin having melted off, but the inside hasn't even gotten involved yet. Change is never over and done—I get poked and worked on and poked a little more, sometimes for years after hard things. I can suddenly get an insight about what happened in 2003 that jostles other stuff I thought was settled, and suddenly I'm sorting piles again.

Like when giant question marks drop into a story we've long ago turned into a bedtime one, since it's so lovely and settled and we know the ending because we're here to tell it, right? We turn out the light. Then the phone rings and it's those questions calling from *inside the chrysalis!* Here is one of the ridiculous horror film tropes that life, in small ways, sometimes imitates to the same effect as in the films: the chainsaw suddenly roars to life again ... *after* the guy who's trying to kill you with it is supposed to be dead. You can think you've learned everything there is to learn from a thing, but don't underestimate its ability to come back to life and insist there are lessons you skipped.

"The child had never known, the girl was never sure, the woman the longer she was herself, was least of all certain,"[26] said Margaret Wise Brown. I, too, know much less than I used to, but in finding my way to this place of unknowing, I have somehow begun to know this: That it is all part of the process—the slow work, the discomfort, the circling back and beginning again, the trying to jump ahead and skip parts but they're still there with no guarantee they won't rear up and insist to be acknowledged later. All of this belongs, and we mustn't try to give it back. It's the kind of gift we didn't want and also never knew we needed, but that doesn't make it any less ours.

Listening to a podcast on my walk the other day I heard comedian Marc Maron say, "It's the human thing, man. This is part of it." And I stopped to write it down, because I realized in that sentence, he was talking about everything.

In her book, *Somehow*, Anne Lamott says to a friend, "I love you, honey, but don't talk to me about evolution. I am where I am. I know who I am."[27] I guess that explains why she's been one of my most consistent spiritual mentors: because she's ahead of me. Unlike Anne, I'm not really sure where I am sometimes, let alone who.

I do get glimpses though, like I'm suddenly somewhere high above myself and I can locate my little star on the mall directory that says, "You Are Here." They're glimpses because a moment later I'm generally back to wandering around looking for a map, or trying to figure out how to read the one in front of me.

I had such a flash of insight recently, and it said this: "You're a pretty average grandma. C+." Meaning, I don't quite measure up under my own criteria. I'm used to getting A's or killing myself trying, so 'satisfactory' surprised me, landing with a thud.

I suddenly saw the whole parade of grandmas in my own life: Grandma Myrl, a farm wife whose every moment was her family and who stepped in to take care of us when my parents couldn't quite, so she exists in the literal lifesaver category. (She has god-status, if you figure in her cooking.) Aunt Lillie, my great-aunt who I think signed up to be our grandma because she didn't have any kids of her own, and just happened to live in the bedroom next door to our actual grandma. Grandma Dena was really cut out to be a journalist, not so much a nurturer. She also didn't leave her house much due to crippling agoraphobia and died suddenly when I was only eight. I trace many of my gifts to her, so she's high on the list of people I wish to know better someday—I've pieced her together from her own written records but also my fuzzy eight-year-old lens. There's a moment where Dena's watering flowers in her garden and I'm frozen behind her on a steppingstone, desperately wanting to get a cookie from the kitchen drawer but scared to death of asking. I would a hundred times rather ask Aunt Lillie, because Lillie was the truest-bluest, paper-dolls-and-cookies kind of grandma. On top of that, she was a friend.

So I have three grandmas in that sample set, and I have my own daughters' grandmas. My mother, who struggled with mental illness and had to turn several years of my childhood care over to Lillie and Myrl, then got well, got a career, but sorta forgot to ever come back to nurturing her children or grandchildren. This is not a judgment but the plainest statement of my experience. My dad once said, "Your mother has always been sad that her children never needed her." As her child who became so independent at an impossibly young age to survive, I thought, "So this is how misunderstandings start." She was a grandma who lived far away, who sent big, exciting checks at Christmas and stayed in a hotel when she came to town, traveled the world wearing fancy nails and hair, sending postcards from everywhere. She had a pool at her condo to which there were fun annual visits, but they involved more time swimming than with Grandma. She has always loved her granddaughters fiercely, but her days have been about different things.

On the other side, my girls had Mana, their other grandma, who lived closer for a lucky chunk of their childhood years, and delighted in taking them to amazing educational toy stores and petting zoos, riding hand-carved carousels, reading them all the best stories, and who always came to stay when my husband and I traveled. She made dolls and matching Christmas jammies and generally did all the things the very best (often only imaginary) kind of grandma does.

I always imagined I'd be, if not the too-good-to-be-true grandma, at least a very real "I will always want to spend time with you, take care of you, and be your true-blue friend" kind.

But observing myself with my grandchildren the other day, I had a terrible realization: As a mother, I managed to be the mother I longed for. But for some reason, as a grandma I'm much more like my mother and her mother before her. I'm not the lap they're going to crawl into when they need grandma-love. I know, what kind of grandma I am is entirely within my own power. Well, isn't it? Except that it doesn't feel that way, really. I come from a family so physically awkward at showing love, it's almost unbearable when we pick each other up at the airport. We're not touchy people and we look at our shoes a lot. It's A+ love, somehow stuck in C+ expression.

Also, I became a stay-at-home mother at nineteen and it turns out, in therapy forty-plus years later, that I may have a few *teensy* unacknowledged and unresolved feelings about that. Yes, there are still things I haven't always wanted, or been ready, to understand. Especially about myself.

So now we're to that one fell swoop of sickening realization I had, standing awkwardly watching my grand-littles play the other day, my heart almost breaking with the miracle of them. But also looking at my shoes; loving them fiercely without knowing quite how to get into their inner circle. I realized that I am a person. My grandmothers are mythopoeic gods, the award-winning cast of my own creation story. But I am a regular, flawed, struggly, imperfect, likely-to-die-without-much-improvement person. All the previous evidence I'd been so carefully collecting to make my case to the contrary didn't really change anything. This has always been who, and where, I am.

Later that night, I was telling a friend about how it turns out I'm the off-brand kind of grandma, and how hard processing this new information about myself is, and that I don't know quite what to do about it, if anything. I was a bit weepy, acknowledging how helpless I felt looking at all that truth. Finally I said, "I've had a terrible realization: it's that I am just a person."

And my friend said, "You *are* just a person." I think we both knew for me, it was progress.

Progress—I suppose it is. If you're wondering how realizing you're just like everyone else amounts to progress, after trying so hard on every front in your life to at least appear—if not actually *be*—extraordinary, I guess I'd say keep walking, and maybe someday you'll find yourself in this same spot. I hope our mothers knew this eventually, and our grandmothers too. I don't know many things for sure, but suddenly I know in my bones that to be a person—to be who I am, where I am—and to know it, is enough. In fact, it's exactly what I was put on earth to do. I've achieved it, and I don't have to reach anything higher than this because no matter how high I climb, it will never get me anywhere more real.

Just recently I realized that my fifties were my favorite decade. I had to think about that. I'd had new freedom from home and children and a lot of success with my art in my forties. My mom always promised my forties would be my favorite, and they were exciting and fulfilling, but they were also hard. I was subjected to lessons I never imagined I'd be forced to learn. Looking back, I wouldn't repeat my forties on salary.

My fifties though? There was some kind of new magic afoot in that decade. It didn't involve my own freedom or personal achievement. It didn't involve perfect happiness for anyone in my family. It certainly didn't involve better hair. Instead, my fifties brought one dance with uterine cancer and another with stroke, sudden job instability for my husband, dementia and decline for my parents, a heartbreaking divorce for a daughter that included her moving home and having a nervous breakdown. Put a global-pandemic-cherry on top, and how could those years possibly be my favorite? But they were. I needed to chew on that for a while.

What I've come to is this: Sometime after fifty, I began to change—maybe even evolve—in a way that made it so what was going on in my outer life no longer determined everything about my inner life. I loosened myself just enough to breathe, and suddenly my bottled-up inner life took on a life of its own.

Not so I could retreat into it and ignore all the hard and disappointing things about real life. More like I pulled the door back and this time found peace and happiness I didn't even know I'd hidden there. My fifties felt like a coming-of-age story, one that led me back to my own reliable legs and place to stand, as well as feet with roots, anchoring me in a life that is moving so fast, I swear I can now see the babies age and the trees grow in real time. The tesseract saved me at eighteen, but sixty found me wanting to circle back to include what I'd skipped. To empty my pockets, reclaim every part I removed to make myself fit. I don't have that much time left, and I'm picking up speed. I want to walk every inch of whatever distance remains between A and B for myself.

In her book *Field Notes for the Wilderness*, Sarah Bessey writes: "Claim your whole story. All of your life belongs to you. You might be surprised by the unexpected harvest of this."[28]

Jesus came to turn everything on its head. He says, "You have heard it said ... but I say—" Perhaps He used that pattern to give us a hint about what life was going to do to us. People with authority, including ourselves, were going to tell us things but then our experience was going to come along and show us the truth. I'm in a time now where I feel like God is saying to me about some things in my life, "You've been telling the story like this, but I'm trying to teach you to see it and yourself with new eyes. Pay attention to what I am showing you: you've got to be willing to change the way you think about the things you know, *even the ones you're most sure about.*" When Jesus explained He was the way, the truth, and the life, maybe He was using words that expressed this same thing. Maybe the *way* to our potential transformation lay in the *truth* of our lived experience—our *life.*

I think if I were to ask that completely non-introspective caterpillar what it is sure of, it would be sure it is a caterpillar. Sometimes I wonder if I've been crawling around focused on eating leaves with no idea of not only what's possible, but what is meant to be. Jesus came out of the tomb having been transformed. We don't know exactly what took place on a cellular level. We don't know exactly what that promised rebirth could mean for the cells of our used-up human bodies either. But we can understand that it means *something.* Whether we know what it means for us personally or what it will look like in the end, we can trust ourselves as our lives pull us toward our own transformation. A well-known Quaker adage says, "Let your life speak." Parker Palmer fleshes that out. "Before I can tell my life what I want to do with it," he says, "I must listen to my life telling me who I am."[29] We must each give our life permission to take us in the direction of our own becoming.

I've come across something called 'asemic writing,' and I can't get enough. The word 'asemic' means "without the smallest unit of meaning." Asemic writing is a hybrid art form fusing text and image—your brain will clearly identify it as writing, although there are no letters, which means meaning can occur across, even outside, linguistic systems and understanding. Similar to abstract art, an asemic work can be polysemantic; it may have zero meaning, infinite meanings, or meaning that evolves, depending on the viewer's interpretation. And all of that is why I love it so much.

When I engage with asemic writing, I can know it has meaning without necessarily being able to say—or needing to be sure—what that meaning is. When I see asemic pieces of music, my mind immediately has a clear idea what kind of song I'm looking at without even needing to hear the notes.

This idea of language without specific symbols or music without specific notes speaks to something deep in me I'm continuing to unpack. Through engaging with asemic works and also interrogating my reaction to them, I've been able to find out something about myself: I experience meaning as a kind of magnetic force that I don't need an understanding of to feel pulled by. For me, truth can be compelling without necessarily being clearly defined or comprehended. Asemic writing asks for patience and continued attention. Look today, but also look again tomorrow—because of your own movement and growth, you may understand tomorrow what you couldn't quite make sense of today. If you're willing to keep looking, you may suddenly find great personal meaning in places where you found nothing before.

Zooming out, I can see how the roadmap of my life has much in common with asemic art—I have known it is taking me toward something bigger but have often found no intelligible symbols that spell out the directions. It doesn't tell me a thing looking forward, but if I look back with enough interest—and willingness, because I believe looking for truth when there's no guarantee we're going like what we find requires an intentional kind of openness—I can see how so many things have worked together to bring me to who and where I am now. My life—best and worst—becomes rich with meaning.

Metamorphosis is addition and subtraction in concert. The caterpillar loses a lot of parts it didn't realize it could live without, as it gains parts it never knew existed and isn't sure what to do with. Until it begins to fly. In sudden flight, the caterpillar transformed must realize the story it had been telling itself, no matter how comforting or true, was told through a pretty limited filter. Its entire life so far—creep and eat, creep and eat—was crawled through a glass darkly.

Metamorphosis is not a test for the caterpillar. This kind of transformation is something that can happen *because* you are a caterpillar though. A caterpillar—in your case a person—is enough. You're already qualified.

Coming to understand and accept this—*my caterpillar-ness, my underlying, regular personhood*—means I can stop trying to engineer my transformation. I can stop worrying about building wings. Which is a good thing, considering that as a kid I once jumped from the top of a swing set holding a paper bag above my head, sure that was going to somehow slow my crash to the ground. Not my only bad idea, and remembering it reminds me I cannot make a butterfly happen on my own, no matter how smart or evolved I can prove I am, and no matter what I manage to achieve. But transformation can happen if I am open to the grace of process, to the abundance of my own experience—not how much there is but what it can and will do to and for me, if I let it—to the possibility of rebirth but also acceptance of the deaths that will require, and to the love of myself and others that will ready me to receive what is already mine. What is most essential is that I keep moving toward myself, my wholeness, the willing participant in my own becoming.

Section Notes

1. Taylor, *Leaving Church*, 219.

2. Isak Dinesen, quoted in Hannah Arendt, *The Human Condition* (University of Chicago Press, 1998), 175.

3. Fred Rogers, *You Are Special: Neighborly Words of Wisdom from Mr. Rogers* (Penguin, 1995), 97.

4. In November 2015, the church announced a policy excluding the children of gay couples from ordinances including baptism. The policy also specified gay marriage to be apostasy and grounds for excommunication. It was rescinded in 2019.

5. William Carlos Williams, quoted in Robert Coles, *The Call of Stories: Teaching and the Moral Imagination* (Houghton Mifflin, 1989), 30.

6. "About Us," The Walt Disney Family Museum, waltdisney.org, accessed January 22, 2025.

7. Muriel Rukeiser, "The Speed of Darkness" (1968), *The Collected Poems of Muriel Rukeiser*, Janet E. Kaufman et al., eds. (University of Pittsburgh Press, 2005), 465.

8. Krista Tippet, host, *On Being* podcast, episode 706, "Sitting Together in the Dark," February 28, 2019, 53 minutes. Guest Teju Cole.

9. Chieko Okazaki, *Disciples* (Deseret Book, 1998), 52.

10. Sarah Bessey, *Out of Sorts: Making Peace with an Evolving Faith* (Howard Books, 2015), 88.

11. Michael G. Reed, *Banishing the Cross: The Emergence of a Mormon Taboo* (John Whitmer Books, 2012), 67–85.

12. Jeffrey R. Holland, "Lifted Up Upon the Cross," October 2022 general conference.

13. Richard Rohr, *The Universal Christ: How a Forgotten Reality Can Change Everything We See, Hope For, and Believe* (Convergent Books, 2021), 148.

14. Rohr, *Universal Christ*, 147.

15. Rohr, *Universal Christ*, 156.

16. Kate Bowler, host, *Everything Happens* podcast, season 13, episode 10, "Standing in the Gap," November 5, 2024, 42 minutes. Guest Parker Palmer.

17. Pete Enns, "Desperately Seeking God and Other Cries for Help from the Evangelical Dark Side," *The Bible for Normal People* (blog), February 5, 2016, thebiblefornormalpeople.

18. Richard Rohr, "Transforming Pain, Center for Action and Contemplation," Center for Action and Contemplation, October 17, 2018, cac.org.

19. Margaret Renkl, *The Comfort of Crows: A Backyard Year* (Spiegel & Grau, 2023), 16.

20. Ann Patchett, *What Now?* (Harper, 2008), 20.

21. Fred Rogers, *The World According to Mister Rogers: Important Things to Remember* (Hyperion, 2003), 26.

22. Sue Monk Kidd, *When the Heart Waits: Spiritual Direction for Life's Sacred Questions* (HarperOne, 2016), vi.

23. Rebecca Solnit, "Slow Change Can Be Radical Change," *Literary Hub*, January 11, 2024, lithub.com.

24. Anne Lamott, *Somehow: Thoughts on Love* (Riverhead Books, 2024), 112.

25. Stephen Harrod Buhner, *The Lost Language of Plants: The Ecological Importance of Plant Medicine to Life on Earth* (Chelsea Green Publishing, 2002), 30.

26. Anna Holmes, "The Radical Woman Behind 'Goodnight Moon,'" *The New Yorker*, January 31, 2022.

27. Lamott, *Somehow: Thoughts on Love*, 91.

28. Sarah Bessey, *Field Notes for the Wilderness: Practices for an Evolving Faith* (Convergent Books, 2024), 209.

29. Parker J. Palmer, *Let Your Life Speak: Listening for the Voice of Vocation*, (Jossey-Bass, 1999), 4.

ABOUT THE AUTHORS

Susan M. Hinckley is a storyteller in words and pictures. A longtime exhibitor with the American Craft Council, her art is held in private collections across the United States. She writes and reflects on her faith and church experiences as co-creator of the *At Last She Said It* podcast. She'll travel any distance for good green chile or a glimpse of her grandkids, splitting her time between the Southwest and Midwest. Wherever she is, her heart roams the desert—preferably in a fast convertible.

Cynthia Winward makes her home in Provo, Utah, although she will always be a California girl. Before pouring all her creative energy into the *At Last She Said It* podcast, she was the owner of an online embroidery business. Her kitchen is her happy place, where she enjoys making the world's greatest red-chile enchiladas. She prefers salty over sweet, TV over movies, and early mornings over late nights. She enjoys the good life as an empty nester with her husband, Paul.